. Discovered by Lubitsch and Jesse Lasky
f Paramount in 1929, Lillian went to
ollywood. After appearing with Jeanette
MacDonald and Maurice Chevalier in *The
ove Parade*, Lillian won the coveted role
f Huguette in *The Vagabond King*.

Cecil B. DeMille chose her to play the
en role in M-G-M's spectacular *Madame
an*.

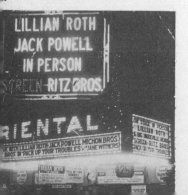

was hailed by
the footsteps of

[continued on back endpaper]

I'LL CRY TOMORROW

I'LL CRY

TOMORROW

WRITTEN IN COLLABORATION WITH

MIKE CONNOLLY   GEROLD FRANK

TOMORROW

BY LILLIAN ROTH

NEW YORK
FREDERICK FELL, INC., PUBLISHERS

Manufactured in the United States of America by
American Book–Stratford Press, Inc., New York

Designed by SIDNEY SOLOMON

PUBLISHED SIMULTANEOUSLY IN CANADA
BY GEORGE J. MC LEOD, LTD., TORONTO

I am grateful to
EARL WILSON
a man who believed in me

TO MOTHER

FOR A LIFETIME OF PATIENCE

AND AN ETERNITY OF LOVE

Unhappy am I that this has happened to me? Not so. Happy am I, though this has happened to me, for I continue free from pain, neither crushed by the past nor fearing the future; for such a thing as this might have happened to any man. . . .

—Marcus Aurelius Antonius

A NOTE TO THE READER

THIS BOOK has been a long time in the writing, and a long, long time in the living. It is the story of a child star who grew up too soon—or perhaps too late—the account of a life which has held a great deal of tragedy, not only for me but for many dear to me. I haven't found it easy to open these doors to the past, to tell things which most people would hesitate even to confide to friends, let alone put in a book for strangers to read.

I recall the mingled hope and fear I felt not so long ago when my story was sketched on Ralph Edwards' "This Is Your Life" program. I was told a television audience of 40,000,000 people would see me as I came on the stage.

I thought then, almost desperately, *"What will they think of me? Will they remember that I was once famous and then infamous? That I was a drunk for so many years? Will they think that I am flaunting my past or making a bid for sympathy? . . ."*

Some of these emotions are mine now. Why *am* I writing this book? The reasons are mixed. For one thing, I believe the very writing will help clarify myself in relation to the world about me. I think it will help reestablish my integrity in my own eyes, and I hope it will help reestablish my integrity and my dignity in the eyes of those who knew me when I had neither.

But I am also writing this book in the hope that it will help others. You will find this easier to believe after you've read these pages and discovered how much others have helped me.

If someone were to ask me, "Lillian, what made you drink?" I'm not sure I could answer the question satisfactorily, even for myself. Unhappy childhood, tragic love affairs, anxieties, deep-seated complexes—such psychiatric labels will come to mind as you read this book. Can the answer be stated so simply? I don't know. I can only present my own experience for what it is worth. I do know that psychiatry, which has an excellent record in mental and emotional problems, reports comparatively small success in the field of alcoholism.

For sixteen years I existed in a nightmare world, one which many enter but not many leave. That *one can come back,* that there is a way out from shame and despair and utter hopelessness—this is the sum and substance of my book. And this, I believe, justifies opening the doors to a past that sometimes—when I look back at it—seems utterly incredible and unbelievable to me who lived it.

In some instances in these pages I have given fictional names to people, but these persons were and are real. All that is in this book is true.

—LILLIAN ROTH

Fort Lauderdale, Florida

BOOK
ONE

CHAPTER I

I HAVE thought of many ways to start my story. I could begin it at a moment of triumph, when as a Hollywood star my escorts to a world premiere were Gary Cooper and Maurice Chevalier, when three of my pictures were running simultaneously on Broadway, and I earned $3,500 for an afternoon's work. That would be a glamorous beginning.

I could begin it at an awful moment, when I stood before an open window, behind me years of alcoholic horror and degradation, about to leap to the pavement eleven stories below. That would be a melodramatic beginning.

Or I could begin it at the age of thirty-four, when as an ex-inmate of a mental institution, I was released to start my life over again. But that might be a puzzling beginning, and difficult for some to understand.

Perhaps, as my husband Burt suggests, the way to tell it is the way it happened, allowing it to unfold in the order dictated by whatever mysterious forces mold us into the persons we become. "That's the only way it will make sense," he cautioned me. "Tell it as it happened."

This is how it happened, then.

My life was never my own. It was charted before I was born.

My parents were hopelessly stagestruck, and as a result, I literally waited for my very first entrance cue in a theatre. My mother, who had firm ideas about pre-natal influence, spent as much time in theatres as she could. She laughed and cried with Eva Tanguay and Nora Bayes and Sarah Bernhardt, delighted to think that in some occult fashion her enjoyment was shared by the child she carried. She wanted me to be a singer; and because her greatest idol, almost to the point of worship, was Lillian Russell, I was named for her when I finally arrived on December 13, 1910.

My father saw another future for me. He dreamed of me as a great dramatic actress. Born Arthur Rutstein in Russia, he had been brought to Boston, my mother's birthplace, when he was four. Handsome, happy-go-lucky, and gifted with contagious charm, he played a bit part in "Peck's Bad Boy" at sixteen. To hear him describe it, he was the star. For years my mother laughingly chided him for never getting over it—and teased him about his voice. Dad's voice was an off-key tenor, and temperamental in the high ranges, but it didn't stop him from teaming up with a friend who played the accordion, and singing on the Boston ferry for coins tossed by the passengers. When Dad took Mother along for the ride, during his courtship, he called it "serenading" her. She would sigh with the memory. "Juliet had her Romeo and I had my Arthur. Sometimes I think I suffered more than she did." Actually, Mother didn't mind, because it meant more money to go to more shows.

Arthur was 24, working in his father's produce market by day and ushering in theatres by night, when he first met my mother, Katie Silverman. They were married soon after. My baby sister Ann made her appearance two and a half years after me.

I have often tried to trace my parents' passionate love for the theatre. Perhaps it answered some deep need in them. Perhaps it was the result of unfulfilled dreams about which I never knew. My mother, a strong-willed but emotional woman, felt that show people—those with real talent, and she was a stern critic—were the chosen of the gods. "We took you to see the greats and near-greats," she told me when I was old enough to understand. "They all had something to offer, or they wouldn't be up there making people laugh and cry." She had a small, sweet singing voice herself. "That's all I had, Lilly baby, but there was a lot of harmony in my soul, and I gave you that."

Dad, however, was always acting, forever putting on a show for us. He gave a song everything: his left hand over his heart, his right outstretched to a cruel unfeeling world, big tears rolled down his cheeks as he sang, "Just a Cousin of Mine," or "Please, Mr. Conductor, Don't Put Me Off the Train, My Poor Old Mother is Waiting, Waiting for Me in Pain." I remember, in a room off the parlor, bouncing on my little bed to the rhythm of his songs. It was Dad who taught me recitations and despite my shyness brought me out to recite before Sunday company.

Whatever the case, the stage was my life and that of my sister Ann as far back as I can remember.

Ann and I were not alike. No matter how miserable I felt when called upon to perform for guests, I never rebelled. Dad would say, "Lillian is so good. She always minds me. Stand up, darling, and do something for us." Ann, however, refused. Dad might plead, beg, threaten—

she would not budge. I was also a silent child, keeping much to myself. My father sometimes worried aloud. "She's so quiet, Katie," he would say. "You ought to find out what she thinks about, what goes on in that little head of hers." Mother would pick me up and hug me. "Oh, Arthur, what can she be thinking of? She's only a baby!"

I thought—and felt—many things. Looking back now, I know that what I felt most during my childhood was fear—and loneliness. I feared my mother's displeasure. Though she loved me, she was a perfectionist. Quick to kiss, she was quick to slap. Her dedication to my career was single-minded: to her the theatre was the magic door to everything she dreamed for her Lilly, and she would allow nothing to get in the way. My sense of loneliness is more difficult to explain. I was lonely for—I knew not what. I always felt inadequate. No matter what I was told, I thought every other child was prettier, more charming, more likable—in short, nicer than I. I never liked the person I was, and later, I found alcohol helped me run away from myself.

In 1916 we moved to New York, to a cold-water walk-up on 43rd Street, between Ninth and Tenth Avenues. Arthur, who was always going to make a million, thought he'd find more opportunities in the big city. Even more important was the fact that New York was the center of show business.

Hearing that jobs were available for talented little girls, Katie used to dress Ann and me each morning near the coal stove in the kitchen, and then make the rounds with us of the producers and theatrical agents. Their offices were invariably crowded. Each was like the other—a desk, a bored girl behind it, and the same answer, day after day: "Nothing doing." Mother refused to be discouraged. One blustery winter's day in 1916 she dropped in with us at Educational Pictures. Yes, there was a job, then and there—for me!

It was to be my first assignment in show business, to pose as Educational Pictures' screen trademark, a living statue holding a lamp of knowledge.

Katie's excitement as she signed me in possessed me too. It was always to be like that. Her wish became mine. In later years I always looked into the wings, where she stood during my act, to see what her face said. A smile meant I had done well. The merest shadow of a frown, that my performance wasn't perfect, no matter what the critics wrote the following morning.

Now, in preparation for my first job, she undressed me and a fatherly looking old gentleman with a cigar clenched in his teeth started to paint me with white body makeup. When lunch time came, Katie left me in his charge while she and Ann went out to buy sandwiches for all of us, including the old gentleman. Left alone with me, he went to the door, looked outside, and locked it. "Cold in here," he said. I had been standing on a box. "Better lie down, where it's warm," he said, taking me in his arms and carrying me to a couch near the stove. He painted my thighs, then worked his brush upwards and began painting me where it made me uneasy.

He daubed me with the brush, again and again, on the same part of my anatomy. The cigar moved from one corner of his mouth to the other, and then back again. "Only five years old," he said. "My, you're a nice little girl."

[17]

I covered my eyes with my hands. I knew there was something wrong in what he was doing, but I couldn't stop him or cry for help. If Katie found out, something terrible would happen. She would scream, her face would contort, and I could not bear to hear her scream or to see her face like that.

When he heard her footsteps in the hall, he hurriedly unlocked the door and stood me up on the box again; he was just finishing my feet when Katie came in and spread out our lunch.

An unknown fear held my tongue. I never told her. But for years afterward I dreamed constantly about a man with a cigar in his mouth, who locked me up in a room and did dreadful things to me. A popular Admiration Cigar advertisement at the time pictured a smiling, moon-faced man with a cigar in his mouth, and he was repeated, cigar and face, on and on into infinity, growing smaller and smaller in the background. Whenever I caught sight of him in subway or trolley ads, I shut my eyes tightly and hid my face in Katie's skirts until all his heads faded away.

Katie learned that Sam Goldwyn was producing motion pictures in Fort Lee, New Jersey, across the Hudson River. If Educational Films could use me, why not Goldwyn? Each morning we took the long trip by bus, ferry and bus again, Katie, Ann and I. Once in the barracks-like studios, we waited hopefully for calls as extras—we two among perhaps a hundred children, with their mothers. We were always cold. Someone distributed tin cups of hot coffee, and Katie hurried about looking for hot water to dilute it for us. We stood, sometimes for hours, stamping our feet to keep warm, until we were called. Our assignment usually was to mill excitedly about, shouting and waving our arms, while the cameras ground. Sometimes Katie was in the same scene.

"What are you doing, Mommy?" I asked her once.

"I'm earning three dollars, too, today. Now I'll be able to buy you that little muffler you wanted."

One day we waited a long time. We grew blue with cold. Suddenly she exclaimed, "The devil with this! My children aren't going to freeze!" She bundled us up, took us all the way back home, and put us to bed under warm blankets. It was like a party, we told each other: we had never been home so early in the day before. "Babies," she said, "I'm going to heat some nice big rolls for you, with lots of butter and hot cocoa, and I'm going to bring it to you right in bed."

After our treat, she read us the Sunday comics until we fell asleep.

Later Ann and I were rewarded with steady acting jobs. While Ann played Theda Bara as a child on one set, on the other I was an angel in white gauze and lace, waiting to be born. We angels stood perched on a high platform facing a row of dazzling Kleig lights. Just before the action began, a man shouted a warning, "Children, don't look at the lights!"

They flashed on. I blinked, then stared, fascinated. As I watched, they changed shape; the slender incandescent spiral in the center became a winged man, then a glowing giant, growing taller and taller yet remaining the same.

We were homeward bound later, and I was trailing Mother, who was carrying Ann, when my eyes began to smart. I shut them tight, but the pain only increased. "Mommy, where are you!" I screamed. "I can't see you."

She thought I was playing a game. "What are you talking about, Lilly?" she asked over her shoulder. "I'm right in front of you."

"Mommy, I can't find you, I can't see you," I wailed.

She put Ann down and grabbed me up. I felt the pounding of her heart. She began to run, crying hysterically. "Oh, my baby, my baby," and I clung to her, my arms around her neck, my eyes feeling as though a million needles were stuck in them.

The doctor called it "Kleig eyes," and prescribed a rest in bed for me. My father comforted me. "Baby," he said, "you'll get used to those lights and become a great actress. Let's start right now." He taught me, "The Making of Friends," by Edgar A. Guest. I still remember the words, for they were my first dramatic lines.

They began:

"If nobody smiled and nobody cheered
    And nobody helped us along,
If every each moment looked after itself
    And the good things all went to the strong . . ."

"What's the use of that?" my mother asked. "She needs ballet, and singing lessons, and so many things—"

"She'll have those, too," said Dad. "But right now I want her to learn this, with all the hand motions, with expression!"

Quite without warning, I had to test my dramatic skill on Dad himself. Katie got word that children were being interviewed for parts in the film, "The Bluebird," and hurried down with me. Several children and their mothers

[20]

were already eagerly on hand. When the casting director came out to look us over, he pointed at a little girl who sat next to me. She rose and walked over to him. "Everybody else excused," he announced.

Katie and I and the others straggled out disconsolately. I sensed rather than knew that Mother was boiling.

It came like an explosion once we were outside. "Why didn't you get up when he pointed at you!"

"No he didn't, Mommy. He wanted that little Violet Mae sitting next to me."

My mother walked faster. I ran along in the snow, frightened, tripping, trying to keep up with her as she strode along. "He pointed at you and you wouldn't stand up!" Turning suddenly, she slapped me. The blow struck me as I tripped forward toward her: I was knocked off balance into the snow.

She cried out with horror. "Oh, my poor baby! What have I done!" She picked me up, and almost beside herself, began to cuddle and kiss me. My left eye was beginning to puff. "Oh, God, look what I've done!" And then, "Oh, my God, what will your father do when he finds out!"

She was rocking me in her arms, both of us crying. I smothered my mother's face with kisses. "Don't worry, Mommy," I managed to get out. "We can tell him I fell against this lamppost, can't we?" I pointed to one conveniently near.

"Oh, he won't believe it," she said miserably.

"Yes, he will. I *could* have slipped . . ."

We memorized our story on the way home. My father was in the kitchen when we arrived. When he saw me he uttered an exclamation. "Come over here, Lillian!

Let me look at that eye!"

I walked over slowly, my fingers crossed behind my back so that I could tell a fib without being a bad girl.

"How did this happen?"

"I slipped and fell against a lamppost, Daddy. It was very icy—"

My father looked up suspiciously at Katie, then back at me.

"Is that the truth?" he demanded.

"Yes it is, Daddy," I said stoutly. "And I can show you the place, too."

He surely knew then that I could not be telling the truth, but he only grumbled as Katie, maintaining a discreet silence, wrung out a cloth in water and held it tenderly to my eye.

I missed the part in "The Bluebird," but Ann and I played Constance and Norma Talmadge as children; then I was Evelyn Nesbit as a child; then we were cast to play General Pershing's daughters in the film, "Pershing's Crusaders."

Dad's dramatic coaching led only to such bit parts until one January afternoon when a crowd of us children were gathered on an icy Fort Lee hillside. We had been instructed to watch the child stars of the picture kiss each other before they tobogganed down the snowy slope. Wesley Barry, the freckle-faced male star, approached his leading lady to embrace her. But the scenarist hadn't reckoned with feminine modesty. Wesley's leading lady wouldn't kiss him.

Instead, she dissolved in tears and refused to go on.

The director threw out his arms despairingly. "What do we do now?" he demanded.

"I'll do it," I piped up. I was astounded to hear myself say it. The idea of kissing a boy was shocking to me. I could feel the shame burning my face as everyone turned to look at me: if I could have sunk into a snowbank, I would have. But perhaps I was inspired by the disastrous memory of what had happened earlier when I wasn't on my toes. In any case, Mother was beaming, and that was the important thing.

An onlooker called me over after the camera had taken its closeup. "What's your name?" he asked.

"Lillian Roth," I said.

He smiled. "My name's Roth, too." He turned to my mother. "I'm casting a show for the Shuberts and I'd like to see your child tomorrow. I think she's just the type. We're looking for a sad, pensive little girl."

Next day I was in his office. "Honey, can you do a little acting for me?" Mr. Roth asked.

"Oh, yes," I replied. "My daddy taught me 'The Making of Friends,' and I could do that for you." I recited it, with expression. When Katie brought me home, I ran to my father and told him the good news. I had been cast for Wilton Lackaye's little daughter in "The Inner Man," a full-fledged Broadway production.

Daddy was jubilant. "See, Katie, what did I tell you!" He picked me up, threw me into the air, and kissed me. "She's going to be a great dramatic actress. A tragedienne —that's what. Why, she'll be making $1,500 a week in no time!"

I had just turned six.

CHAPTER II

RAGEDIENNE or not, I had to go to school, and during the run of "The Inner Man" Katie enrolled me in the Professional Children's School. Classes were held only from 10 a.m. to 2 p.m., but in the four hours you crammed a full day's school work, including diction and French.

After classes Katie took me home, and when we were finished with dinner, made me up for my role as Mr. Lackaye's daughter. I soon discovered there was a great difference between reciting Edgar Guest—even with expression—and performing on the stage. "The Inner Man" called for me to sit on the lap of Mr. Lackaye, who played a criminal finally redeemed by the faith of his little girl. One of my poignant lines was "Daddy, Daddy, won't you PULLEASE come home with me?"

Mr. Lackaye gave me my first professional dramatic lesson.

"A play tells a story and you must pretend it's really happening," he explained. "You must pretend there's nobody in the theatre—no audience, no one back stage—just you and me and the other actors. You must pretend I'm your real father. And remember—never, *never* look at the audience."

He said this last so solemnly that my skin crawled.

What awful terror lurked out in that vast unknown? After the second day I couldn't hold my curiosity. For a breathless moment I lifted my eyes and looked directly into the forbidden darkness.

I almost screamed. Before me, as far as my eye could reach, was a weird ocean of pale, disembodied heads floating in a gray, ghostly dusk. I buried my face in my stage father's shoulder, and tried to catch my breath. There was something about Mr. Lackaye that was strangely comforting. I snuggled closer: the odor of tweed, the fragrance of talcum, and through it all, the familiar, sweet scent of whiskey—why, I thought, it was just like being on my real daddy's lap!

The Professional Children's School was made to order for those of us already working. If you had rehearsals or matinees, your schedule was arranged accordingly, and there were even correspondence lessons if you went on tour.

As at other schools, the mothers waited outside for classes to let out, but since they were stage mothers, their conversation was studded with Broadway names and punctuated by the rustle of newspaper clippings passed from hand to hand. My classmates' rollcall read like a theatrical *Who's Who* of the future: Ruby Keeler, Patsy Kelly, Milton Berle, Ben Grauer, Helen Chandler, Gene Raymond, Penny Singleton, Helen Mack, Marguerite Churchill, Jerry Mann, and many others.

Sometimes I got out earlier than the other students and overheard the mothers on their favorite subject—the talent of their offspring. For example, Mrs. Grauer: "I really think my Bunny has one of the finest speaking voices I've ever heard."

"Don't I know?" This from Katie. "Didn't I hear him recite 'The Midnight Ride of Paul Revere'? He was wonderful."

Or Sarah Berle, with whom mother often played casino: "Katie, you should have heard Milton at the benefit last night! He tore the house down. When he did Cantor, you'd have sworn it was Cantor. And when he got down on one knee to do Jolson—"

Mother would interrupt: "Shubert came to him and said, 'Get down on both knees, and Jolson goes!'"

They all laughed. They were proud of their children, and if Katie carried no clippings in her purse, it was because, as she once told me, "I didn't have to carry proof, Lilly. Your name was up in lights."

Milton Berle, who was several grades ahead of me but delighted in teasing me, did impressions, and even in those days he was accused of stealing someone else's act. Katie had taught Ann and me to save our acting for on stage: off stage we had to be perfect little ladies, like the little girls on Park Avenue. I couldn't understand this, because Milton acted all over school. The moment the teacher left the room, he was running up and down the aisles, clapping his hands a la Eddie Cantor, and sending the rest of us into gales of laughter.

The prettiest of my schoolmates, I thought, was Ruby Keeler. I admired her slim, tapering hands. Mine were stubby, and looked even worse because I bit my nails. I was so self-conscious of my hands that I hid them when I talked; so nobody could see them, I snatched at pencils and books, succeeding only in dropping everything so often that I was nicknamed "Butterfingers." Dr. Coué was the rage then, so I pulled hopefully at my fingers and recited, "Every day in every way they're getting more tapering and more tapering, like Ruby's." Critics today, interestingly enough, speak of the way I use my hands to put over a song. I had to learn graceful gestures to draw attention away from my hands.

As I hid my hands, so for a long while I hid my voice. I knew Katie wanted me to be a singer, and I tried. Dad was always singing about the house. I followed suit. One afternoon, I was singing at the top of my voice, "I'm Forever Blowing Bubbles," the current hit, when Katie looked up from her copy of *Variety*. "Oh, Lilly," she said, "that bubble really broke. That last note was way off key." She shook her head. "Just like your father—you can't even carry a tune."

I never forgot her words.

After that I sang in secret, practicing in the bathroom where I turned the taps on full strength in the tub to drown out my voice. The rushing water became my orchestral accompaniment: it became drums, oboes, bass fiddles. I *would* be a singer when I grew up. I would make Katie proud of me.

Katie, to be sure, overlooked few chances for me. After "The Inner Man" closed, a stock company put out a call for a little boy, and I was turned down. Katie hurried me home, dressed me in a velvet Lord Fauntleroy suit borrowed from a neighbor, and rushed me back. "This is my son, Billy," she said. I felt utterly disgraced, but I got the part.

Then Katie got word that Henry W. Savage was casting "Shavings," and had interviewed scores of children for a 50-page part. She had to be with Ann, who was playing in "The Magic Melody" that day, so she dropped me off at the producer's office. She'd learned the play was about a toyshop, and she briefed me. "Now, do your best, baby," she said. "And don't be shy."

Under orders, I approached the "Nothing doing" girl timidly, but with determination. "I would like to see Mr. Henry W. Savage," I announced. She peeked over the desk to find me. "I'm sorry, little girl, but you can only see Mr. Savage by appointment."

"Oh, well," I said. "I have an appointment."

She coughed to hide a smile, disappeared into the next room, and returned a moment later to say Mr. Savage would see me.

I walked into the adjoining room and stopped, transfixed. Behind a desk an enormous man was getting to his feet, rising taller and taller, until when he reached his full six feet four he seemed to tower over me like the giant in *Jack and the Beanstalk*. He was tremendous—massive, broad-shouldered, white-haired—with a voice to match. It boomed out, rattling the ashtrays on his desk. "Good afternoon, young lady. I hear we have an appointment."

I forgot all about my fib. "My mother told me you want a little girl to play a part in a toy shop," I managed to stammer.

He looked down at me from his awful height. Suddenly he said, "How would you ask me, 'Are you the windmill man?'"

All at once it came to me. That's who he looks like—Thor, the God of Wind and Thunder. "Are *you* the *windmill* man?" I asked, in great awe. For all I knew, he was.

Mr. Savage said, "You have the part."

[28]

"Shavings" put my name in lights for the first time. Just turned eight, I was billed as "Broadway's Youngest Star." Interviews with me were syndicated throughout the country. Wherever I turned, my face stared back at me, for photographs of Lillian and her one-eyed rag doll Petunia were placarded on subway pillars, telegraph poles and billboards.

Neither my photographs nor the growing scrapbook my parents kept meant much to me. What was exceptional about doing what you were told? Often I felt I'd have more fun with Ann playing Red Cross Nurse, helping the poor Belgian children orphaned by the Germans, a game all the other neighborhood children played. Now and then I stood in the wings and watched the rest of the show, but my eyelids would grow heavy, and Katie would take me into a dressing room, spread my coat over two chairs, and I would nap there until I was due onstage again.

Our home life, what we had of it, held little but inde-cision—and quarrels. My success, and Ann's during our early years, only stressed our insecurity. We seemed either to be transients, away on tour, or, when we were at home, caught in endless bickering between our parents.

When Dad courted Katie, he was known as the hand-somest boy on the block, she as the girl with the most personality. My mother was not beautiful, but she had an enchanting smile, and an immediate, warm sympathy that made her everyone's confidant. Arthur's charm was unmistakeable. Away from home he was merry and fun-loving, immensely popular. He began as a good-time drinker; then it developed into a problem, although liquor never took over his life as completely as it did mine.

Dad had big dreams. He tried his hand at everything, but never succeeded in becoming the man he wanted to be in the eyes of his wife and his children. He sold produce, then greeting cards, then men's clothing; he was a stock and bond salesman; he even operated a waffle shop. One failure followed another. Each time he tried to pass it off lightly. "Well, Katie," he would say, "that wasn't for me, anyway." And he would take a drink to forget it. I am sure, now, that ambitious as he was for us, his ego must have been hurt by the fact that Ann and I earned more than he, and that he was always going from job to job.

In time his drinking made him irritable and suspicious. Once, I remember, he accused Katie of poisoning our minds against him. She snapped, "If you ever saw yourself when you're full of whiskey—how can they love you when you frighten them to death?" I watched, terrified of the blow that might come: once I had seen him strike her. I knew how explosive their tempers were.

As it worked out, however, we were separated from Dad for long stretches from my 9th to my 15th year. For after "Shavings" Ann and I became vaudeville headliners on the Keith Circuit, and Mother travelled with us. This meant three to four months on the road, then back to New York for a brief layoff, and back on the road again. Our act was "Lillian Roth & Co." Ann was the "& Co." until her great sense of comedy caused Katie to change the billing to "The Roth Kids."

I did dramatic impersonations—impressions of Ruth Chatterton in "Daddy Long Legs," and of "Pollyanna," which I abhorred because she was "always glad all over." My greatest thrill came in my impersonation of John and Lionel Barrymore in the duelling scene from "The Jest." Here I could be the extrovert on stage that I could never be in real life. First I was John, taking my duelling stance, rapier in hand, my eyebrows cocked. "Methinks thou art a cur!" Lunge, and back again. "Thou buzzard!" I roared. Jab, and dance away. Then, in an instant, I whirled about and became Lionel, transformed into the wily, cunning cackling-voiced swordsman who parried John's violent thrusts with consummate disdain . . . The audience watched, silent and intent, and I was in raptures. I knew power, I glowed with the magic of the theatre, I felt the audience in the palm of my hand.

Then, bathed in perspiration and triumph, I bowed to thunderous applause and turned the stage over to Ann. My sister proceeded to throw herself into a brilliantly hilarious satire of my act. She burlesqued me down to the contemptuous curl of my imaginary mustache. The audience howled, and I suffered. The tragedienne in me was deeply hurt.

We played on bills with such headliners as Georgie Jessel, George Burns and Gracie Allen, Ben Bernie, and the Marx Brothers, and Katie taught us to curtsy to all of them, as was only proper with older persons. Rosie Green of Keno & Green, a comedy song and dance act, carried her baby, Mitzy, around in a little basket, and I often stopped to coo at her as she lay backstage laughing and gurgling.

"See my baby," Rosie once said to me. "She's going to grow up to be a great impersonator, too. Just like you, Lillian."

"Like me? Gosh," I said, flattered. I was all of 10 years old.

Once, in Washington, D. C., Ann and I were told that the President of the United States was in his box that afternoon. After the show the stage manager hurriedly knocked at our dressing room door. "The President wants to see you, kids!" he exclaimed.

Still in our costumes, we rushed out the stage entrance into the back alley, and there they were, President Wilson and the first lady, sitting in a huge open touring car. The President asked us to get in. Ann sat on his lap. I sat shyly between him and Mrs. Wilson.

"What a serious little girl you are, both on and off the stage," the President said to me. "You know, I am going to make a prediction, young lady. Some day you will be a great actress." Then he turned to Ann. "And you, my dear, you were utterly delightful. Mrs. Wilson and I haven't laughed so much in a long time."

I found my voice and thanked him. Ann, busy examining and fingering the interior of the luxurious car, piped up, to my mortification, "Ooh, what a big auto! My daddy has a tin lizzie." The President smiled and turned to Mrs. Wilson. "Shall we take our little guests for a ride around the block?" Away we drove. When we emerged into the street outside, it was jammed with people held back by police on both sides. They waved and applauded as we passed by, and then we were brought back to the stage entrance again.

"Goodbye, little girls, and stay sweet," Mrs. Wilson

called back to us as their chauffeur drove them away. I thought, as we went to our dressing room to put on our street clothes, it was just like a beautiful fairy tale—like Cinderella's ride in the pumpkin coach.

Mostly, however, vaudeville on the road was a hard life, made up of lonely train rides (even now a train whistle fills me with haunting sadness), lonely nights in strange hotels, and lonely cities in which we knew no one. "The Roth Kids" in lights in town after town meant little to us. Wistfully Ann and I looked out the train windows, watching the endless procession of backyard gardens flow by, catching a glimpse of little family groups, of children playing with their pets, of mother and father contentedly together on a back porch. We yearned for a home, a garden, a hammock, a sense of belonging.

Like prisoners Mother, Ann and I counted off the days until we got back to New York. "Where do we go next, Mommy?" I would ask. Katie would produce a long slip of green paper. "Hattfield, for three days." "Then where, Mommy?" "Pittsfield, for a split week." And so it was—four days, three days, and week stands, month after month.

But when we returned to New York—and Dad—there were only arguments after the affectionate greetings of the first few hours. For added to Dad's uncontrollable temper was his jealousy.

"Did Mother ever leave you alone between shows," he would ask, taking me aside. "Was she with you all the time?"

I knew Mother went nowhere. Time and again I awakened to see her sitting beside us, reading by the little table light, reluctant to slip into bed with us because of what terrors the night might hold. She feared the darkness, and often in a hotel she saw—or thought she saw —a man peeking over our transom.

Once she was sure of it. She woke us, frantically. "Babies—babies—get up, hurry up, there's a man after us!"

She could hardly dress Ann in her panic. My fingers were all thumbs as I tried to button my clothes. I was sick with the terror on my mother's face. I went into a cold sweat. My heart pounded in my ears. I was sure something monstrous was breathing in the room.

Then we were rushing out and down the stairs into the dimly lit lobby and Mother was screaming at the lone desk clerk—not knowing but that he might have been the man himself. Then we were running through the dark streets, my mother shrieking for help, until we found another place to spend the night. But there was no more sleep.

Once I woke to find her brushing things off us. "What are you doing, Mommy?" I asked sleepily. "Get out of bed," she said excitedly. "It's full of bedbugs!" Minutes later she had us dressed and furiously rushed us out of the hotel.

The streets of the small towns were always deserted late at night when we walked from the theatre to our hotel. What might not be lurking behind every tree, every shadow? Sometimes we heard footsteps behind us. We hurried, and the footsteps quickened, and I was limp with fear until we reached the bright lights of the hotel.

Back in New York the arguments grew more bitter. I was in an agony of shame when my father began his accusations, sometimes behind the locked door of their bedroom. I became hot and cold, I tore at my nails. How could I face people who heard them screaming at each other?

Once, a quarrel broke out between them in the kitchen. They began to struggle, and something exploded in me. "Stop it!" I screamed hysterically. "Stop it, I can't stand it!" I grabbed my glass piggy bank and threw it with all my might between them, trying to separate them. It crashed against the wall. My parents, startled, turned to me, and a moment later I was in Katie's arms, and we were both sobbing.

Dad was all remorse. He took a quick drink and then another. "How could I do this to my Katie! To my Lilly!" He began to cry. "They can string me up from a tree if I ever lay a hand on you again, Katie!"

My mother could only shake her head. "You and your crocodile tears." She wept, and took me into the bedroom, where Ann slept, undisturbed.

On another occasion, at a gathering, a handsome man engaged Katie in a long, bantering conversation. Dad's face grew pale. He was in an ugly mood when we came home. For a while he drank silently.

Then—"Will you be good enough to tell me—" he began, grinding his teeth as he always did when he was about to explode.

"Arthur. The children . . ."

Praying they would not fight, I tiptoed to bed. But suddenly I heard piercing screams. I leaped out of bed and ran into the kitchen. My mother lay on the floor, blood trickling from the corners of her mouth, her eyes puffed, her face bruised. She was rolling wildly back and forth, screaming uncontrollably, catching her breath, then sobbing and screaming again.

My father, a long red gash on his face, was in his bathrobe, slumped in a chair, his eyes glassy, a bottle beside him. He moaned to himself, "Oh my God, Lillian what did I do?"

He rose, as if to go to my mother, but she shrieked, "Don't come near me—don't touch me!" He fell back into his chair.

I pulled her to a couch and cradled her head in my lap, while my father repeated dully, "Do something, Lillian, do something." I was sick to my stomach with fear and horror, and with a compassion I could not put into words. My mother moaned and wept, and my father slumped in his chair, looking at nothing.

I spent the remainder of the night running between the living room, where my mother lay weeping, and the kitchen, where my father sat staring at the wall, and drinking. Katie fell asleep, finally, but I was in the kitchen every few minutes, tugging at my father's arm, shaking him, imploring him, "Please don't fall asleep, Daddy, please, please!" I did not know what I feared, but I knew he had to remain awake, he *had* to remain awake.

For years afterward there were many nights that I could not fall asleep until daylight came through my bedroom window.

CHAPTER III

I was twelve when Katie, seeking new stage personalities for me to impersonate, took me to see Lenore Ulric in "Kiki." I fell in love with her. What fire and passion in her performance! Oh, I thought, if only I could be like her!

At Katie's suggestion I took enough courage to write her a note, and she invited me to her home. I trembled as I rang the bell.

Miss Ulric herself opened the door. I was overwhelmed for a moment by this exotic, vibrant personality, dressed in beautiful black satin pajamas.

"Oh, Miss Ulric, I'm Lillian Roth who wrote you about impersonating you," I burst out.

"Good heavens," were her first words. "You look enough like me to be my twin. A little twin!"

"Oh, thank you, Miss Ulric," I said breathlessly. "That's what many people tell me, and you're my idol!"

She put her arms around me and kissed me. Then, to her maid, "Bring in some cake and milk." She turned to me. Was there any scene in the play I would like to do?

I told her it was the scene in which Kiki, brandishing a stiletto, turns on the society lady who seeks to steal her lover and cries, "I am a Corsican! My father is Corsican!

My mother is Corsican! And when we are angry, we
know how to use the knife. We do it like this—"

I seized the cake knife and launched into her scene.

"Wonderful! Wonderful!" she applauded. "*Very, very*
good. But you must lower your voice deep into your
throat, and you must run your hand wildly through your
hair." She did the scene several times for me, and then
later said, "If you feel you haven't the characterization
just right, come back."

I added Helen Mencken, Judith Anderson and Jeanne
Eagels to my repertoire. How electric Jeanne Eagels was
in "Rain," how alive—every move, every turn, a picture.
Oh, I thought, to be a dramatic actress! What was vaudeville compared to the legitimate stage—a full three hour
show in which you felt so deeply, in which you reached
out and touched people's *souls*.

Suddenly Dad was in the big money. While we were
on tour, he had gotten a job as head salesman for a Fifth
Avenue clothier and earned as much as $300 a week. He
used much of it, plus some of our money, for "invest-
ments." He was always going to hit on something that
would bring us a fortune overnight. Then, he promised,
he would buy us everything we wanted, including the
house and garden.

Now that he was doing well, Katie was finally able to
realize one of her dreams—a private school for us. She
decided to take us out of show business for a year, so
that I could attend Clark School of Concentration, a fash-
ionable cram school. My one term here, as it turned out,
completed my formal education.

I entered Clark like the little lady Katie wanted me to

be. She bought me a $1,000 wardrobe. Overnight, my socks and oxfords were discarded along with my childhood. I had been skipped several grades at the Professional School, and was only thirteen when I received my diploma. Now, at Clark, I found my classmates were three and four years older than I. On the threshold of fourteen, I was a grownup without even having known what it was to be a child.

Today when I come upon John Held, Jr's drawings of flappers in the fabulous 20's, I see myself. Silk blouse, dangerously short skirt; rolled stockings, red garters with bells, long fluffy bob (after Ulric), and a vanity case piled high with makeup and cigarettes. I didn't smoke. But the advertisement read, "Be nonchalant. Light a Murad." And I wanted to be nonchalant, I wanted to be sophisticated.

But I knew the picture I saw of myself was wrong. For I was anything but nonchalant. I was impatient, impatient for I knew not what, driven by an energy I could not control. I seemed to have a clock ticking in me faster than any one else's: time itself could not move swiftly enough. I was full of anxieties—whether people liked me, whether my acting was adequate, whether I was as good as I should be.

Often I discussed this with my best friend, Minna Gellert. She was a year older, a shy girl who wrote poetry. Until I met her, at 13, I had not even had a close friend. I envied the serene atmosphere of her home, and I envied her poetic ability. That, I thought, was real talent. And although I was busy with rehearsals, dancing, music, acrobatics, I felt they were mundane accomplishments. I was discontented, tormented by an inner compulsion to be the prettiest, the best, the greatest. When things became too hectic for me—when it seemed I wanted to leap out of my skin, stop all the clocks, loosen all the bonds—I would confide in Minna. "Why am I so tense?" I would ask, despairingly. "Why can't I slow down!"

"Lillian," she would reply in her slow, calm way. "It's only that you have all that creative ability in you. Just give yourself a chance. You haven't found yourself yet." And so she soothed me.

The classmate I was most interested in at Clark was Leo Fox, a tall, dark, curly-haired boy of 17. I concentrated the Ulric look on him in history class one day, and soon he was taking me for ice-cream sodas and Saturday night movies. He was my first flame. The girls tagged him "Lillian's sheik." Another schoolmate was Carl Laemmle, Jr., whose father was president of Universal Pictures. He called for me in a chauffeur-driven Stutz Bearcat, the last word in rakish automobiles, and we talked about the movies of tomorrow. On our first date he put his arm around me and in a warm, confidential voice, murmured, "You know, Lillian, some day I'll be a big Hollywood producer." "Oh, yes," I said, deftly extricating myself. "My father always says, 'Talent will out.'" Junior took the hint.

Besides, hadn't a critic in the New York *World* written: "Thirteen year old Lillian Roth is a real find. She has a dramatic sense unusual in one so young, a dramatic intensity which bids fair to see her go far on the road to stardom."

Toward the end of my school term, Willie Howard, the

comedian, saw me at a benefit performance. He took Katie aside. "She's too big to be doing kid stuff," he said. "Why don't you try her out for a show?"

He jotted something down on his calling card. "Here," he said, "Tell Lillian to take this to Jake Shubert and say Willie Howard sent her."

The following Monday, having cut classes, I was ushered into Mr. Shubert's presence. After all, Willie Howard had written: "Dear J. J. This is Lillian Roth. Star material."

Mr. Shubert looked on either side of me, then caught me in a swift, sidewise glance—a habit of his—and asked softly, "What can you do?"

"I'm a dramatic actress," I announced.

"Sorry, little girl." He turned away. "We're casting for 'Artists and Models.' I need singers."

"I sing, too," I said, my fingers crossed.

"All right," he said, after a moment. "Come back at nine o'clock. I'll hear you."

At the appointed hour I found nearly 200 persons—the entire cast—onstage. Was I to audition before all of them? Mr. Shubert walked into the empty theatre. "Go ahead," he flung over his shoulder. "Sing!"

Standing in the midst of the cast, and still in hat and coat, I sang "Red Hot Momma." Mr. Shubert was somewhere out in the darkness, but I couldn't see him. Well, I thought with a sinking feeling, I guess Katie was right about my singing. I began to leave the stage.

"Where are you going?" came his voice. "Let's have another number."

I tossed off my hat and coat and gave everything to "Hot Tamale Mollie."

Silence. Then Mr. Shubert's voice rumbled, "How old are you?"

"I'm going on fifteen."

"Wait around. I'll talk to you later."

After the auditions he asked if I knew the regulations of the Gerry Society, which looked after juveniles in the theatre. I was too young to sing or dance in New York. But, he said, "I'll put you in my Chicago company. We can change your age there. From now on, you're 18, Lillian."

I ran all the way home and barged into our apartment. "Mom," I shouted, "meet your 18-year-old singing soubrette—the star of 'Artists and Models!' "

My mother almost fell off her chair.

I was not, of course, the star of "Artists and Models," but I was a singer—and being paid for it. The joy, however, was not quite what I expected. For Mr. Shubert might change my age, but I was still 14—and "Artists and Models" shocked me. It introduced me to nudity—and to headaches, the kind of headaches I suffered later whenever I couldn't cope with a situation. I shared a hot, sticky cellar dressing room with 20 showgirls who posed in the finale uncovered from the waist up. I had never undressed before another girl, and the nonchalance with which they strolled about backstage with hardly a stitch on, and the equal near-nudity of the chorus boys, who called each other "Betty" and "Mildred," distressed me.

When I complained of headaches, Marie Stoddard, a kindly woman who played character parts in the show, took me in hand. "Christian Science can help you," she said. She gave me a copy of Mary Baker Eddy's *Science and Health with Key to the Scriptures,* and a small Bible, and showed me chapters in both to read every night.

"Lillian," she said to me one afternoon, when my head seemed gripped in a vise and I had to hold back the tears, "your pain is only a dream. Try to understand that, dear. You are part of God's mind, and God's mind sees no evil and feels no evil." She sat beside my cot and was so gentle and persuasive that often my headaches seemed to vanish. She spoke constantly of Jesus Christ. "Many of the Jewish faith read Christian Science," she assured me. "It doesn't interfere with their creed. It merely tries to prove that we are all part of one mind—the mind of God."

As I once tried Dr. Coué for my hands, I now invoked Christian Science for my headaches, wandering about repeating, "I have no headache . . . My headache isn't real. . . ."

The chorus boys liked me and used to protest to Katie that she wasn't letting me grow up. "Why don't you get her out of those skirts and blouses? Her figure is developing beautifully." They showed me how to bead my eyelashes and even whipped up a sophisticated dress for me. "Never laugh at the way they act or talk," Katie warned me. "They're born that way. They have a marvellous sense of humor and they can be wonderful company."

Since there wasn't anyone my age in the show and I was lonely, it wasn't surprising that Katie allowed me to go to a company party one Saturday night. Immediately after the show the full company piled into half-a-dozen automobiles. I was taken by the stage manager, who promised he'd bring me back safe and sound. We drove for miles until we reached a huge barn-like house near River Forest, which had been rented for the occasion.

Once inside, I gaped. Were these men—or women? They wore hats pulled down to one side, carried canes, wore monocles, cigarettes dangled from their lips; they wore stiff collars and ties, tight, narrow skirts, low-heeled shoes, three quarter coats. Then I got it. These were chorus boys in reverse! But boys were there, too. The girls called other girls "Bob" and "Johnny," and the boys whistled and shrieked at each other. Nearly everyone got drunk. For most of the party I sat in a corner, wide-eyed, drinking sasparilla and taking it all in.

A boy wiggled himself into a beaded outfit and did the shimmy. A girl danced nude on a table. Women danced wildly with other women; then every few minutes a pair would disappear to another part of the barn, out of sight. I felt a little ill. Vaguely I knew there was something dark and wrong here, but nothing quite crystallized in my mind.

I asked my escort, "What are they doing? Where are they going together?"

He laughed, and shrugged it off, and the mystery remained.

When I came home Katie asked sleepily, "Did you enjoy yourself, baby?"

"Fair, Mom," I said. "Nobody asked me to dance."

I didn't know how to begin to tell her.

Shortly after this Katie took me out of the show, pleading illness. My headaches had become worse, and the best the doctors could advise, finding nothing organically wrong, was a change of scene. It was just as well, Katie said. "Artists and Models" was no place for a girl my age.

We returned to New York.

"All you need, darling," said Katie, "is a good rest."
And then she placed balm upon my head. "You've proved
yourself a singer, you dance beautifully, you act well—
you're going to become a big musical comedy star!"

CHAPTER IV

IF ANYONE typified the years in which I was coming to womanhood, it was Texas Guinan. Those were the years of Harding and Coolidge, of marathon dances and the Charleston, of Peaches Browning and Rudolph Valentino and Lucky Lindy.

I had just finished a Keith tour in which I had introduced "How Many Times," "When the Red Red Robin Comes Bob Bob Bobbin' Along" and "Ain't She Sweet," when two of Texas' backers heard me rehearsing at Irving Berlin's offices. They were putting up the money to bring her famous nightclub review, "Texas Guinan's Padlocks of 1927," to Broadway. They asked me to audition for her.

I was sixteen and shy—I thought I knew all the answers (after all, I *had* been in "Artists and Models")—but I was still a little girl who played "Spin the Bottle" at parties and kept company with Leo Fox when his parents allowed him to go out with a wicked actress like myself. La Guinan, raucous and uninhibited, was something special for me.

Meeting Texas was like meeting a hurricane head on. I walked into Shubert's 44th Street Theatre and the first sight I saw was a well-proportioned five-foot six blonde on the stage, with blue mascared eyelashes, scarlet cupid's-bow lips, and beads hanging from her neck to her hips. She was storming at everyone about her. For a moment I was petrified. Suddenly she saw me, and stared.

"I'm Lillian Roth," I said meekly.

She looked me over. "Well, kid," she rasped, in a voice like a man's, "I hear you're pretty good. Let's hear you sing."

Halfway through my number she interrupted me. "Where's the life in you, kid? They told me you're a dynamo. What's doing?" Then, to no one in particular, "I thought this kid was a bombshell." And to me, again, "If that's all you're going to do on the stage, it stinks!"

My face burned, but I became Jeanne Eagels. "I'm sorry, Miss Guinan," I said icily. "I have just finished my B. F. Keith Circuit and I can go right back to it. In addition, you sent for me, I didn't send for you." I began to stalk off the stage.

Texas relented. "Come back, kid," she said, "don't get excited." She put her arm around me. "Just live up to your notices, and we'll be friends."

Never my best at rehearsals—even today I must have an audience—I became more and more jittery. The night before dress rehearsal, I got laryngitis: I was left with a croak. Texas shifted her gum from her left to her right cheek. "I just knew something like this would happen." Then to me, "Well, kid, I sure hope that by tomorrow night it comes back, because it looks like the finish if you don't make it by then."

I went home in tears. "I'm not ready for it," I cried. "I'll be awful." Even Katie became doubtful. But Dad took control. He hurried to the medicine cabinet and returned with an armful of sprays, syrups and lozenges.

"Look, baby," he said, "stop putting fears into yourself. You're going to be the best thing in that show and I'm telling you—your voice is coming back!"

He dosed me with medicines, sprayed my throat, poured hot tea into me, and packed me into bed under a mountain of blankets. I sweated through the night. Whatever the case—Dad's first aid, Marie Stoddard's Christian Science, or an inner compulsion to please Katie—my voice came back, strong and clear.

Since I appeared only in the first act, Katie and I went home early to wait for the morning newspapers. Friends dropped in to keep vigil. Katie bustled about nervously, serving ice cream and cake, and I sat biting my fingernails. The telephone rang. It was Milton Berle.

"Golly," he said, and there was awe in his voice. "Lillian, you ran away with the show! Wait until you see the *American.* Let me read it to you!"

The critic of the New York *American* had written: "This little girl comes through the curtains shortly after nine o'clock to smash across three songs in the outstanding performance of the show . . . She does a number of things marvellously well, and she has more personality to the square inch than any musical comedy actress seen by this reviewer this season."

Milton and his mother hurried over. We celebrated until dawn, every newcomer bursting in waving a copy of the *American.* Dad all but strutted. "Well, I told you, Katie!" And my mother: "Oh, Arthur, you really know my Lilly. O. K., you take the bows!"

The road up became glamorous. Winnie Lightner, by all odds the top song comedienne of the day, was expected to leave Delmar's "Revels" because of illness. Frank Fay, co-starring with her, Bert Lahr and Patsy Kelly, told me about it when we met on Broadway shortly after "Padlocks" closed. "You work a lot like her," said Frank. "Why don't you catch the show. I think you'd be fine in her part."

"Oh, gosh, Mr. Fay, would I?" I had my doubts, and they increased when I watched her perform that night in all her magnificently hoydenish style. I can never be that great, I thought. It was a long way from doing a specialty with Texas Guinan, and filling the shoes of the great Winnie Lightner. But I took home her lyrics and studied them that night.

I was in the audience the following afternoon just before the curtain rose. There was a tap on my shoulder. It was an usher.

"You're wanted backstage, Miss Roth."

Winnie was sick. I had to go on immediately.

A few minutes later I was singing her song, "I Love a Man in a Uniform." I floated off the stage on waves of applause. Her smash hit had become one for me, too.

The "Revels" grand finale thrilled me as nothing before. Whereas the finale of "Artists and Models" seemed inane to me, with its nudes and waving hands, this was pure theatre. Frank Fay stood on stage at the left, and announced the cast as they paraded, one by one, down a long center staircase.

First came the chorus girls, then the smaller principals, then the principals, and then the stars, Patsy Kelly and Bert Lahr. Then Frank's voice boomed out: "And now— Miss—Lillian—Roth!" I appeared, to a fanfare of trumpets, and descended the steps to the tune of "I Love a Man in a Uniform," with six handsome boys dressed as West Point cadets on either side. The suspense until I appeared, the regal quality I was invested with, the growing crescendo of applause leading up to the thunder when I appeared—I really cried for joy on the stage. The knowledge that Katie, standing in the wings, was almost ready to burst with pride—this was it!

It was only a step from "Revels" to Earl Carroll's "Vanities of 1928." At 17 I was signed, at $400 a week. The new show had a fabulous cast. Sidney Skolsky was press agent, Herman Hover, later manager of Ciro's in Hollywood, was stage manager, and Busby Berkeley, choreographer.

The afternoon of the opening I came to rehearsal and found the marquée blazing with names. There they were: W. C. Fields; Ray Dooley; Joe Frisco; Dorothy Knapp, the most beautiful girl in the world; Barto and Mann; Vincent Lopez and his band. But the name of Lillian Roth was nowhere to be seen. I read the marquée twice, to make sure. Then I walked into the theatre and stalked across the stage to where Earl Carroll stood talking to others in the cast.

"Mr. Carroll," I said in a trembling voice, "I see the lights are going up. I'm one of the principals. You have every one on that marquée outside but me and the man who sweeps the stage."

Mr. Carroll focused his pale blue eyes on me.

"Who do you think you are?" he asked softly.

I told him. "I'm Lillian Roth, Broadway's youngest star. I was 'The Roth Kids.' I was a star on B. F. Keith's Circuit. I replaced Winnie Lightner in the 'Revels.' I was in Texas Guinan's 'Padlocks.' I was a star at the Chateau Madrid. And, Mr. Carroll," I went on, my voice rising as I reached a familiar line, "you sent for me, I didn't send for you."

There was a shocked silence. Mr. Carroll looked at me thoughtfully, as if seeing me for the first time. I met his eye defiantly. He stood there, a tall, thin, baldish man with long whispy hair, a worn gray artist's smock over his frail body. There were two things he could do. He could take me over his knee and spank me, or he could kick me out of the show.

Instead, he grabbed my arm and dragged me off the stage, through the stage door and out into the alley into 50th street, crowded with people. "I'll show you how many people know you," he muttered. When I caught my balance, he was buttonholing one passerby after another, demanding, "Do you know Lillian Roth? Have you ever heard of Lillian Roth?"

Some, taken aback by this startling apparition, halted for a moment, then hurried on. "What are you talking about?" one man exclaimed, shaking himself loose. Another went along with what he thought was a gag. "No, who is she?" But he didn't wait for an answer.

Mr. Carroll wheeled on me. "All right, young lady, now you know. Remember this: the people who go to see you in vaudeville don't pay seven-seventy, and the people who pay seven-seventy to see my show don't know you."

I was undismayed. "Well," I retorted furiously, "if you'd asked them if they knew Winnie Lightner the way you asked them if they knew me, they wouldn't know what you're talking about, either. I'm leaving. Goodbye!"

[51]

I was heartbroken. I cried all the way home, and when I arrived there, Katie folded me in her arms. "You're right," she declared. "You've worked all your life. If you don't fight for what's yours, who will?"

"Oh, Mom," I wailed through my tears, "imagine, Earl Carroll's 'Vanities'!"

Reality came quickly in an ultimatum from the theatre. If I wasn't back before the performance, injunctions would be brought against me by both Mr. Carroll and Actor's Equity. I'd never work a Broadway show again.

Mother and I tearfully talked it over. We were beaten. My contract had no provision for featured billing.

But if I failed to make the marquée lights, I had the "Vanities" to thank for Beryl Halley, "The Form Divine," one of Mr. Carroll's featured show-girls. She took me under her wing. I weighed 135 pounds. Beryl, who was my height, weighed only 118. The reason for the difference wasn't hard to find.

Like all the principals, I had a maid. The maids did little but straighten your makeup table and hook up a few dresses. They were there for prestige, mainly. My girl, though, had a special job. Every few hours she vanished in the direction of the corner soda fountain and returned with a hot fudge sundae or a banana split buried in whipped cream.

One day while I was devouring one of these, Beryl came into my room. She watched me silently for a minute, until I came up for air. Then she spoke. "Lillian, you disgust me."

"Really," I said complacently. "Why?"

"Look at me and look at you! I could slice you in half and you'd still look better. Don't you ever want to be anything in the profession? Don't you ever think of star-dom?"

"Oh," I said, "I've known some fat stars. There's Sophie Tucker and Belle Baker—they're doing all right."

"But your face calls for something else. Don't you see yourself playing the love interest in motion pictures some day?"

"Me? I'm no beauty," I replied, flicking a blob of whipped cream off my nose. "They have people like you to be beautiful. I just sing songs."

Beryl sighed. "Oh, Lillian. Take a good look in the mirror. You've got potentialities if you wouldn't stuff yourself like a little pig."

I looked in the mirror. There might be something in what Beryl said. I went on a diet, under her guidance: apples, oranges and lamb chops. In addition, Mr. Carroll had installed a vibrating machine for the girls in a corner of the rehearsal room, and I dutifully strapped myself into that. I was in its grip one night, shaking vigorously, when Mr. Carroll strolled in. "Well," he said, "you're really taking care of yourself." He walked up to me, lifted my face to his, and kissed me, a far-from-ethereal kiss, while the vibrater vibrated me and him along with it, giving me the oddest sensation. "You're such a little girl," he said, his words trembling with everything else. "This kiss is a little present from me." And he went on to his office.

As I unhooked myself from the machine, I thought: this is the first time Earl Carroll has given me more than casual notice since the day I walked out on him. I began to understand. Perhaps it wasn't the talent you had, or the personality—it was the form divine.

[53]

After all, I had slimmed down from 135 to 116.

Perhaps it *was* the form divine. A few days later the William Fox Picture Company asked me to make a screen test. "What did I tell you?" demanded Beryl, triumphantly. "You were just hiding your potentialities."

As we viewed the test later, the director said, "My dear, if I were you, I'd forget all about a picture career."

My heart sank. "Why?"

"Don't you notice anything about your smile? Your smile is crooked. In pictures," he said, in the voice of a man stating a law of nature, "in pictures one must have perfection. Nothing less will do." I could not know that a year and a half later I was to be engaged by Paramount because—among other reasons—my smile, being crooked, was full of personality.

I was so discouraged I went home and ate a chocolate eclair.

CHAPTER V

I HAVE a vivid memory of my first drink. I had just turned seventeen. A few minutes before midnight, 1928, I stood excitedly in my new formal at the "Vanities" stage-door. Inside, the cast were wishing one another a riotously Happy New Year. (Only an hour before the performance W. C. Fields almost broke us all up by grabbing a broom and chasing a process-server up and down the empty aisles, yowling at the top of his voice.) I was waiting for Leo Fox to pick me up: Katie had given me permission to stay out late that night for a New Year's Eve party with our classmates from Clark, and to greet 1929 with a class breakfast.

There was Leo, jaunty in a new tuxedo, holding open a cab door. "Come on, Lil. We're late."

"Gosh, you look slick, Leo," I said admiringly, and I thought how lucky I was, because all the girls admired him, but he had eyes only for me. On the way over in the cab, Leo pulled out a flask. "Lil, I've got something here. We've got to catch up with the other kids."

Leo and I had never drunk anything but ice-cream sodas together. But this was an occasion. He put the flask to my lips. "Have a nip." I took my first drink. It burned my throat, and I felt the blood rush to my face.

"Gee, Leo, that's great. What is it?"

"Fermented prune juice," he said. It was his own pro-
hibition home-brew, he added proudly. I thought, it's
probably good for my complexion. Sure speeds up the
circulation. I felt warm all over. As we stopped before
the hotel, I said, "I think I'll have another one of those
just before we get in, Leo."

When we reached our table, someone said, "Have a
drink." I drank. This was much stronger. I coughed and
sputtered, but again I felt wonderful. Suddenly the sirens
sounded, the bells rang, the horns tooted: it was midnight. People hugged and kissed each other. Gaily colored streamers shot through the air, the orchestra became alive, and the lights went out.

I loved everybody. My shyness vanished. The clock in
my head slowed down. "Oh, this is glorious," I thought.
"I'm walking on air. I'm going to hug every person in this
room and disappear. I'll vanish. Leo will have to search
for me." I began to weave my way through the enormous
ballroom, amid the flying streamers, the voices shouting
"Happy New Year," the music rippling and throbbing
and cascading all about me. At each table it seemed my
arm was grabbed. "Come on, little girl, down the hatch!"
I drank with everybody and I drank everything they gave
me. I glowed; an indescribable sense of freedom, a desire
to open my heart and enfold the whole shining rapturous
world overwhelmed me.

The room began to spin. Then I was sitting in the
dimly lit lobby, violently sick over my beautiful dress,
over Leo's new tuxedo. The music was far away, in the
ballroom two flights above, and a bellboy was trying to
help Leo clean me up. I was utterly ashamed.

"We'd better go home," Leo was saying.

"What time is it?" I asked dazedly.

It was 12:50. In fifty minutes I had gone through an entire gamut of emotions, and passed out. My experience wasn't unusual, I know now. Other girls my age, drinking as much as I had for the first time, would have reacted much the same. There wasn't the slightest hint, that New Year's Eve, that between alcohol and me there would soon develop a bond so overpowering that until almost the very end I believed only death could break it.

Leo managed to get me into a cab. Minutes later we rang our doorbell. "Home so soon, baby?" my mother's voice came sleepily. "Oh, Mom, go back to bed," I said. "I had a little accident. I'm going to change my dress and we're going right out again." I said it gaily. I was confident that however sick I was, all I needed was will power to conquer it.

I sat on the daybed for a moment, Leo beside me, holding me up. Then it was daylight, and Katie was shaking me. We had fallen asleep, fully-dressed, half stretched out, half-propped up against the wall, shoulder to shoulder. My mother gave Leo coffee and sent him home.

"Oh, Mom," I said. "I sure don't know why Dad likes to drink. It's awful! I feel terrible—if for those few minutes of fun I could get this sick—I'll never touch that stuff again."

Katie laughingly bathed and rubbed me down, then sent me off to bed.

My father wasn't there to give his expert advice. He and Katie had separated—permanently.

Florenz Ziegfeld sent for me, just as "Vanities" was

about to close. He sat at his big desk with half a dozen miniature elephants on it, and Gene Buck, his Man Friday, sat off to one side. "I'm told you're a talented little lady," Ziegfeld said quietly. "Let's hear what you've got." He called in an accompanist, and we did one of my favorites, "Gimme a Little Kiss, Will You, Huh?"

Not once did Ziegfeld look up. He sat there, thumbing through papers, doddling, and rearranging his elephants. I thought, bravely, if you can sing to J. J. Shubert's back, you can sing to the top of Mr. Ziegfeld's head. My song over, I bowed a "Good afternoon, Mr. Ziegfeld," and began to leave.

He looked up then. "When is the show closing?"

"Next week," I said automatically.

"Then we start rehearsing next week—my new Ziegfeld's 'Midnight Frolics.' You'll be the ingenue lead."

I was engaged, at $500 a week.

There was no question that Ziegfeld's New Amsterdam Theatre Roof was the smartest nightclub in New York. After they finished "glorifying" the Follies in the theatre downstairs, Ziegfeld's gorgeous show girls trouped upstairs to appear in the Frolics. It was a glittering show. Ted Husing was master of ceremonies, and Paul Whiteman conducted the orchestra, opening with "Rhapsody in Blue," with Henry Busse at the trumpet. Ziegfeld's girls paraded to "A Pretty Girl is Like a Melody" after which Ted brought me on for a song and dance. In the cast were Helen Morgan, the Duncan Sisters, and the Rhythm Boys—Al Rinker, Harry Barris and Bing Crosby.

As Lenore Ulric had once been, now Helen Morgan became my idol. Her exquisite beauty, her charm even when she had been drinking, worked their magic over the audience. Perched on her piano, singing her plaintive melodies in that sad, husky voice, twisting her handkerchief in the bitter-sweet anguish of her song and her life, she sang straight into your heart. She had just finished a long run in Ziegfeld's "Showboat," and was still the toast of Broadway. But something was happening to her, and presently Ruth Etting was brought up from "Whoopee," and took Helen's place.

One of my worst nights was when Ziegfeld let Rinker, Barris and Crosby go. I had a quiet crush on Bing. I loved his casual singing style, the way he clashed a cymbal as though clashing one was the last thing he wanted to do. Ziegfeld, just back from a European tour, apparently decided the cymbal didn't fit in with the lofty tone of his show. The Rhythm Boys had to go.

Offstage, Bing was mild-mannered and quiet, a rather lonely person who seemed to need mothering. When he crooned in the style that later made him famous, shivers ran up and down my spine.

Often, after the show, knowing Katie's fear of the night, Bing walked us through the lonely streets to a well-lighted section near where we lived, bade us a gallant goodnight, and sauntered off. Katie had a way with lonely people; they liked her, and she was comforting to them. After the trio was let out, I asked Bing what he thought he might do next.

"I don't know, honey," he said. Then, thoughtfully, "We might go out and take a look around Hollywood."

CHAPTER VI

Wᴴᴇɴ my big break came, it came suddenly. Al
Jolson's "The Jazz Singer" burst upon the world and
launched the "Talkies." It sounded the doom of vaudeville; and it also posed the question: how many ways
could the human voice be used on the screen?

Shortly after I opened in the Frolics, Jesse Lasky of
Paramount tested me for something new in films—one
and two reel singing shorts. I went before the camera and
sang some of my popular songs directly to the audience,
trying to achieve a rapport with them until they actually
sang in their seats.

The test was successful. "Why these short subjects
then?" I asked Mr. Lasky. "Why can't I get into a big
picture?"

"It doesn't work that way, my dear," he explained. "A
director must see you and send for you. They must want
you for a part out there." He added kindly, "But I'll keep
an eye open and if anything happens, I'll let you know."

A few weeks later I hurried down to the Criterion
Theatre to see the premiere of my first short, in which I
sang, "Ain't She Sweet!" On the same bill was Maurice
Chevalier's first American picture, "Innocents of Paris,"
and I was eager to see that, especially since Mr. Chev-

alier himself was a guest celebrity at the Frolics that week.

My hopes were dashed a moment after my short flashed on. Was this how I appeared on the screen? How could I ever dream of being another Garbo or Barrymore? I wrinkled my nose, I screwed up my face, I blinked, my smile was definitely crooked . . .

Then Chevalier's picture. I was entranced. His charm and gaiety filled the theatre. That night I stood in the wings at the Frolics and saw the great French star sing "Valentina," wearing his famous straw hat, grinning his captivating and oh-so-crooked smile, letting the magic of his warm personality work its wonder on us. The audience cheered itself hoarse.

Yes, I thought, as I returned to my dressing room, you always know when you're in the presence of a great. Either you had it, or you didn't—

"Miss Roth—"

It was a stagehand. Mr. Jesse Lasky and Mr. Ernest Lubitsch were in the house and would like the pleasure of my company at intermission.

Mr. Lasky introduced me to a little man with a big cigar, who seemed to whistle under his breath as he rose. "Mr. Lubitsch," said Mr. Lasky with a twinkle in his eye, "is interested in you, Lillian. He saw your short film this evening and he's been watching you perform here. He'd like to talk to you."

Almost breathless, I sank into a chair. This was Europe's greatest director. To be given the "Lubitsch touch" meant stardom. Mr. Lubitsch looked at me. Then he removed his cigar and said in a thick German accent: "How would you like to go to Hollywood?"

I found my tongue. "I'd love to!" For a moment I thought melodramatically—it means leaving Leo, but I must choose quickly between love and a career.

Lubitsch pulled reflectively at his cigar. "I am making Mr. Chevalier's picture, 'The Love Parade.' I think you would be good in it."

Me, play opposite Chevalier? "Oh, Mr. Lubitsch!" I gasped.

On the ground that my Hollywood experience would enhance my value later, Earl Carroll gave up an option he had on my services. Paramount signed me to a seven-year contract: $600 a week for the first six months, $750 for the next six, then $1,000 a week, then $1,500, then $2,000 and, in three years, $3,200 a week!

Chevalier was on the same Super-Chief that took Mother and me to the West Coast, but I worshipped him from afar. I dared not approach him. I only dreamed of the great love scenes he and I would play under Lubitsch's magic direction. My heart was breaking a little for Leo—and when I was not wandering through the train hoping to catch a glimpse of Chevalier, I was writing tearful letters to Leo.

The publicity drums began booming. I posed for photographs in net stockings and the highest of heels, and with a garter peeping out from the ruffles. This was the same star buildup the studio had given Clara Bow and Nancy Carroll before me.

Mr. Lubitsch greeted me with a smile when I arrived on the set. There, before my awestruck gaze, was Maurice Chevalier, the beautiful Jeanette MacDonald, and a little man with expressive, merry eyes, Lupino Lane, a British actor.

Mr. Lubitsch introduced me. "Do you remember me?" I ventured to ask Chevalier. "I worked with you in the Frolics."

He flashed his inimitable smile. "Of course—I remember—how could I forget?"

Lubitsch passed out copies of the script. "Now, will you please sit there, Mr. Chevalier—" He pointed to a bench. "And Miss MacDonald—" He stopped. Script in hand, I was floating ecstatically toward Chevalier's bench.

"No, Miss Roth. I want you to sit on the other bench with Mr. Lane. You're playing opposite him."

I was crestfallen. How naive could I have been? Who else but lovely Jeanette MacDonald would play opposite Chevalier? And I—and Mr. Lane—what were we to do?

I soon found out.

"We have two identical sets here," Lubitsch explained. "Mr. Chevalier and Miss MacDonald will sit on that bench. You, Miss Roth, will sit with Mr. Lane on this bench. He is Mr. Chevalier's butler. You are playing the maid to Miss MacDonald's princess. They are having a love affair; you and Mr. Lane are having one, too. You two are to parody everything your master and mistress do. When they kiss, you kiss. When Mr. Chevalier declares his love for Miss MacDonald, Mr. Lane will declare his love for you. Get it?"

I got it. As Chevalier pursued Jeanette, at a high point in the scene, Lupino was to pursue me, bringing his face so close to mine that I was to gaze cross-eyed with love at him.

I had to hold back my tears as Lubitsch sketched the

ridiculous role I was to play. But I went through my lines.

Lubitsch chewed savagely at his cigar. He began to whistle under his breath. "That's terrible, Lillian! Where's all that zip and zoom you had on the Ziegfeld roof?"

"Oh, Mr. Lubitsch," I wailed. "I'm so disappointed! I thought I was going to play the love interest opposite Mr. Chevalier. I'm not a comedienne!"

He put his cigar back into his mouth grimly. "When I am finished with you young lady, you will be. Get off that bench." I obeyed. He sat down next to Lupino Lane. "Now, Lillian, watch!" He clasped his arms passionately around Lupino, and cigar in mouth, looked at him with such soulful cross-eyes that the entire company roared.

"That's the way to do it!" he growled. "Come here a minute." I walked up to him. "Let's see you cross your eyes." I tried, unsuccessfully. He put his forefinger a few inches in front of my nose. "Watch it," he ordered. "Don't take your eyes off it." Slowly he brought his finger nearer and nearer the bridge of my nose, until it was an inch away. I felt my eyes move inward: I stared, cross-eyed.

"Perfect, little lady!" he said, and chucked me under the chin. "Now sit down and make love!"

Chevalier was extremely kind to me during those delirious, free-wheeling early days. Sometime later I went to San Francisco for a film premiere. Gary Cooper, then even more silent and taciturn than he is today, was my escort.

At dinner after the show I found myself seated between Chevalier and Cooper. I sat stiffly between the two men, still very much in awe of the great French entertainer. All at once I felt something against my left knee. The table leg, I thought, and I moved my leg— and the table leg moved. I blushed, and looked up. Chevalier was grinning at me. He'd been nudging me with his knee. "Would you like to dance?" he asked.

For an ecstatic three minutes I was in his arms. I cud- gelled my brain for scintillating conversation, but nothing came. The best I could manage was, "Wasn't the audience enthusiastic tonight?"

He nodded: "And you are enthusiastic, too?"

"Oh, yes," I sighed. "I get pleasure out of everything."

We danced in silence for a moment. "You have very beautiful eyes, Miss Roth," he said, and his smile made my heart pound. "You must be careful that they do not get you into trouble."

That was my romance with Maurice Chevalier.

Shortly after I signed at Paramount a German actress arrived—Marlene Dietrich. She was lonely and unhappy. We shared the same make-up girl—Dot Pondell—who years later became Judy Garland's confidante. It was Dot who was always after me to take off weight, just as M-G-M nagged at Judy for her plumpness. I gained weight as we shot "The Love Parade" and Lubitsch or- dered me to take off ten pounds. I wasn't too successful; and since he shot the story backward, I was heavier at the beginning of the picture than at the end. I tried every method to lose weight, even gathering courage one day to accost one of Paramount's top stars who seemed to be able to melt pounds away at will.

"How do you do it?" I asked. "What's your secret?"

"No secret at all, Lillian," she said. "Just take a glass of half-and-half—half gin, half lemon juice—every morning for breakfast." Her method was far too drastic for me then. (Years later I tried the plan, improving on it by eliminating the lemon juice, but then the idea had nothing to do with diet.)

One morning Dot said, "Why don't you drop in on Marlene? She'd appreciate a visitor." I went to her dressing room, and whether because of my youth or my obvious hero worship, she confided in me. She was unhappy in Hollywood, she said, lost in the swift, impersonal rush of America, and heartsick for her little daughter, whom she had left in Germany. I adored Dietrich, her charm, her deep voice, her warmth. As we chatted, I surreptitiously glanced at her legs again and again, for she was to be my competition: according to Paramount publicity, I had the most beautiful legs in Hollywood. This was not actually true: Lubitsch nurtured the legend by ordering me to wear shoes and hose of the same color, and coaching me how to walk and place my legs when I stood or sat. Dietrich never worried about such details—no matter how she walked or sat or stood, her legs were beautiful.

I was not too happy myself in Hollywood. My social life was dull. Letters to Leo every few days; now and then one to Ann, who was attending boarding school, and to Dad, who was living in Boston; the movies with my mother, when I wasn't too tired; a visit or two with Mr. Lasky, who had moved to the West Coast offices of Paramount. My hours were long. Sometimes I began work at 6 a.m., when I had to be on set for makeup, and returned home after midnight. I went out a few times with Junior

Laemmlc, now a producer at Universal. I was working too hard to be out much, or to indulge in any of the wild Hollywood life I'd read about. Nothing had much meaning until David came along.

CHAPTER VII

I HAD only a waving acquaintance with David Lyons at Clark. I was fourteen, then, and he was nineteen. But he was to become important to me during those first few months in Hollywood.

Junior Laemmle phoned me one night and asked me to go for a drive. On the way he said, "I forgot to tell you—you know, we've got a school friend living over in North Hollywood. He's been under the weather lately, but I know he'd like us to stop in and say hello."

David sat up in bed when we walked into his room. His curly blue-black hair was tousled, and he was pale, but he flashed a cheerful, contagious grin that had me smiling back without realizing it. "Hiya, Lums!"

"What a funny name," I said. "Nobody ever called me Lums."

"That's short for Lillums," he said. "And Lums sort of fits you, too."

"My name's Lillian," I said a little tartly. "My mother always said everybody must call me by my full name, Lillian. Not Lilly. And not Lums."

His smile lit up the room. "Well, I'm sorry, but you're Lums to me. Now, if you'll just skidaddle out of here and wait a minute, I'll get some clothes on and we'll talk about school days."

When he came into the living room a few minutes later and draped his slim, five-foot-ten over the arm of my chair, I began thinking that perhaps Leo wasn't the only boy in the world. David was brimful of personality, and exuded charm and good spirits—an exuberance you could not withstand. He was working for Junior as an assistant director, having recently come from a six-month stay in Arizona.

We talked about Leo, whom he knew and liked, and about Clark.

"You used to be standoffish, if I remember," I said. "You drove a big yellow Packard—"

"And I wore a raccoon coat—"

"That's right," I said, suddenly remembering the dashing appearance he made, and how I had been too shy to try to know him better because he was so much older. "And you were going to study law."

He nodded. "I went to Syracuse University. But now I'm out here—and at this particular moment," he said, looking at me meaningfully, "I don't mind telling you I wouldn't change for anything."

I must have raised my eyebrows at that, for he hastened to add, "Look, Lums, don't get me wrong. I feel toward you like I would toward a sister. I know you go with Leo, but suppose you were my sister. You'd let me take you to a movie, wouldn't you?"

I nodded.

"Well, believe me, that's the way I feel about you. And I'd like to take you out tomorrow night. May I?"

He might get off his high horse and feel about me as a boy feels about a girl, I thought, a little annoyed. But I welcomed his friendship. I was in glamorous Hollywood, and nothing particularly glamorous was happening to me.

A few nights later David took me to the opening of Junior's first picture, which starred Alberta Vaughan. "Now, you'll be brought to the mike and asked to say a few words about Junior," David warned me. "After all, you're going to appear in 'The Love Parade' and you're a personality."

I planned to say how glad I was to be there. Instead, I began talking about Junior's activities at school, and went on until David all but pulled me away. I had made a fool of myself.

David sought to console me during the ride home. "I feel about you as I do about my sister," he said, "and if she were sad, I would do this." He pressed a cool kiss on my forehead. That irked me. The more often he called me his sister, the more annoyed I became—and the easier it was to forget Leo.

My letters to Leo became fewer: his answers to me, more infrequent. Soon David and I were meeting wherever possible. It wasn't always easy, because Hollywood's infamous caste system kept us apart. The studio insisted that I was a star, and ought not be seen too often with David, for he was only an assistant director. Thus, he was never invited to the studio parties to which I was asked, although those who extended the invitations knew we were going together. David took it in good spirit. He always waited outside until the party was over, and then we had a little time to ourselves. The nightlife we knew consisted of a brief visit to BBB's, a nightspot off Hollywood Boulevard, where we sipped soft drinks, or a dance at the Roosevelt Hotel.

"I don't feel at all about you as I do about my sister,"

he finally confessed. "But I don't want to be a heel taking away another fellow's girl."

I reassured him. "That's over now. You're not taking me from Leo. My romance with him was puppy love, David. I know it now. It's the real thing with you."

" 'Lums, darling," he would say. "If you only knew how much I love you and how happy I want to make you!" He would kiss me then, and I would forget everything else. Only with David, it seemed, could I be myself. He loved me as I was. I needed no pretense, felt no need to justify myself to him. He alone spoke about making me happy; everyone else spoke about making me famous.

We began to talk about marriage. I would leave the profession when I was twenty-one; I would work hard, meanwhile, and save my money, and he would work hard, and save his money, and then we would be married.

As the weeks passed, Katie grew more and more concerned. She upbraided me. David wasn't the right boy, she said. Anyone who would allow me to give up my career couldn't really have my interests at heart. In any case, at eighteen what right had I to contemplate marriage? I was only at the beginning of a career that could take me to unknown heights. "Oh," she cried, "when I think of the youth and beauty and talent you're ready to throw away for that boy—." She grew hysterical. "I can't bear to see it," she wept. "If he must be with you all the time, take another apartment. I just can't bear to see him around you all the time!"

I was torn. Everything Katie had built up for me, all the dreams she had had for me even before I was born, were crashing before her eyes. And she *was* right: I was too young to think of marriage. But to turn away from

[71]

the one person who made me feel whole—I didn't know what to do. The headaches that tortured me in "Artists and Models" came back. I had never disobeyed Katie. . . .

In desperation, I moved into another apartment in the same building, but two weeks later Katie and I were friends again, and I had moved back. We lived in a state of undeclared truce. Katie's apprehension, in part, stemmed from a fact more evident to her than to me: how seriously ill David was. I did not realize it until one afternoon when he suffered a violent coughing spell and spat up blood. The doctor, after examining him, took me aside.

"Don't you know?" he said. "This young man is tubercular. He'll have to remain in bed for a while."

I was shocked. David *was* sick. And because he was, and needed me, I loved him the more.

The following night I had a social engagement with Paul Bern, the M-G-M producer whose suicide, a few years after his tragic marriage to Jean Harlow, so stunned the film world. I could not break the appointment: it was an unwritten law in Hollywood that you didn't break appointments with producers. Mr. Bern took me to the theatre. As we sat there, my mind was with David. Desperately I wanted to be at his bedside taking care of him. The old impatience came upon me. Suddenly I felt a horrifying sensation as if ants were crawling over my skin! I squirmed, almost beside myself. (Not until later was I to learn what bizarre forms anxiety could take.) And what would Mr. Bern think of me? He pretended to notice nothing, and finally the seizure passed.

Later, driving me home, he said, "I'm going to tell you

something, little girl, as you start off in life. You have a great career before you, providing you meet the right man. You're going to be on top of the ladder, or at the bottom. You're just a bundle of emotions, Lillian; the wrong man will degrade you—the right man will uplift you."

I should have remembered his advice.

David and I were now all but inseparable. Late one afternoon I started a particularly tough dubbing chore. I must have sung one song twenty times. By nine o'clock the scene still didn't suit the director. David had been waiting for me since six. I committed the most grievous sin of all in the eyes of a studio executive. I pretended I heard the director say I could go home, and I walked off the set.

That night David and I went away, across the border to Tijuana. Perhaps I would break the promise I'd made to Katie that I wouldn't consider marriage before I was 21: I wasn't sure. We stayed away that night. But we did not consummate our love. I knew little about sex, and what I knew confused and frightened me. My memories were tied up with lecherous old men and back-stage obscenities. And David, no more experienced than I, was ill, racked with coughing spells, and I mothered him through the long hours to dawn.

We had it all planned: one day we'd have three children, two boys and a girl, and they would have the home and garden, the parents in love with each other, and the sense of belonging I never had.

David knew I knew he was sick, and worried about him. But when, for weeks on end, he was so full of energy and good humor, so vital in all he did, his illness seemed as remote and unbelievable as a bad dream.

Suddenly, Jesse Lasky waved his magic wand again. He called me into his office one morning.

"I've just had a letter from your father," he said. "He certainly writes extravagantly about you. But there may be something in what he says."

Arthur, he went on, insisted that I was a great dramatic actress who had never had a chance to show my talent. Well, continued Mr. Lasky, Paramount had tested nearly 150 girls for the role of Huguette, in "The Vagabond King," the studio's major production. He explained that Huguette was a woman of the streets, about 32, and the sweetheart of the poet Francois Villon, to be played by Dennis King. Some of the top stars in Hollywood coveted the role.

"Now," he said, "maybe your father knows what he's talking about, even if you are only 18. I want you to go across the lot to Ludwig Berger, who's directing the picture. Tell him I want you tested for Huguette."

Dressed as I was, in sweater, pleated knee-length skirt, tam o'shanter, golf shoes and socks, I hurried to find Mr. Berger.

"Mr. Lasky told me to see you," I told him breathlessly.

He glanced at me impatiently. "For what reason?"

"To test me for Huguette."

"What!" he exclaimed. "My God, I ask for another Pola Negri and they send me a Louise Fazenda!" He stared at me. "Not only that—but look at you. You look fourteen years old. You're a little girl. This calls for a woman with fire!"

I stepped forward, stung to the quick. "I can be very fiery, Mr. Berger," I said acidly. "Why don't you test me and see?"

Mr. Berger all but tore his hair, what there was of it. "I don't know what's going to happen in Hollywood next," he groaned. "Go to the wardrobe department and get fitted and be here tomorrow night at nine o'clock."

I woke next morning with a fever of 101 and a voice that was more like a croak. The chance of my life awaited me, and I had grippe! Was the Texas Guinan jinx at work here, too? If only Dad were on hand to help me!

Shortly before nine o'clock, a raging fever banging at the base of my skull, I appeared on the lot. I waited. Ten o'clock. Eleven o'clock. At midnight I found a blanket in a corner and crawled under it, shivering with chills, alternately dozing and waking. At two a.m. Mr. Berger shouted, "Miss Roth!"

I staggered over to him. "All right, this is your scene." A hand stuck a script in my face. "This is a death scene," said Mr. Berger. "Let's see you die."

That was exactly what I wanted to do. Dennis King's stand-in took me in his arms, I recited my lines in a sepulchral voice, closed my eyes slowly, and died.

"*Wunderbar!*" Mr. Berger threw his arms around me and kissed me. The role of Huguette was mine. I was the new dramatic find of the year. Next day Jesse Lasky exulted over the telephone, as delighted as if he'd been my uncle. "Lillian, the rushes were wonderful. You've got the role of the year—the plum part in the first all-musical technicolor!"

I was ecstatic. I had found myself at last! Tragedy was

me—not cross-eyed comedy. I was on top of the world. Nothing disturbed me—not even Mr. Berger's order that I must put back the ten pounds I took off for "The Love Parade," so that I would look older and sexier.

David, now working as night director at Universal, shared my delight. His hours were from 10 p.m. to 6 a.m. So that I could spend more time with him, I bought my first car, a Chrysler 77; and toward midnight every night I drove the fifteen miles to his studios in North Hollywood. We got very little sleep, but we were rapturously in love, and all was well no matter how much others might disapprove.

Each morning I came bouncing to rehearsal. In my little skirts and blouses and flat shoes, I must have looked ridiculous going through my part. Time and again I caught Dennis King and his co-star, Jeanette MacDonald, exchanging smiles as they watched me.

Also observing me with some interest was a famous British actor who was completing a Robin Hood production on an adjoining lot. Tall, handsome, debonair, Robin Hood, too, doubted my qualifications. He asked me to lunch. "I've been talking to many of your Hollywood stars," he began, "and they agree that it's quite odd to have an 18-year-old girl play Huguette."

"Why?" I asked. He smiled down at me. "My dear, how would an innocent like you, with no experience in love, portray the fire and passion that is Huguette?"

"Why, that's absurd," I retorted. "I'm very much in love, as it happens, and I have plenty of warmth."

He looked at me pityingly. "No, Lillian, you need a good love affair. And I could teach you the art of love—then, I assure you, you'd be the personification, the epitome, of that fiery wench."

I giggled.

A few days later he approached Katie on the lot, and in a gallant manner that quite enchanted her, said, "Mrs. Roth, I'd deem it a privilege if I could take your daughter to dinner one evening."

Mother urged me to go. "You've been working hard. He'll take you to some lovely spots. And it'll do you good to go out at least one night with someone other than David."

Perhaps because I was 18, and curious to see what would happen, I agreed. I could take care of myself. Hadn't Albert, at Clark, learned that the hard way? I was 14, he was 16, and I had told him he must be smoking secretly because I smelled tobacco on his breath. "Is that so?" he demanded. He pushed his face teasingly next to mine, and unexpectedly kissed me on the mouth. I slapped him with a roundhouse right that I brought up almost from the floor. It swung him halfway around. He kept his distance after that. Of course I could take care of myself.

On the appointed evening Robin Hood, and his secretary, Sidney, called for me and we drove to Venice Beach, an amusement park. "We'll have a bit of fun here," he said enthusiastically. Pretty harmless fellow at that, I thought.

He escorted me into the front seat of a roller coaster. As it swept into its first dip, he grabbed the safety bar in panic. "Ye Gods!" he squealed. "This is the end! We'll never get out of this thing alive!" As we roared on, he forgot all about me. His face was frozen: he put his head between his knees, and moaned. This was the swashbuckling hero unafraid, Hollywood's great romantic lead, who dashed through Sherwood Forest in his tights, his mustache quivering, avenger of the innocent and unprotected. . . .

"Never again," he breathed fervently when we jerked to a stop. Until 11 p.m. we enjoyed ourselves on milder amusements, while Sidney trailed behind us, carrying the ice-cream cones and popcorn, and souvenirs I won. Then I suggested it was time to go home.

"Righto!" said Robin Hood. We drove toward home. "What say we stop at my apartment for a moment—there's no use having Sidney come all the way into town," he said. "We'll drop him off there."

Why not? Nothing dreadful was likely to happen with Sidney there. When a woman housekeeper answered the door, I felt doubly reassured.

Once inside, Sidney served us champagne. Robin Hood sat at the piano and accompanied himself in a romantic ballad while I sipped the champagne. It was the second time I had ever had an intoxicating drink. The bubbles tickled my nose delightfully, and I liked the vinegary lemony flavor. "It tastes like citrate of magnesia," I exclaimed. "It won't feel like that, my dear," said Robin Hood, stopping long enough to refill my goblet.

Now the victrola was playing, and I was dancing and singing happily. Suddenly Robin Hood's strong arms were around me, he was dragging me into an adjoining bedroom, trying to pull my clothes from me. I was dizzy, but not helpless: I fought him off, tearing and scratching and screaming.

"My God, you're a little hell-cat!" he exclaimed. "How you excite me!" But I fought and bit and kicked, and

[78]

then Sidney was in the room, fixing his master's face where I had dug my nails, and muttering worriedly under his breath, "Don't you know she's under age—she's jail-bait?"

As Sidney led me to the front door I managed to get out a parting word: "I told you I had fire!" I screamed, and burst into tears.

Sidney silently drove me home. Robin Hood's picture was held up for three days until his face healed sufficiently for makeup to hide his wounds.

When the time came for Huguette's death scene to be put on film, my temperament and physical disability conspired to help me. The heat that day was almost intolerable; the city sweltered in a temperature of almost 103 degrees, and under the technicolor lights, the mercury hit 110. We repeated the scene so often that I became hysterical, and had to be given sedatives. As I rested in the first-aid room, Mr. Bachman, the producer, rushed in. "Lillian, you've got to go back for one more take."

"No, I can't!" I couldn't control my sobs. "I just can't do it again!"

They cajoled, they pleaded, they insisted, and finally, they helped me back and the scene I played then was that used in the film—when I returned to work before the camera, exhausted from the heat, from weariness, from hysteria.

CHAPTER VIII

THE NEWS I brought to David from the mail room was startling: my fan mail was pouring in second only to that of Clara Bow, the "It" girl, and Paramount's reigning queen. And I hadn't even been starred in a picture!

"Darling," David said jubilantly, "that's the way you're really made in Hollywood. Not by the studio, but by the public!"

Paramount promptly capitalized on my popularity by casting me in "Honey." The song I sang, "Sing, You Sinners!" became a tremendous hit, and was identified with me for years afterward. It's a favorite with audiences even today.

In Paramount's next film, "Paramount on Parade," Buddy Rogers and I sang another hit: "Anytime's The Time To Fall in Love."

Now Cecil B. DeMille, looking for a siren for his new extravaganza, "Mme Satan," borrowed me from Paramount, and I found myself reading my lines to the master himself. DeMille then was a compact, balding man who wore riding pants, shiny black boots, an open-collared shirt, and was never seen without a riding crop. He was brisk and impersonal.

The plot of "Mme Satan" called for me to steal Reginald Denny from Kay Johnson, who played his wife. We were supposed to be attending a masquerade ball on a zeppelin. At the height of the festivities, the zeppelin cracks up and begins to sink. Kay Johnson, clinging to her husband, begs frantically, "Oh, if we ever get out of this alive, please, please, give my husband back to me."

I retort, "On one condition. There are only two parachutes left and three of us. I'll take a parachute and you take your husband."

DeMille liked my reading. "Fine," he said. "Go to the wardrobe department and tell Adrian I want him to take your measurements."

Hollywood's famed dress designer had prepared a startling costume. I was to come to the ball as a pheasant —iridescent golden bra, iridescent golden shorts, and stemming out behind, tremendous pheasant feathers. Adrian wrestled with the bra. "You'll never fit into it," he said, annoyed, looking at me as if I had betrayed him. "I've designed it for a boyish figure."

We consulted Mr. DeMille. "The girl isn't supposed to be made to fit the bra," he said sharply. "Make the bra fit the girl." Adrian scolded and fussed, but did as he was told.

After DeMille obtained an interior shot of me in the zeppelin, he said, "Tomorrow you're going to jump. The zeppelin will be breaking up. You'll jump from there."

I followed his pointing finger, and stared, open-mouthed. More than 200 feet above our heads was a narrow ledge. Far below it was a net. "Me, jump from up there?" I gasped. "Into that net? In these high heels and feathers? Oh, Mr. DeMille, I couldn't possibly!"

He scarcely looked up from his notebook. "I'll see you at nine o'clock in the morning, Lillian."

I got to a telephone as fast as I could and rang up Walter Wanger, in charge of Paramount production. "I can't do it," I protested. "I'm frightened. I'll break my neck making a jump like that."

Mr. Wanger was sympathetic. "Don't worry, Lillian, you're too valuable a property. I'll ask Mr. DeMille to get a double."

Nine o'clock next morning, Mr. DeMille said, "All right, Lillian, here's where you jump."

I jumped, thinking of things to say to Paramount if I survived. DeMille had a way of saying "jump"—and you jumped. Not once, but five times before he was satisfied.

Almost as appalling was the scene that followed. I was to rebound out of the net and crash through the glass skylight of a men's Turkish bath. Perched on a narrow ledge, where I was held by a stagehand so I wouldn't tumble, I was to plunge through a large sheet of candy glass, which photographed like the real thing, but supposedly was far safer.

Again I protested. "Mr. DeMille, in 'The Love Parade,' Lupino Lane was so excited by one of my kisses that he jumped right through candy glass and he was all cut up. It might happen to me, too."

DeMille said nothing. Instead, he strode over to a pane of candy glass leaning against the wall, lifted it high over his head like a platter, and brought it down hard on his skull. The glass smashed and shattered all about him. "If it didn't hurt my old bald head," he said caustically, walking away dripping splintered glass, "it won't hurt your young back end." I jumped on schedule.

Suddenly, everything seemed to go awry. While making a short with a rotund comic, the cameraman told me my face couldn't be seen in a close-up kiss. "Ask him to turn aside so that we see you for a moment," the cameraman instructed me. I followed orders, only to have the actor suddenly mutter under his breath as he held me close, "Who in hell wants to look at a little Jew like you?"

I walked off the set in tears. "I won't work with that man," I managed to say when I was called on the carpet. And I wouldn't—or couldn't—tell why.

The front office issued an ultimatum. Go back and finish the scene—or be suspended. I finished the scene.

I came home nights to argue violently with Mother. I simply must stop seeing David, she cried. It was affecting my work and my health. He had no real interest in me, or in my career. She would rather break my contract with Paramount, she wept, then see us married.

She was under great pressure because David's parents had telephoned her several times from New York. They were deeply concerned. The hours David and I kept, trying to be together despite his night shift, were only making him more ill, they insisted. But beyond this, they made clear, they would never permit their son to marry a girl in show business. This was unthinkable. If we dared marry, they would annul it.

Everything was being done to break up our romance. David and I clung together. "They'll come around," he would say, trying to comfort me. "You'll see. They'll all come around in the end."

But worse was on tap. A switch in the top echelons at Paramount brought B. P. Shulberg to the Coast to replace Jesse Lasky. I quickly discovered a new hand was at the helm. One night as I danced with Mr. Shulberg at a party given by David Selznik, he said casually, "You haven't been easy to handle lately, have you, Lillian?"

"What do you mean?" I asked uncertainly.

Well, he went on as we danced, each of us smiling and nodding to others, it appeared I had once deliberately walked off the set; I had complained about Mr. DeMille; I had caused a scene over an insult, real or fancied, in a close-up shot; and I was temperamental and difficult.

"We're sending you back to New York to be kicked in the rear by the Marx Brothers until you learn how to behave," he concluded casually.

I was stunned. I left him standing on the floor and ran crying into another room. But his word was law. I was to play a love interest in the Marx Brothers' new picture, "Animal Crackers," being shot in New York. What neither my mother nor David's parents had been able to accomplish—separating David and me—was done by a one-sentence ultimatum from Paramount's front office.

Mr. Shulberg later salved my wounds. When I returned from New York, a wonderful part would be awaiting me: playing the romantic interest in the new Chevalier picture!

If anything made bearable my separation from David, it was the zany experience of making a film with the Marxes. It was one step removed from a circus. First Zeppo, the youngest, sauntered into the studio, about 9:30. At 10 somebody remembered to telephone Chico and wake him. Harpo, meanwhile, popped in, saw that most of the cast was missing, and strolled off. Later they found him asleep in his dressing room. Chico arrived about this time. Groucho, who had been golfing, arrived somewhat later, his clubs slung over his shoulder. He came in with his knees-bent walk, pulled a cigar out of his mouth, and with a mad, sidewise glance, announced, "Anybody for lunch?"

Work resumed at mid-afternoon, and then it was five o'clock, and they were finished for the day.

Every scene took longer than the director planned, for the ad libs came thick and fast, and the budget soared as the laughs increased.

Groucho and I had a scene that had to be shot over at least ten times. In this instance I was the culprit. We were supposed to be hunting a thief who had stolen a valuable painting from Margaret Dumont, who played the society dowager Groucho chased. My line, when we stumbled on a fake painting, was, "Oh, if we could only find the real painting!" Groucho's line was, "I know who the thief is. Here's his signature." "Who is it?" I asked. "Rembrandt," he said. "Don't be silly, he's dead," I retorted. Groucho snarled, "Then it's murder." I burst into giggles every time he said that, ruining the take. The line itself wasn't so hilarious, but I knew Groucho was going to say it with the big cigar jutting from his clenched teeth, his eyebrows palpitating, and that he would be off afterwards in that runaway crouch of his; and the thought of what was coming was too much for me.

We were running far over schedule, and I was eager to get back to David and the Chevalier picture. Word came from the coast: the film was already under way! Then, a reassuring report—Paramount was using a girl who resembled me in some of the long shots. There had been many newspaper stories reporting that I had won the role opposite Chevalier.

Finally Katie and I were on the train bound for the coast. During the ten-minute stopover in Kansas City I bought a newspaper and read: "UNKNOWN TO PLAY CHEVALIER'S LEADING LADY." They ran a picture of the girl, Frances Dee. I died a thousand deaths between Kansas City and Los Angeles.

The parting of the ways was inevitable. It came after I made one more picture—"Sea Legs," with Jack Oakie. The final straw was my discovery that when Paramount sent me out on personal appearance tours, they received nearly five times as much for my services as they were paying me.

Both Katie and David—separately—agreed that I should go out on my own.

"Lums, you have box-office appeal," David argued. "You can sing and dance. Most Hollywood stars come out on the stage, say, 'How do you do?', and take a bow. They've had no stage training."

David had so much faith in my potentialities that he joined an agency office to book me. He offered me to the Balaban and Katz Theatre Circuit in Chicago; they engaged me at $1,750 a week, more than twice my Paramount salary. And I was held over for seven weeks, playing north, west and south Chicago, and the famous Loop.

No question of it—we'd made the right decision. Mounted police held back the crowds as I emerged from the stage door between and after shows. Bids came pouring in. David, delighted, flew to New York to handle them.

Then, a long distance call from him: "Darling, you're set to headline at the Palace in November! The Palace—and top billing! And four Paramount short subjects in Astoria, at $3,500 a short!"

I was overjoyed. David was wonderful!

Even Katie had to admit that he really was interested in my welfare.

We arrived in New York to find three of my pictures running simultaneously on Broadway. (First nighters had paid a record $11 a seat to see "The Vagabond King.") Happily I bought Katie a mink coat, Ann a kidskin outfit, and myself a leopard coat trimmed in seal. Dad came in from Boston to greet us.

But the joy of reunion was turned to ashes by word that David was suffering violent spells of vertigo that puzzled his doctors. The day I opened at the Palace with Lou Holtz, David was taken to the hospital for tests. I saw him every possible moment. "To think I have to miss you at the Palace!" he lamented. "How I would love to be out front, watching you! But I've thought of a great plan—a repeat at the Palace—and I'm going to see about that booking right from this bed. I'll be in the first row next time."

No matter how badly David felt, he seemed to be able to forget his pain when I was there. It was difficult for me to realize how ill he really was. As in California, he pushed his sickness aside. "Just nervous headaches," he said. He was gay, charming, lovable.

After the Palace I went on tour, carrying out bookings he had arranged for me, flying back between engagements in Buffalo and Washington to be at his side. When I opened at the Palace the second time, two months later, co-headlining with Walter Winchell and Harry Richman, David was still in the hospital. Walter and Harry soon knew about him, and like good troupers they bolstered me through several shows, but I don't think either knew David's illness was as serious as it was.

After three exploratory operations, the verdict of his doctors was brain abscess. Now David was incoherent much of the time. His nurse, a big, motherly Irish woman, sought to calm me. "They always talk a bit disconnected after brain surgery, dear," she said. "Don't worry —he'll come out of it."

One morning he was scheduled for still another operation. It was Sunday, and I remember telling the interne early that morning that I had three shows—at two, six and nine—and would he telephone me if David wanted me? I gave him the backstage number.

Intuitively I knew the call that came at 5:45 p.m. was for me. I was putting on my makeup for the second show. "Oh, God." I prayed, "don't let anything happen to him." On the telephone I heard the interne's voice, low and grave. "You'd better get down here quickly, Miss Roth. David is going."

I left the receiver dangling. I was running barefoot out the stage entrance when I felt someone grab my shoulders and whirl me around. It was Harry Richman. He dragged me struggling back to my dressing room and threw me sobbing into a chair. "Stop it!" he shouted, and slapped me. "Where do you think you're going?"

"Let me out of here," I wept. "Please. David's dying. Please!"

"Don't you realize," he went on inexorably, "they're playing the overture and two thousand people are waiting out there for you?"

Winchell hurried into the room. "What's going on?" he demanded. "We're due onstage!"

"Oh, some damn fool has told her that David is dying," Harry said distractedly. "What a stupid thing to do! They don't say things like that on the telephone, do they, Walter?"

I looked at Walter. He couldn't answer. He was pulling at his fingers nervously and his eyes were tear-filled. I thought—isn't that odd? He's reacting just like me.

They kept encouraging me while my maid dressed me, and then I was before the audience, singing the ridiculous words of "I'm Flying High, But I've Got a Feeling I'm Falling." How can they expect me to sing a happy song? I can't stop crying. I got through my act and came off the stage for a moment. Then I would have to return to do skits with Harry and Walter. Harry hugged me. "Listen, Lil—keep it up—you're doing swell!"

Then I was onstage again, alive in a nightmare.

When the show was over George Wood, Richman's manager, rushed me to the hospital in a cab. Now David's parents can't try to separate us any more, I thought dully. Nobody can do anything to either one of us any more.

David's mother looked up as I ran down the corridor, and turned away sobbing. When I opened the door to David's room, I stared—the bed was made, but he was not there.

I fled from the room. "No, no, no, no, no!" I screamed. "I don't believe it! I don't, I don't, I don't!"

His nurse led me to an adjoining room—a nursery—full of empty cribs. "Oh," I cried, "we're never going to have our babies now."

She helped me to a chair. "Lillian, dear. Please, now
. . . you mustn't cry for David. He's with our Lord."

I turned on her. "Don't talk to me about God!" I
shouted. "David's dead. How could God take him away
now? He was so young, we had so many plans—"

She tried to comfort me. "Maybe you'd like the lifetime plant your mother sent him," she said. "No," I said,
"the plant will live forever and he's dead."

I heard George's voice. "It's time to go back, kiddie.
You're on in half an hour."

When I returned to the theatre Harry and Walter were
waiting at the stage door. Walter put his arms around me
and led me to a chair. Then he broke down and had to
walk away.

Harry talked to me. "Listen, Lil," he said gently. "You
know you're a great artist. You're going out before that
audience and do what you always do to them. You're
going out there because David's watching. He wanted
this for you. You can't fail him."

I went onstage again. I sang the Huguette waltz, and
something of my youth went from me in the words that
night:

> "Never try to bind me, never hope to hold,
> Take me as you find me, love and let me go,
> Though the loves we leave behind us
> Change and fade away
> Never mind, we'll have our love some day."

CHAPTER IX

ADELE ROGERS ST. JOHN wrote a syndicated piece about my tragedy that tore one's heart out. It was titled, "Take Your Happiness and Love While You May." Its moral was that youth was the time for romance.

I wouldn't let David go. Somehow I managed to complete my week at the Palace. Every entertainer can pull himself together on the stage, even if he collapses a moment later in the wings. Offstage, reality came, and hysteria. I wanted to die. I went into tantrums of self-reproach. Vainly Katie tried to comfort me. "I never realized he meant so much to you," she wept, and her guilt made me even more despondent.

I imagined I suffered David's vertigo, David's headaches. Dad came to New York and did all he could to cheer me up. Nothing helped. A family friend, Ted Reiner, who had been waiting for me to "grow up," hoping against hope that I would marry him, also tried to console me. Finally, Mother and Ted hired a psychiatric nurse for me. I was in hysterics most of the time. Everything tortured me: the mournful sound of the ships on the Hudson River, the rasp of automobile horns in the streets below. I could not sleep. I raged about the apartment convulsed with tears.

My parents called in a neurologist who recommended several months' rest in a sanitarium. "I can't sleep even a few hours a night at home," I screamed. "How can I spend months in a sanitarium?"

David, from his hospital bed, had arranged a three month tour for me of the Paramount-Publix theatres through the South and West. "Very well," said the physician. "Let her go on the tour. She ought to get away. She's had something close to a nervous breakdown. But see that she doesn't have time to brood. Have her take up bridge. It might keep her mind occupied."

I went on tour. My trunks were full of David's letters and his photographs. In every town I had his pictures tacked on the dressing room walls, pushed into the frame of my dressing room mirror. With me went Ellen, the psychiatric nurse, a tall, compact girl who was to care for me, and Katie, who wasn't sure whether it was wise to come along, but came when I insisted.

Time and again I woke in the night screaming that David was in the room with me. Katie and Ellen had their hands full. "He's alive," I wailed. "He's in the room now." The same vivid dream came night after night. David lay in his hospital bed, his tousled hair as before, talking to me. "When the nurses come in here with the doctor," he whispered, his eyes twinkling, "they'll tell you I'm dead. But you know I'm not, Lums. Don't believe them. They can't prove it." Then the nurses and doctor, all sad and sorrowful, walked into the room, and David lay dead, his eyes closed, his head bandaged, his face waxen. "He's dead, go out of this room," they chanted. "He's dead, go out of this room." Then the nurses and doctor shook their heads in unison, as if to music, and together filed solemnly out of the room, ignoring me as if I weren't there. Suddenly the bedcovers moved and David was sitting up again, his eyes open and sparkling with all his wondrous vitality, grinning as he said, "See, Lums, they're wrong. What did I tell you? I'm not dead!"

I tried to lose myself in activity. Ellen established a routine. As soon as we arrived in town, the management arranged for bridge players to be in my dressing room between shows. I came off stage, removed my makeup, and sat for a little while at my dressing table, staring at a photograph of David. I always had a fresh flower in a glass before him.

Ellen would slip in silently. "All right, Lillian, our guests are here." I would rise like a sleepwalker, walk into another room where a bridge table had been set up and a man and woman were already seated, two decks of cards before them. I would acknowledge the introduction automatically, sit down, and immerse myself in the game.

Nothing helped. My dreams tormented me. When I did not dream, I lay awake. Ellen tried—with little success—to read me to sleep. David, I sobbed, always knew how to cheer me up. Even when he was in his sick bed, he could do an impression—a hilarious, double-talking salesman selling the Brooklyn Bridge; Douglas Fairbanks leaping across the boudoir of a Persian princess, only to discover he'd left his sword on the window-seat just as the prince bounded in, scimitar in hand; the corner newsdealer doing a slow burn at a man who read the newspapers but never bought them. Even in our most trying times, when our families were so hard on us, we laughed together. He had been my only shield against melancholy —and now he was gone forever.

I sought to keep his memory fresh. He had died at 6:20 p.m., Sunday. Each Sunday at that hour, in whatever city I found myself, I went to my room and remained alone for a little while.

We played Minneapolis. Then Des Moines. In Kansas City Katie left for Chicago, to join my sister Ann, who had returned to show business briefly with Benny Meroff's act. Katie was almost as despondent as I: she was convinced that she had only made me feel worse by coming along. Chicago—and Ann—seemed a sensible idea.

Goodman Ace, then dramatic critic for the Kansas City *Journal-Post,* reviewed my opening night favorably. He wrote sympathetically of my courage in performing so soon after my great loss. Later he telephoned me. He and his wife Jane conducted a Sunday radio program, "The Easy Aces." He had heard I was a bridge enthusiast. They talked about bridge on their show: would I like to be his guest this Sunday at 6 p.m.?

Reluctantly I agreed, for I had no heart to meet strangers. Before the program, the Aces chatted briefly with me. Then Mr. Ace said, "By the way, what will you sing this evening?"

I looked at him is dismay. "Oh, I can't sing on your program, Mr. Ace," I said. "Not on a six o'clock program on Sunday."

Perhaps I failed to explain it well. But next day in his column, under some such title as *"Mourning Becomes Roth,"* he took me apart. I couldn't sing on his program because of my bottomless grief, he wrote, but I could dance at a nightclub the very same evening. What gave with Roth? What kind of phoney publicity play was she trying to make out of her fiance's death?

I threw down the newspaper and burst into tears. This was the unkindest cut of all. "And I didn't even want to dance," I cried over and over again to Ellen. "I didn't want to dance."

What happened was easily explained. After the show Ellen and the theatre manager, in an attempt to cheer me up, persuaded me to go out to supper. "It will be good therapy," Ellen assured me. Later, our escort asked me to dance. I begged off. "Oh, snap out of it, Lillian," Ellen said. "Go ahead and dance!" Too indifferent to make an issue of it, I danced—and one of Mr. Ace's informants had seen me.

I got through my show, but by midnight I had worked myself into near hysterics. Nothing Ellen could do helped put me to sleep. Finally she decided to do something not found in the psychiatric rule book. "Listen, Lillian," she said, going to her bureau drawer and returning with a bottle, "I want you to take a little drink. It will make you feel better about everything."

I took the drink she gave me. Then another. A third— and I was off to sleep, my first dreamless night in many nights. And when I woke, rested, I thought: if this is all I must do to get sleep, I'll do it. It's wonderful. I enjoyed the taste no more than when I drank on New Year's Eve with Leo. No matter. I could sleep, and that was a blessing.

The drink Ellen gave me was the fifth I had ever had.

Kansas City. Houston. San Antonio. And nightcaps each midnight to bring sleep. One night Rose Thurston, a chorus girl in our vaudeville unit, Ellen and I went for

a stroll alongside San Antonio's pretty lagoon. We came
to a drug store, went in and ordered sodas. Standing at
the counter were two aviation cadets. One was tall, with
laughing blue eyes, blond hair and a winning smile. I
couldn't actually say that he looked like David, but his
smile was engaging and had the same boyish quality.

"Lillian, the tall one is for you," Rose said, trying to
cheer me up. I fell in with her mood. "And the short
one's for you, Rose. You know I'm not interested."

"He's looking at you, Lillian," Rose said, but I refused
to glance up from my soda. On the way back to the hotel,
Ellen spoke. "I know how you feel about David's memory, Lillian, but it might help you if you became interested in someone else. You can't hug a ghost to yourself
forever."

At noon next day I found myself introduced to Willie
Richards, air cadet, stationed at the San Antonio barracks. He had telephoned my room that morning, talked
persuasively to Ellen, and arranged to meet me.

He was a long way from his home, Pittsburgh, he said,
and lonely. Would I go dancing with him some night or
maybe flying some day? We dined together and he told
me about himself. His father was a lumber merchant, but
he expected to make his career in the Air Force. He spoke
excitedly about his experiences in training; he was gay
and uncomplicated and likable and I found I welcomed
the chance to get out of myself for a little while.

He had to be in his barracks each night at 10 o'clock;
but for the rest of that week we dined together. I wasn't
the most delightful company. I was reading the philosophies of Nietzsche and Schopenhauer in Will Durant's
Outline of Philosophy, and trying to practice each phil-

osophy in turn, as years ago I'd done with Couéism and Christian Science. Now I was Superman—aloof, beyond good or evil, pain or pleasure. Now I was charming, sophisticated, cynical. Now I was pure soul, ethereal and mad as Ophelia, lost in a remote, beautiful other world with my dear, dead David.

"You're a funny girl," Willie said at one point. "I can't make you out but I sure like you."

When we were about to leave for Galveston, our next stop, he became serious. He couldn't bear to think of San Antonio without me. I was in his blood: he loved me. He knew it, he said, holding my arm and looking adoringly at me. He understood the place David had in my heart, but I was young, and he was young, and together we would make happiness ours. He could not live without me.

I was in my Superman mood. "I've had to learn to live without the man I love," I said tartly. "You'll have to learn to live without me."

Rose and I had a farewell double date our last night in San Antonio. We were to go to the theatre. The four of us stopped in Rose's room for a quick pick-me-up of Texas corn liquor. I had three drinks and blacked out— the second time in my life. Ellen came, and between them I was helped back to my own room.

In Galveston the telephone rang every few hours. It was Willie. He was desperately in love. Yes, we'd known each other only a short time, but love was like that: this was it. He was ready to resign his commission in the Air Force, fly to meet me in Atlanta, the last stop on my tour, and marry me. All I had to say was yes. Even a whispered "Yes" would do.

What under other circumstances would have been ridiculous suddenly seemed a good idea. I must break with the morbid past and begin a new life. And why not with Willie? He was decent, clean-cut, he would not interfere with my career, he was the kind of fine young man with whom Katie could find little fault. And he loved me—wasn't he ready to give up his career for me? I said finally, "All right, Willie. Come ahead."

When I told Ellen the news, she took it quietly. I learned only later that she telephoned Ted, who caught a plane for Atlanta and when we arrived there, was on hand to plead his own case.

Ted listed the reasons against my marriage. The boy had no money; he was too young; it was too soon after David's death. I had seen Willie all of four—or was it five?—times, and anyway, he, Ted, mature and understanding, could take care of me as I needed to be cared for.

I wouldn't listen. A few hours later Willie arrived. He walked into my room. I was dressed in my Huguette costume, posing for a German sculptor who had been assigned to do a bust of me for the German Hall of Fame in Berlin. Willie walked in—wearing a ready-made brown suit with sleeves too short and shoulders too narrow. I had not seen him in civilian clothes before. I thought, panicky, "Oh, no! What have I done? I surely can't love this boy!"

Ted was right. But how could I tell Willie? When Ted dropped in later, I introduced them. "Mr. Reiner has come from New York to take me home," I said. "He's a friend of the family."

"Honey, I know what you've been through," said Willie, "but leave things to me and I'll make you forget." He held me close.

Confusion was added to confusion. The two men argued over me. "Can't you see she's a sick girl?" Ted demanded of Willie. "She's going back to New York and a psychiatrist, and I'm taking her."

Willie bristled. "You and what army?" he retorted. "She'll be all right when she marries me. Why, you're an old man!"

While they argued, I slipped out. My David was dead, I thought bitterly, and these two men are fighting over me as though I were something inanimate, without heart and mind and wishes of my own. What are they trying to do to me? Why don't they leave me alone!

I walked the streets, distraught. Then I recalled that an actor I'd known in Hollywood was also in Atlanta, making a personal appearance in connection with one of his films. I telephoned him: I was in trouble, I said. "Two men are in love with me, and I'm completely disgusted with life and don't know which way to turn. I don't want to marry either of them."

He met me twenty minutes later at a bar. I poured out my heart to him—how wretched I was. One drink followed another. I blacked out: and sometime in the night I found myself in my room, but quite unable to remember how I had gotten there—or what had happened before. A cold sweat broke out on my forehead: what *had* happened? I raged inwardly, and then I was fitfully asleep, then awake, then asleep.

Slowly, a soft, steady knocking penetrated to my brain. I struggled awake. I was 5 a.m., and Willie, on the other side of the door, was pleading in an insistent whisper, "Come on, honey, let's skip and get married before anyone knows what's going on."

As though drugged I rose, dressed, and let Willie take me to an all-night restaurant. We might charter a plane and fly to another state, Willie said, since I was underage to be married in Georgia. He hurried to a pay station telephone and called the airfield, while I waited dully at the table. The gray dawn began to come through the window.

Willie returned a few minutes later. The ceiling, he said glumly, was too low to fly.

"O. K. We'll get married here," he said masterfully. "You'll fib about your age."

On the outskirts of town, as the milkcarts clattered by, he awakened a minister, whose wife and two daughters stood sleepily at our sides as witnesses. When we got back into the waiting cab, Willie took me in his arms. "Honey," he murmured exultantly, "we're married!"

The words struck me with almost physical force. What had I done now? Why? The first time in my life I had made a decision on my own, without Katie—and look at what I had done!

When we broke the news at the hotel, Ellen stormed at me. "You're completely out of your mind!" she cried. "David dead three months, and you married! Ted is right. You do need a psychiatrist!"

What now? The most sensible procedure was for all of us to go to New York. That night I lay in my berth while Willie shaved, making himself handsome for me. Now and then the train whistle sounded—remote, haunting, infinitely sad. I thought of David, how close we had been, the vows we had exchanged, the sweet plans we had had.

I jumped up, threw a robe over me, and ran through half a dozen cars until I reached Ellen's compartment. "I can't, I can't go through with it," I said wildly. "I can't do it."

Ellen called Ted, and they comforted me. "We can still handle it," said Ted. "You stay with Ellen tonight. We'll annul the marriage soon's we get to New York."

Five minutes later Willie was pounding on the door. "Where's my wife?" he demanded. "Darling, what happened to you?" I sat staring out the window into darkness. Willie wasn't to blame. I had said yes. He had quit the Air Force. How could I do this to him? I stood up. "You'd better open the door, Ellen," I said. "I'm going back with him."

In the dining car next morning we sat down to breakfast. Ted said to Willie, "You'll have to keep the marriage secret or it will ruin Lillian's career. What will her public think? David dead three months and she married."

"You've got to cooperate, Willie," Ellen said. And Willie agreed.

But as we got off the train, the newspapers thrust in my face had the story: "LILLIAN ROTH MARRIED SECRETLY TO FLYER."

Katie came flying in from Chicago, Arthur from Boston. There was a family conference. I was ill, no question of it. I would be taken to a psychiatrist, one of the most eminent in the country, Dr. A. A. Brill, author of *Basic Principles of Psychoanalysis*.

Meanwhile, for whatever it might mean, I could brood over the fact that so far as the New York *Daily Graphic* was concerned, the two major news stories of the day were the abdication of King Alfonso of Spain, and my marriage to Willie. Between us the King and I took over the entire front page of the newspaper. "Throne gone through his abdication, former King Alfonso of Spain today faces problem of all ex-kings—what to do with free time," read the caption beside the King's photograph. Under mine, the words read: "Lovely Lillian Roth, who left town in tears when her fiancé died, returns today smiling, accompanied by her husband, William C. Richards, son of a Pittsburgh lumber magnate."

Dr. Brill saw me after talking in turn to my father, mother, Ellen and Willie. When I entered his office, he greeted me with a smile. "You're not at all the wild woman I expected to see," he remarked, and told me to sit down. He looked at me searchingly. "Suppose you tell me what this is all about?"

"Haven't the others told you already?"

He chuckled. An elderly, paternal man, with a short goatee, he had an air of complete relaxation about him. "Yes, but they're a little upset. You look like a sensible girl. You tell me."

"Doctor, I'm all mixed up." I told him about David, of the romance not consummated, of the almost hypnotic hold his memory had. I told him of my dreams, my uncontrollable tears and tantrums. I told him of the pent-up energy that made me, sometimes, feel I would burst. I told him of my feelings toward men: I was physically attracted to men, but repelled by intimacies. I told him of the man who had painted me when I was five, of my confusion about sex. We spent hours reviewing my childhood, my relationship with my mother, my sense of being everywhere and belonging nowhere.

"You don't love Willie, do you?" he asked.

No. But he was sweet. I liked him.

"You married him before you recovered from the shock of David's death," Dr. Brill observed. "You weren't ready for marriage. Suppose we get Willie reinstated in the Air Force. Then you could get an annulment and Willie, from what I've seen of him, won't be too badly hurt by this brief episode."

The reinstatement, however, didn't go through. Dr. Brill called me in again. The best thing to do for the time being, he said, was to go away with my husband. "You're a nice little girl basically," he went on. "But you've had a couple of bad shocks and a great sorrow. You can afford a trip to Europe, can't you?" I nodded. "Well, then, take it. Get away from your family and from nurses for a few weeks. Then come back and see me."

It was sixteen years before I saw Dr. Brill again. He sent me to a mental institution then.

CHAPTER X

HAD I not been drinking, would I have married Willie? I was not much of a drinker then. When I took liquor, it was for escape—or, as I liked to say, medicinally. Without knowing it, I was being given my first lesson in the witchcraft of alcohol. For after a drink or two, liquor made me the kind of girl I wanted to be— free of repressions, unfettered by conscience, able to take love and life in my stride.

When I first saw Willie, an idea floated temptingly on the far edge of my mind: *Wouldn't it be glorious to go off with such a dashing, handsome, soldier-flyer?*

But Lillian, my sober conscience warned me, that isn't right. You're in mourning. You mustn't, you mustn't. . . .

It was the drink—the quick drink or two—that made me forget this pious thought. The quick drink opened all the closed doors.

Dr. Brill had told us to get away as soon as possible. However, I had personal appearances to do in Toronto and Montreal, and Willie was eager for me to meet his parents, so we stopped off in Pittsburgh en route to Canada.

In Pittsburgh I discovered that I was pregnant. I was

almost beside myself. Ought we to go to Europe, now that I was to have a baby? Ought we have a baby, in my mental condition? If it couldn't be David's baby, I wanted no one's. Desperately I took medicines.

After my Canadian engagements we stopped for a week end in Atlantic City. I still carried David's pictures; they were on our dresser where Willie couldn't help seeing them. He was miserable, and I was miserable. One rainy night we both became gloriously drunk. We walked, arm linked in arm, on the boardwalk, reeling and singing, the rain in our faces, stopping every little while to drink from the bottle of bourbon Willie carried on his hip.

Later we staggered to our room. Depression seized us. Gusts of rain pattered against our windows. The roar of the surf was in our ears. It was a night for high deeds and final acts. I found myself telling Willie that I could never love him: my heart was still with David. I cried, and Willie broke down, too. I was no good for leading him on and he was no good for making me marry him. And now the baby was on its way to complicate matters still more.

"We could kill ourselves," Willie said. "That would be final. That would settle everything."

We wept for our young lives that were to be snuffed out so soon. But how? Would it be more in the great tradition to join hands and walk into the ocean to our death? Or should Willie charter a plane and crash-dive us to eternity?

We woke next morning with excruciating hangovers. We looked at each other, slowly packed, and went on to New York. I bought Willie half a dozen suits at $165 each and we sailed for Europe, in the bridal suite of the *Ile de France*.

I lay ill at the Prince of Wales Hotel in Paris. We had done the French capital swiftly and madly, sleeping all day, playing all night. I was ill not only from drinking, but from all I had attempted to prevent an unwanted baby from coming into the world.

One afternoon I managed to go with Willie to the Grand Prix at Deauville. I fainted during the third race: Willie rushed me back to Paris. I lost our baby on the operating table at the American hospital.

I was very ill. I feared I would die. I wanted desperately to see Katie. Though I had scarcely enough strength to speak, I telephoned her in New York. "Mom, I miss you terribly," I said. "Come over here. You always wanted to see Europe, and now you're going to see it."

Her happiness bubbled over three thousand miles of cable. "Lilly, I'll be on the next boat! With bells on!"

Suppose I should not last until she arrived? The doctors, suggesting wine as a blood builder, had prescribed a glass of red wine for lunch, a sparkling Burgundy for dinner, and a pint of champagne before retiring. I tripled the dose.

When Katie arrived, we drove to meet her at Le Havre. In the following weeks we took her everywhere: the Louvre, the Eiffel Tower, the Folies Bergere, Maxims. We drove to Versailles and Fontainebleau. Ill as I was, I enjoyed her delight, for she was like a child in fairyland.

After Paris, Geneva. The doctors had ordered me to avoid strenuous exercise. I disregarded their orders: I went riding daily, even learned to jump hurdles. I wanted to live hard and fast. I drank heavily. From fits of wild gaiety I sank into deep melancholia. It was the same in Brussels, in Berlin, in London. David began to reappear in my dreams. One night I knew: I'd had enough. I said to Mother and Willie, "What do you say we go back home?"

We returned to America, arriving in New York in late August, 1930. The trip had taken two months. It had cost me $25,000.

Now I was earning a great deal of money, but it was meaningless. In addition to my appearance in the new Earl Carroll Vanities, I made short subjects for Paramount. Among these were the Fleisher cartoons in which I led the audience in songs while a ball bounced from word to word of the lyric as it flashed on the screen, a verse at a time. I sang "Down Among the Sugar Cane," "Honeysuckle Rose," and "Let's Fall in Love." Every song was an ironic parody of my own state of mind.

Willie and I threw at least two big parties a week in our new terrace apartment overlooking Central Park. We hired a secretary, maid and butler-chauffeur. I bought a custom-built ruby-red Hudson, a display model that had cost the Hudson people nearly $10,000 to manufacture, but which they sold me for $4,800 in consideration of my appearance in their ads.

The car would have delighted an Indian prince. It was upholstered in beige lambskin. The handles were 14-carat gold. An ivory vanity with gold-trimmed mirror was built into the horn of the steering wheel. In the back was an ivory French lacewood bar. The car also held compartments in which were fitted a motion picture camera and an overnight case. My Filipino chauffeur had beige uniforms that matched the color of the upholstery.

I bought more furs for Katie and myself: minks, ermines, Persian lamb, silver fox capes. I did a Lubitsch, all in gray—gray suede suit, gray kidskin boots trimmed with gray fur cuffs, gray stockings, gunmetal gray Russian hat. I had a similar costume in black Persian. I had a $10,000 diamond ring, a $1,000 wedding band, gloves monogrammed in diamonds. I spent wildly. David and I had saved so frugally to have a home. But David was dead, and why save money now?

Nothing consoled me. Night after night, after Willie fell asleep, I cried for David, thinking, if only he were lying close to me.

When I worked, my drinking was subconsciously timed. No more than four whiskey sours each night, after the show. On Sundays, however, the secret strategist hidden in my brain plotted it more elaborately.

Although I was never too happy in furs and jewels, they were expected of a star, and so on Sundays I bedecked myself with them, and Willie and I made our appearance at our first port of call—Toots Shor's Five O'Clock club, where everybody who was anybody was always found at Sunday cocktail hour. Toots himself, whom I had met when I was fifteen, in Philadelphia, always gave us a warm welcome. We sat at my favorite post, a table near the entrance, where we could see everyone and everyone could see us.

Par for the course here was three old-fashioneds: four, if you were in the mood; I always was. Experts explained to me that old-fashioneds gave you the lift to swing into a scintillating evening. Their tartness awakened one's palate, too.

The hand of the clock moved on; and presently we were making our gay goodbyes and adjourned to the Stork Club, where everybody who was anybody was always found at Sunday dinner. Again our entrance, properly timed and skillfully executed: Lillian Roth, star of stage, screen and radio, and her adoring Willie, six feet of blond, handsome manhood.

Naturally, it was not *comme il faut* to order dinner directly: the tang of the old-fashioneds had mellowed, and—so the best authorities held—nothing quite picked you up again as well as a straight rye—with a water chaser. That guaranteed an honest-to-goodness *bon appétit*.

Then one ordered—steak chateaubriand for two, and a *salade* which your own lovely hands (stubby fingers forgotten) would mix, with just a *soupçon* of garlic. And while you waited—for Sherman Billingsley was undoubtedly standing at the broiler, stopwatch in hand, to assure the exact degree of succulence—perhaps a second rye, straight. A second rye went exquisitely with the crisp, gleaming celery, the delightfully bitter olives, the radishes red as your own flushed cheeks.

Reluctantly, since all good things must come to an end, you turned to your food—and wines. Naturally you ordered sparkling Burgundy because everyone knew red wine complemented good red meat.

For dessert—when the huge newspaper-size bill of fare was thrust into your hands and your eyes finally focused on the print—what else but cherry jubilee? Followed, as

every gourmet knows, by a demi-tasse—with Benedictine.
No sugar. Certainly no cream. *Never* cream in a demi-
tasse, even if Willie wanted it.

The violins sobbed, and the Huguette in me stirred and
woke. How sweet, how tragic, how bitter-sweet we all
are, everyone of us, in a world we never made! How
warm I feel! How wonderful to float away on rivers
mysterious as poems whose words just escape you, to
float away, serene and queenly, into unseen beauties of
heart and mind and soul. . . . The hum of voices, the
warmth, the glow, the white tablecloths, the red wines,
the walls, the sobbing violins, all begin to spin. . . .

"Honey, I better take you home. Right now!" It's
Willie's voice, from far away. A strong right arm to help
me rise, unsteadily. How much I love the world! "Willie,
I'm so hot!" Maybe I would make it to the ladies' room,
maybe not. But I doubt if I was as beautiful in my exit
as in my entrance.

Willie worked out a plan. If we were to buy a plane—
a three-passenger Curtis Wright, costing about $2,500—
he could fly packages for a department store. I bought the
plane. Willie had several forced landings while flying
about seeking the contracts that never materialized. We
argued hotly. I didn't like him to fly. He might be killed
and I would hold myself responsible.

"O. K." he said dejectedly. "I'll go back to Pittsburgh
and see if I can't work out something in Dad's lumber-
yard."

I drove him to the airport and saw him off. After he left,
I thought, poor Willie. I wouldn't let him accept a pilot's
job, and that was the one thing he had been trained for.

I was ruining his flying career, and our lives were all mixed up. Our marriage will never work out, I thought, as I drove back to town.

At night, after my performance, I drank heavily. I was out to forget something. I wasn't sure it was David anymore, though I broke down thinking of him every night. But I continued my work, and shortly went on tour of a number of Paramount's Eastern Theatres.

The day I was to open at the Newark Paramount, Katie and I passed the front of the theatre on the way to morning rehearsal. My name was up in lights as the headliner. When we returned, however, a large pennant fluttered conspicuously above the marquee. In enormous gold letters against a black field, it read: MILTON BERLE—IN PERSON!

Katie stopped. "Where is he 'in person' from?" she demanded. "He's never made a picture." She walked backstage to find Mrs. Berle. "Sarah—I mean Sandra—" she said. "Where in the world did you get that flag?" Mrs. Berle laughed. "Oh, Katie, we always carry Milton's flag with us."

Mother and I went into a fit of laughter in my dressing room. "Shall we ask the manager to take it down?" I asked. Mother dismissed the idea. "If Sarah—I mean Sandra—can drag that flag about, let her have it. The audience knows who's the headliner."

CHAPTER XI

A COURTEOUS little man in a gaberdine coat was waiting when I returned late one night from Newark. "Miss Roth?" he said, and presented me with an envelope. In it was a summons to appear in municipal court. I owed a garage bill of $232 for repairs and storage for my old car during my trip abroad. I had refused to pay it, contending that all I owed was $32 for storage, since I had not requested any repairs. The summons was the garageman's answer.

Katie and I appeared in court the day I was to open at the Paramount Theatre in New York with Georgie Jessel, Burns & Allen and Bing Crosby. I was twenty, and although I looked the picture of innocence in a little black princess dress with big white organdy collar, and a little white, off-the-face hat, I was suffering from a violent hangover. My mouth felt as though it were lined with absorbent cotton.

Waiting for the case to be called, I grew impatient. "Oh, Mom, let's pay the money and get out of here," I exclaimed. But Mother decided we ought to see it through. She added, "Look at the judge, Lilly. Doesn't he look young to be sitting up there?"

I was too bleary-eyed to see him clearly, so we moved

up several rows. It was Judge Benjamin Shalleck, and he was young and good-looking, with warm, brown eyes. "Mom, I think I'll stay," I said.

When my case was called, I went before him, and began, "Your Honor, I—"

He interrupted me. "You have a lawyer to speak for you, Miss." Well, I thought, isn't he nasty! My lawyer requested an adjournment, pointing out that I would be busy for the next three weeks.

"Is this so, Miss Roth?" His Honor asked. "Yes, Judge," I said meekly. He looked at me for a moment, and then smiled—a captivating smile that made him look almost boyish. "There's a great deal of unemployment about today, and if the young lady has work, we certainly don't want to keep her from it. Case adjourned until three weeks from today."

For the first time since David's death my heart felt lighter. "Oh, Mom," I whispered as we walked out. "I've just got to meet him. Isn't he adorable?"

She squeezed my arm. "He certainly is, darling."

Georgie Jessel, who was on the Paramount bill with me, didn't know the judge. Neither did Burns and Allen, nor Bing Crosby, nor anyone else in the show whom I asked. Nearly three weeks later I came across Taps Shaurnstein, an agent, who knew him. "I see him in Lindy's every night," he said.

"I've got to meet him," I said breathlessly. "He's the most adorable thing I ever saw."

Taps laughed. "Tell you what. After the show tonight, drop into Lindy's casually with your mother and I'll introduce you."

Lindy's restaurant, on Broadway and 51st Street, was

then as now one of Broadway's most popular rendezvous for show people. That night it poured, but Mother and I arrived in style in our magnificent Hudson. Neither Taps nor the judge were in the restaurant. We waited for nearly an hour. Then a telephone message came for me.

"We're up here at Pomerantz'," said Taps. "He changed his mind."

We hurried out, hailed my chauffeur, and drove wildly through the rain to Pomerantz', another restaurant some thirty blocks north on Broadway. When we entered I saw the judge at a table, and my heart began to thump. I began twisting my handkerchief like a 15-year-old.

"I want you to meet Miss Lillian Roth and her mother," said Taps, doing the honors. "This is Judge Shalleck and his brother Joe."

The judge had a little smile as he shook my hand. He knew I had come up in the downpour to meet him. There was silence for a moment. Joe Shalleck, who I'd heard was a well-known criminal lawyer, began the conversation.

"Who are you?"

"My name is Lillian Roth."

"I know that. But what do you do?"

I stared at him coldly. "I walk a tightrope," I said.

"I see you bite your nails," he went on blandly. "What are you so nervous about? Look what you're doing to your handkerchief."

"That's just a little idiosyncrasy of mine," I retorted. "And anyway, look how you chew your cigar." I was furious. I wanted to get up and walk out.

"You've got a case coming up before my brother—tomorrow, isn't it?" Joe pursued. I said, "Yes." The judge, who had been sitting back smoking a cigar, spoke for the first time. "Is that what you wanted to talk to me about?"

"No," I said, ready to cry with mortification. "What's $232 to me?"

"It seems strange that we should meet the night before."

I rose. "I'm leaving. Can I drop you anywhere? I have a car outside."

They strolled out with me. "Is that your car—the red one?" demanded the judge, in a tone of disbelief. "I wouldn't be seen riding in that fire-engine! Why, it's the gaudiest thing I ever saw."

"It's not red, it's iridescent ruby," I said icily. "As far as I'm concerned, you can both walk. It will do you good." With that parting shot I assisted my mother into the car and followed regally; our chauffeur tipped his hat, and we drove off.

"I hate men like that!" I almost wept. "I won't go into that courtroom tomorrow."

In the morning, however, I was there, as I knew I would be. Judge Shalleck ruled against me; by the time I paid my lawyer, the case had cost me well over $400.

The judge called me before him. "Are you satisfied with the verdict?"

"Should I be?"

"Well, if you want to be technical, perhaps not."

"You mean you're having doubts about your decision? Isn't that a strange admission for a judge?"

He reddened slightly. "Miss Roth, you are morally responsible for this debt, even if you are a minor. And you're able to pay it."

"That's perfectly all right with me," I said curtly. "Goodbye."

"Now, now, wait a minute," he said placatingly. "I'm just reading about you—in Winchell's column." He had the New York *Daily Mirror* spread open before him. I leaned over to read: "Lillian Roth and her flyer spouse are straining at the handcuffs."

"Well!" I said with some spirit, "no wonder I lost my case if you're reading a paper while it went on!"

He grinned. "Seriously," he said, "is there any truth in it?"

I drew on my gloves. "Well, in a way it's so."

He picked up his gavel and toyed with it. "Be home tonight," he said. "I'll call you."

"Is that a court order?" I retorted.

He laughed, and I laughed.

We drank beer at a speakeasy the following evening. I felt as self-conscious as a little girl. I had headlined with famous personalities, I had seen police holding back crowds struggling to see me, I had signed hundreds of autographs—yet I was in awe of this 34-year-old judge of the municipal court bench.

On the way home he asked, "When are you going to be divorced?"

The question was completely unexpected. As a matter of fact, I hadn't thought about divorce. "Well, I really don't know," I replied.

"My brother can handle it for you," the judge said. "Why don't you see him tomorrow?"

We were at the entrance of my hotel. "Good-night," he said, and kissed me. It was April, the first anniversary of my marriage to Willie.

Joe Shalleck was helpfulness itself. A Mexican divorce could be arranged. All I was required to do was telephone Willie in Pittsburgh to sign the necessary papers.

"I can't do that," I said unhappily. "I just couldn't break it to him."

Joe Shalleck understood. If that's the way I felt, he would handle that, too.

Two days later a heartbroken Willie was in my hotel room, weeping. How could I do this to him? I wavered, on the verge of calling off the divorce. After all, I liked Willie and he was in love with me. The telephone rang. Judge Shalleck was in the lobby, waiting to take me for a drive.

"Please," Willie begged. "I'm sick, Lillian, I need you. I've lost twenty pounds, Lillian. I've got tuberculosis."

I knew he was playing on my sympathy, but I had too much experience with illness to dismiss his words. "All right, Willie," I said "I'll call your mother tonight and if what you say is true, I'll go back with you."

I went out with the judge. Willie took a room at the hotel.

His mother told me there was nothing wrong with Willie, when I called her. She understood my position: she agreed that we were not meant for each other.

CHAPTER XII

I F JUDGE SHALLECK wants me to divorce Willie, I reasoned, he must want to marry me. He was one of the town's eligible bachelors, I knew. He had only recently been elected to the bench. He was proud of the telegram he showed me not long after our first meeting, from Governor Franklin D. Roosevelt, congratulating him. "From what the Counsel to the Governor has told me of your ability and experience and qualifications," it read, "I am sure you will make a very splendid record." Ironically, years later, in 1949, Ben Shalleck was defeated for Congressman on the democratic ticket by Franklin D. Roosevelt, Jr.

I day-dreamed. I would be a judge's wife. I would have a home, and children, and a warm family circle. My life would take on meaning and stability.

The divorce went through on schedule. As a parting gift I gave Willie the plane he loved so much. I began seeing the judge almost nightly. His courtship was nothing to fill a girl's diary. He arrived around nine o'clock, the *Mirror* and *Daily News* under his arm, and two nickle packages of mints for me. He greeted me, settled himself comfortably on the sofa, and lost himself in his newspapers. Once a week he took me to a fight or a hockey game.

My grand passion began to subside. Was this how a man treated a woman whose divorce he had arranged? I felt like an iniquitous woman, for he never spoke of marriage.

I went on a two-week tour. When I returned a friend told me the judge had been dining a girl he used to go with. I was furious. He rarely dined *me*. I was the girl he visited! Where was he now? In Chicago, at the Democratic National Convention, with his pal, Jimmy Hines, democratic leader in New York.

I took the first plane for Chicago, marched into his hotel and rang him from the lobby. "This is Lillian. I'm downstairs."

"Come up," he said calmly.

I walked into his room. Before he could get the cigar out of his mouth to kiss me, I demanded, "Is it true you've been taking someone else out while I was away?"

He looked at me for a moment, and slowly replaced his cigar. "Do I ask you who you go out with?"

"I haven't been going out with anyone else, but if that's the way it is, O. K. Goodbye!" I strode toward the door.

"Wait a minute," he said. "Wouldn't you like to stay over for the nominations? Here with me?"

I whirled on him. "No!" I screamed. "I nominate you Cad of 1932! You and your gavel and your cigar!" I slammed the door behind me.

I took the next plane to New York, threw myself into my work, and tried to forget the judge. I was to open almost immediately at the Capitol Theatre, making personal appearances with Abe Lyman, Milton Berle and Bette Davis. As I hurried up Broadway to the Capitol, I saw that Milton's name was above mine on the marquee.

This was too much. The friendly feud we'd had through the years was all very well, but enough was enough. My contract called for first billing, and suddenly I was the Lillian Roth who walked out on Earl Carroll years before. I laid down an ultimatum to the Capitol management: I wanted my top billing.

To those not in the profession, it may seem childish to take billings so seriously. But you work hard to become a star: you fight to keep the position you've won. When you drop from it, the thud echoes from Broadway to Hollywood.

Inexplicably, Milton came down with a heart flutter in his dressing room. He was sure he couldn't go on. It took high finesse to meet this crisis. While Milton rested in his room, an emissary was sent to me. Would I consent to split billing? My name would be first on the side of the marquee facing downtown. Milton wanted his first on the opposite side—facing Lindy's restaurant.

"All right," I said. "Let Milton's friends at Lindy's see that he has top billing. I'd rather be first in the eyes of the people coming up from the subways."

The judge returned to New York and began telephoning me once a week. My feeling toward him had chilled: our conversations were almost impersonal. "Well," he concluded each one, "I guess I'll be seeing you around sometime." "That's right," I replied coldly. "You'll see me around—unless I see you first."

I was not at a loss for dates. On the rebound from the judge, I met a tall, dark, handsome magician, Fred Keating, who was on the bill with Russ Columbo and me at the Brooklyn Paramount. Fred was gay, witty, ready to do anything for a laugh: we were both out for a good time, and we had it together. I told him he had the magic to make me forget: he told me that not since Jeanne Eagels had a woman affected him so. Yet, inwardly I fumed. I wanted my revenge on the judge. Here I had lost Willie; and now the judge, who had encouraged my divorce, acted toward me as if I were just another casual love affair. Neither Fred nor drinking helped me put the judge out of my mind: I decided to return to Hollywood and resume my movie career.

When I walked into the judge's court to say goodbye, he called me up on the bench beside him. "I'm going to California," I said without preface. He laughed. "I don't believe it."

I swallowed my pride. "Ben, I don't have to go. You could keep me here. But once I leave, you'll never see me again."

He ruffled some papers in front of him. "I don't like to make decisions for you," he said noncommittally. "Shall I see you to the train?"

"No," I snapped. "Someone else is seeing me off." I almost ran from the courtroom.

That night Fred Keating kissed me goodbye, and I was enroute to Hollywood. Almost upon arrival, I was cast with Barbara Stanwyck in "Ladies They Talk About." In it I sang, "If I Could Be With You One Hour To-night."

Liquor, I thought, was no problem at this time. I could take it or leave it. Mostly I took it—though not while the picture was shooting. I drank to forget. The judge had ruined everything. Why hadn't I stayed with Willie, sweet, likable Willie? Or gone along with fun-loving

Fred? Why was I out here alone? It helped little that the judge wrote every few days. Like his telephone calls, his letters asked nothing and promised nothing.

The men with whom I now went out in Hollywood were interested only in one-night romances. I drank heavily. Frequently I blacked out, waking foggily at four or five in the morning, with no memory of what had happened. That frightened me. Where was all this leading to?

Warner Brothers, seeing the rushes of "Ladies They Talk About," promptly offered me a three-year contract at $1,500 a week. I spent several days in agonized indecision; and then, fortified with bourbon one night, I telephoned the judge.

"Hiya, Judgie," I greeted his voice, gaily. "There's a decision I want you to make—in my favor."

"What a nice surprise," he said, and his voice was cool over the wire. "But you shouldn't be spending your money on long-distance calls."

"Listen, Ben," I rushed the words. "Warner's are ready to give me a three-year contract. If I take it, I stay out here. I've been getting your 'Dear Lillian-Sincerely, Ben' letters. I really don't know what to think anymore. Ben—do you want me or don't you want me? You must make up your mind."

There was silence at the other end. Then: "I'll take a couple of weeks off at Christmas and come out there and we'll talk about it," he said.

When I hung up, I knew I had to settle this. I took another drink, packed my bags, flew to New York, and telephoned Ben. I was in New York, I told him. I would be over immediately. His apartment was fifty blocks from my hotel, and a snowstorm raged, but I walked the entire distance, the snowflakes melting on my burning face, before I trusted myself to speak to him. *I had gotten a divorce for that man: he was going to marry me,* I vowed.

When I entered his apartment, Joe Shalleck was there, too.

"Hello, Ben," I said. "I see you have your legal counsel with you. When do we set the date, boys?"

Ben carefully lit his cigar. Joe spoke: "Yes, Ben, why don't you name the day?"

"All right, John Alden," I snapped. "Let Ben speak for himself. He's pretty good, when he tries."

There was a silence. Ben drew pensively at his cigar. "Well, I don't know," he said finally. He looked at me, and his voice took on a judicial tone, as though he were summarizing a case. "You're certainly not the most beautiful girl in the world. You're certainly not the most brilliant. But there's something about you—maybe the way you crinkle your nose—or maybe I love you when you're angry—but you set the date."

"As far as I'm concerned, we can be married tomorrow," I said.

Joe spoke up again. "I'll order the invitations," he said. "The wedding's on me."

It was set for January 29, 1933.

The newspapers treated our nuptials with the dignity befitting a judge's wife-to-be. Wrote the New York *Sun,* on December 13, 1932: "The engagement of Miss Lillian Roth, stage and screen actress, and Municipal Court

Justice Benjamin Shalleck, will be formally announced by her mother, Mrs. Catherine Roth, tonight at a birthday party at the jurist's apartment, 444 Central Park West, when the thirty-fifth anniversary of Justice Shalleck's birth and Miss Roth's twenty-second will be celebrated.

"The wedding will take place in January. Miss Roth will give up the stage and make her final public appearance at the Broadway Theatre on Sunday night for the James J. Hines Christmas Fund, the proceeds to go to buy Christmas dinners for the poor . . ."

"You understand," Ben had said, "you'll have to forget your career." I knew that. I wanted a normal life. I didn't like myself in California. I didn't like the kind of men who took me out, nor the drinking, nor the blackouts. What had Paul Bern told me when I first arrived in Hollywood, stardust dazzling my eyes? The men in my life would make or break me.

Without misgivings I gave up my career at high tide. M-G-M phoned me from Hollywood. Paramount wanted me for an important part. Warner's offered to co-star me with Loretta Young in "She Couldn't Say No."

To them all, I could—and did—say no.

The elaborate wedding reception at the Savoy Plaza was at four, the ceremony at nine, the train for Florida left at ten. Mother was tearful but happy, my father drank toasts to everyone. I was gay over repeated goblets of champagne. The guest list of 1,000 was a rollcall of stage and political personalities: Jimmy Hines, New York Democratic leader, Judge and Mrs. Samuel Rosenman, Justice John J. Sullivan, Basil O'Connor, former law-partner of President-elect Roosevelt, Benny Leonard, Father Thomas O'Neil, Mr. and Mrs. Jesse Lasky, George White, Earl Carroll, Abe Lyman and many more. Ben stood up and read telegrams as they poured in. One he read before he realized it was addressed to Miss Lillian Roth. It said, "Better luck next time." It was signed, "Fred Keating."

When Ben and I left, Dad was asleep in a chair in the lobby. I bent over and kissed him. He lifted one eyelid. "Take care of my baby," he mumbled, and fell asleep again.

The moment Ben and I were alone in our drawing room, butterflies struck my stomach. I was locked in. It was as it had been with Willie, all over again. *Now what have I done? Why did I pursue this? I don't love him. . . .*

Desperately I wanted a drink. "Isn't there any more champagne?" I asked Ben. "You won't need it, darling," he said, as he pulled me to him.

After he fell asleep, I lay awake as the train sped through the night, listening to the long, haunting whistle at the crossings, staring out the window at the stars. The moon rode high and clear; the nearest stars were all but invisible. But farther up the sky, they shone large and bright. Was it true that each person who dies has a star to look out from? Was David looking down at me, and what was he thinking?

Our second night in Miami the judge heard me rummaging in my trunk. He came into the bedroom. "I've been looking everywhere for some papers," he remarked.

"Do you suppose your mother packed them in your trunk by mistake?"

"I don't think so, Ben," I said hurriedly. "I'm sure she didn't.

"Let me look." He searched my trunk and in each drawer he found a quart of liquor hidden under the lingerie.

"What have you all this for?" he asked in astonishment.

"Well," I said nervously, "I thought—well—I thought we might give some parties here—"

"Oh, Lillian! You know liquor is available here."

I tried to make clear that I wasn't going to drink the liquor, I just had to know that it was there.

"Why do you have to know it's there?" he asked.

"I don't know, Ben!" I said wildly. "Let me alone. I just have to know it's there!"

Many friends from show business were in Miami that week—Sid Skolsky, Jack Benny, Walter Winchell—but it was a stormy week for Ben and me, with tears and arguments over my drinking. We went on to Havana, where I fell in love with Presidentes, cocktails heavily laced with absinthe. I passed out several times: absinthe was powerful, but it wasn't going to beat me. I drank more Presidentes, and lay most of the day in a stupor on the beach.

In the train back to New York, Ben asked, "Is this the way our married life is going to be, Lillian? Are you just going to continue to drink?"

"I don't do anything wrong, Ben," I replied miserably. "And I'm really not drinking so much. Don't I really behave all right? But if it worries you, I promise it'll be different when we get back." I would be a real judge's wife to him, I vowed: "We'll have a beautiful home and maybe we can have a baby right away."

Our apartment—with an extra bedroom for the baby we hoped to have—overlooked a magnificent vista of Central Park, with its blue lake gleaming like a jewel in a green setting. I indulged in a spree of decorating, and I was proud to think that I was one of the first in New York to use bold white and black: white walls, black velvet couches, zebra-striped pillows, white leather seats, a modern bedroom with spun-glass walls. I had everything a woman could want: youth, position, a handsome, respected husband, and I was financially independent— money I had earned, a bank account of more than a quarter of a million dollars. What more could I desire?

"Why not," I suggested to Ben some weeks later, "why not have open house once a week? I love to watch people have fun and I want to help you politically."

Thus began the tradition of the Shallecks' Saturday night parties. They were successful from the start. Besides Mother and Ann, our steady guests included many who had been at our wedding, as well as such friends as Georgie Jessel, Lita Gray Chaplin, Milton Berle and Nino Martini.

Ben was delighted after the first party. "You were a wonderful hostess, darling," he said. "I was proud of you. You hardly drank."

"Of course not, Ben," I said, and I believed it. "When I have exciting things to do, I never think of a drink."

He was unaware that I had fortified myself before the

guests arrived. "You know, Lillian can't drink much," he commented one night. "She takes one drink and it lasts her all night. Look at her, bouncing around full of energy." He could not know that as I made the drinks in the kitchen, I sampled them; or that long after the last guest had left, the maid and I began our own drinking party as we emptied ashtrays and cleaned up . . . while Ben slept the sleep of the innocent.

Ben could not know how I dreaded going to sleep. Strange memories and fears assailed me. David had died paralyzed and blind. My father had been virtually paralyzed that night as he sat in a drunken stupor after beating Katie. I had lain paralyzed when the old man with the cigar painted me, so long ago. So many nights, lying next to Ben, I closed my eyes and thought I slept, yet strangely, I was awake . . . I must be awake because I could look across the room and see the dressing table with my perfumes on it. I could see the chair opposite our bed—first its legs, then the judge's shoes and socks, then his trousers neatly placed across the chair, then his shirt and jacket carefully placed above the trousers—all precisely, meticulously laid out, ready for the next day. "All that's missing is his gavel," I thought, and giggled. Or was I giggling? Was I awake? I couldn't move. Invisible chains bound me. I tried to scream, but no sound came. My throat was locked. *Now I'm screaming but he doesn't hear me. Easy, easy . . . this will pass. You'll have it again, but it will pass. . . .* Then, unexpectedly, I could move. I would get out of bed, my heart thumping madly, my body soaked in perspiration, and with a shaking hand pour myself a drink, and then another, and then another, from the bottle I now had hidden in the clothes hamper

[128]

in the bathroom. Then I could go to sleep and the paralyzed dream, the screaming trapped helplessness, would
not come again.

When a woman wants a child and cannot have it, her
yearning can become an obsession. Motherhood, I
thought, would bring me the peace I sought. It would
dull that indefinable ache, the loneliness that was my
other self, the something I wanted I knew not what.
Perhaps I would find contentment if I had a child of my
own upon whom I could pour the love locked in my
heart, the love I could give to no man save David and his
memory.

In vain Ben and I consulted physicians. No babies
came. Had the child been a boy, his name would have
been Charles; a girl, Anna—both named for Ben's father
and mother. We had it all arranged. In the end, I resigned myself to being childless.

Yet I had to keep busy. Perhaps mothering other
people's children was the answer. Soon I was taking a
score of orphans to my home of an afternoon, arranging
little parties, serving ice cream and cake, and surprising
them with little gifts. I took them on auto trips to the
zoo and sometimes to the circus.

With Molly Minsky, wife of the burlesque impresario,
I founded a philanthropic organization, the Charlanna
League, named for the children I could not have, to raise
funds for the Second Street Day Nursery. I held lunch-
eons and cocktail parties which sometimes began at three
p.m. and lasted through midnight. There was a kitty on
the bar; at the end of the party I found many $50 and
$100 bills.

Others in our group were Mrs. Berle and her daughter Rosalind, Lita Chaplin, Mitzi Green and her mother, Florence Lustig and Ruth Bernstein, old friends, and Ben's sister, Estelle Milgrim. We held bazaars and rummage sales, and raised considerable amounts of money. A glass of beer kept me amiable for hours at the sales. After I came home, however, I had to take several straight drinks, and even a stronger nightcap to ward off my fearsome dreams.

In the few years my League was in existence, I resigned three times. Some new members resented the strict parliamentary rules I insisted upon at meetings. (Ben had taught me this.) I was high-handed, they complained. Perhaps I was. I worked hard, and never failed to fortify myself before a meeting.

What particularly incensed me was the charge that I engaged in charity work for publicity. At one meeting I announced:

"I've been glorified internationally and I don't need the glory of a hundred women. If you think I'm doing this for personal publicity, I'm resigning. I'll do my own charity work."

High-handed or not, apparently I could raise money, and each time a resolution was passed to invite me back. The final straw came during a particularly cold February when nearly all the members were wintering in Florida. I called a meeting of the handful in New York and we voted $1,000 from the treasury to buy shoes and snowsuits for needy youngsters.

When the sojourning members returned, they put me on the carpet. "These children managed to live all these years without you," one woman snapped. "You had no right to spend this money when we were away."

I was too hurt to answer. I resigned for good, and went home. Couldn't I get along with anyone? Couldn't anything work out right for me?

Although beer by day and liquor by night satisfied me while I was busy in the Charlanna League, now my nerves demanded more. I switched from a morning beer to a jigger of liquor first thing after I awoke.

It seemed a good formula. I improved upon it by pouring two ounces of bourbon into my breakfast orange juice, so the judge was none the wiser. One afternoon I was shopping at Saks-Fifth Avenue with Ruth Bernstein. I stood examining charm bracelets at the counter, when the store began to spin. Sweat streamed from my forehead and splashed in large drops on the counter before me. My knees began to buckle. I couldn't swallow.

I clutched Ruth. "Get me outside."

I leaned against the storefront and the cold air revived me. I caught my breath. "Oh," I said. "But that was a bad moment. Must be something I ate." We continued shopping. A few minutes later, while Ruth was trying on a hat in another store, it happened again.

She managed to steer me outside, where the people and the traffic and the noise of the avenue rushed headlong at me. She hailed a cab and opened the windows. "Should I take you to a doctor?" she asked anxiously.

"No—I can't swallow—get me water, quick!" I gasped.

The knowing cabbie, who overheard us, stopped before a bar. The bartender took one glance at me.

"Water, hell," he exclaimed. "She needs a drink." He poured out a tumbler of rye. "Here, get this down, Miss."

I reached for the glass. My hand shook so violently the liquor spilled. Ruth held the glass to my lips.

The bartender watched me. "These spells come often?" he asked casually. I shook my head. "Take a tip, Miss," he said, "carry a shot or two with you in the future."

I realized that I could never go out of the house again without liquor. Orange juice and bourbon in the morning was not enough. The physical demand was growing. I would need liquor more often—not because I wanted it, but because my nerves required it. Since I was a judge's wife, I couldn't be seen dropping into bars: I must carry my own liquor. That day I bought small two-ounce medicine bottles in the drug store, filled them with liquor, and thereafter was never without a couple in my purse.

Soon I was slipping down doorways, vanishing into ladies' rooms, anywhere I could gain privacy, to take a swift drink to ward off the spells that came upon me with increasing frequency. The two-ounce bottles graduated to six-ounce, and then to a pint, and in the last years of my marriage to the judge, wherever I went, I carried a fifth of liquor in my bag.

"Lilly, darling, aren't you drinking too much?" my mother worriedly asked one day. Neither she nor Ben had any idea of how much I consumed daily; but they knew of my nervous spells.

"Oh, Mom, I can stop when I want to," I said irritably. "When I have work to do, don't I do it? When I have to run a charity affair, don't I handle it well? Don't I behave all right in public?"

Once, driving down Tenth Avenue with my sister-in-law, Estelle, I said, "I don't know why I'm so unhappy.

I have everything in the world. And yet . . . Estelle,"
I said somberly, "I see myself very poor someday. I see
myself deserted. Something awful is going to happen to
me. I'm going to be penniless and my great fear is, what
will I do? And what will happen to my mother?"

"How can you cry carrying cake in both arms?" she
said, marvelling.

I went on the wagon. After all, I could stop drinking
when I wanted to. On the third day, I found myself
pacing back and forth in my apartment, crying out,
"Why am I so nervous?" I bit my lips until they bled,
trying to control my trembling body. "What *is* this?" I
asked, in desperation. "I haven't had anything to drink in
forty hours. What's happening to me? Maybe my mind's
giving way." I threw myself into a chair and sat there,
shaking. My skin began to itch with crawling things that
weren't there. I struck at my body, my thighs, my legs.
I scratched until the blood came. I'm going mad, I
thought. I'm going to burst right open. I can't stand what
I'm going through. In desperation I hurled myself against
the spun-glass walls of our bedroom, raised my hands
high against the wall and slid them hard across it, lacerat-
ing the palms, moaning with the pain. They oozed blood
in a hundred places. Maybe the hurt would drive away
the horror, the tingling, the panic, everything. . . .

I gave in. I took the drink I didn't want to take.

CHAPTER XIII

THERE WERE some happy moments in the years with Ben. One of the brightest was when I rented and furnished a small apartment in the same building for my mother, so that we could be near each other; another, to see her joy when I surprised her on her birthday with a $10,000 check for a trip to the French Riviera.

There was the thrill of returning to work in pictures. I was offered a part in "Take a Chance," the movie version of a Broadway hit starring Ethel Merman. The film was to be made in Astoria. Ben was doubtful about the idea.

"You don't know what it will mean to me, Ben," I pleaded. "I simply have to do something. And you know I never drink when I have things to do."

He agreed. I worked in the picture with old friends— Buddy Rogers, Jimmy Dunn, June Knight, Lillian Bond and Cliff Edwards. My big song numbers—"Come Up and See Me Sometimes" and "Eadie Was a Lady"—were hits. When the film opened in Washington, D. C., I went along to make a personal appearance, accompanied by Katie.

For an entire week I was blissful. I drank nothing. I was away from Ben, I was with my mother, and we loved being together.

We returned to New York.

I let myself into our apartment. It was three p.m. I sat down and waited for the judge. I glanced through my mail, thumbed through a few magazines—and the old nervousness possessed me. I had no desire to drink, but I was bored, and I wanted to be gay and relaxed when Ben arrived: I wanted his eyes to light up when he saw me. I went into the bathroom and to the clothes hamper, where I kept my own liquor. Ben, by now, was marking off the amount remaining in our decanters on the sideboard, to check how much I drank.

When he came in at 5:30, I was slumped in an easy chair, glassy-eyed.

He stood over me. "Have you been like this all week?"

"Honest to God, Ben, ask my mother," I said thickly. "I only had a couple."

He took me into his arms. "Why did you do it, Lillian?"

"I don't know," I sobbed. "I don't know why I did it, I won't do it again, I promise, I won't."

"Maybe she ought to have something to occupy her mind," said Joe Shalleck, bringing home several law books. "You've got a good brain, Lillian. There are only a few women lawyers. If you were smart, you'd take up law. With our help you'd finish high school and be practicing law before you're thirty."

"Why should she do that?" Ben asked. "She's a good wife, she's a good hostess, and if she didn't drink so much, she'd be a great help to me."

At times Joe defended me. "Ben, she really hasn't had time to sow her wild oats. That's why she drinks. If you'd drink with her and get gay, that would help."

Ben tried.

"Lillian," he would suggest, "let's not drink anything until Saturday night. Then we'll drink and you can get as high as you like." Or, "Let's spend Thursday night alone. We'll drink a whole bottle of sparkling Burgundy together, just you and me."

That sounded fair. "Isn't this nicer," he would ask, settling down in his easy chair with his glass of wine, "than going out and causing talk by drinking too much?"

But Ben did not realize that I was tortured. The slow drinking, the small amounts, only added fuel to the fire. I needed more, my body needed more. I kept jumping up, vanishing into the bathroom, taking a quick drink, and running back to chase it down with wine.

Burgundy and Southern Comfort—to which I had now switched—produce a startling effect when mixed. After he finished his glass, Ben would look at me and exclaim, "You see, Lillian, actually you can't drink. Two drinks and you're woozy."

He tried other strategy. When we were ready to retire, he would say, "Would you like a little drink, baby, before you go to bed?"

"I'd love it!" This was made to order for me. Now I could drink all I wanted without worrying about the odor of liquor on my breath.

We had a drink or two together. Between drinks, I leaned over and kissed him. "Benjie, you're really sweet," I said. "Let's have a little music. Turn on the radio—I feel like hearing Cab Calloway."

We sat, drinking, leisurely listening to the music.

"Now, darling, you get ready for bed and I'll take a quick shower," I said. "I'll be out in a few minutes."

I vanished into the bathroom and reached for the bottle, meanwhile turning on the shower full strength.

"Coming, dear?" This from the judge.

"Coming."

The shower poured down, its steady thrum sounding a pleasant background accompaniment as I finished my bottle. Sometimes, in half an hour, I drank an entire fifth.

"What takes you so long, darling?"

"I'm making myself beautiful, Ben." At the moment I was rinsing my mouth with Chanel No. 5. It burned terribly, but it made my lips smell sweet.

When I emerged, Ben threw aside his newspapers. "You know," he said, "you're not the most beautiful girl in the world. You're not the most brilliant girl in the world. But there must be something about you I like. Do you know that?"

I laughed merrily, and ran to my husband.

Ben's routine when he returned from court in the afternoon was always the same. He came in, hung up his coat and hat, washed his hands, walked into the living room, and kissed me. But some afternoons I drank: and when he kissed me he knew it. Then he would walk away and sit down, looking straight ahead.

Silence. I could not endure it.

"I'm sorry, Ben," I would say abjectly.

"All right. Let me know when dinner's ready." He buried his face in a newspaper.

He was silent through dinner and in silence we returned to the living room. He sat down and again looked straight ahead.

"Ben, I said I was sorry."

"I know."

"Why don't you talk to me?"

No answer.

"Oh, Ben, please, I'm sorry. It won't happen again. I'm just so nervous!"

Silence.

"Ben—let's go to a movie."

Silence. Calmly he undressed, donned his robe, brought out the bridge table, and began dealing himself a game of solitaire.

"Benjie—" I ventured tentatively.

Still silence.

Then it would happen. My jangling nerves would explode. "If this goes on I'll kill myself," I'd scream. "I can't stand it. I can't stand doing nothing. I'm going mad!"

One night I raced into the bathroom, tore open the medicine cabinet, and swept an entire shelf of bottles crashing to the tile floor.

No sound from Ben. I pushed open the bathroom door and peeked out. Methodically he was playing his game, placing a red ten on a black Jack.

I grabbed a bottle of iodine and lifted it to my lips. "I'm dying," I shrieked, "I'm dying."

Iodine causes a purple froth at the mouth. Ben glanced up, saw me, and quickly called the house physician. The latter examined me. "Not much went down, did it?" he asked, almost with a wink. I shook my head. "It burned too much," I whispered to him.

He told me to drink two glasses of milk and forget it.

The second time I did a better job. While Ben lay in bed reading the *Daily News*—Columnist Ed Sullivan only a few days earlier had written of the "radiantly happy

Judge Shallecks"—I nicked the veins of my wrist, gargled with iodine and emerged from the bedroom a frightening sight, frothing at the mouth, my hands stiff before me, my wrists dripping blood.

"You'll be sorry," I gasped. "Oh, Ben!" I fell dramatically to the floor at the entrance of the bedroom.

Ben continued reading. He did not even deign to look up. I scrambled to my feet like a madwoman and rushed at him, ripping off the covers and screaming, "You're a brute. You have no heart. You don't care if I die!" I worked myself into such a fit of hysterics that this time he cradled me in his arms. "All right," he said. "All right, now."

I wept. "I don't know why I do it, honest to God, Ben, I don't know why I do it."

I tried week-ending at milk farms. On one occasion Milton's mother, Sandra, accompanied me, and we took a room together. I tossed and turned all night.

"What is the matter, Lillian?" Mrs. Berle asked, time and again.

"I'm all right," I said. But I got out of bed and opened the windows because I was hot, and then I was chilled and got out of bed and closed them again.

In the morning the house physician dropped by. Mrs. Berle, he said, was concerned about me. I was a sick girl, she told him. How did I feel now?

"Really?" I said. By this time my jitters had gone. "I had a restless night and so would you if you were as darned hungry as I was. I'm fine."

He looked at me for a moment, then leaned close. "If I were you, Mrs. Shalleck, when you get back to town you ought to tell Milton that his mother is a very nervous woman. She was really agitated this morning. She insisted you were ill."

"Oh, no," I laughed. "I feel fine."

As a matter of fact, by the time I returned to New York, I felt fine. But when I came home, the judge was not there. Once again I had to wait for him. I went into the kitchen where my liquor was disguised in vinegar bottles, and drank myself into helplessness.

Ben talked to me. "You're sick, Lillian. You must see a doctor." I agreed. The physician who examined me minced few words. Unless I stopped drinking, he warned, "you won't live another five years."

"Oh, Doctor, that can't be," I insisted. "I just drink to soothe my nerves. I have no aches or pains. Besides, I can always stop when I want to."

Later I was taken to a second physician. "Judge, she's a high-strung girl," he said. "Temperamental. Not enough to occupy her. Let her drink a few brandies now and then. They'll relax her."

I switched to brandy. The doctor had said a few, but I overdid it. The brandy worked less quickly, yet it made my heart thump and gave me a sense of impending doom. I switched back to scotch, bourbon and gin.

Among the judge's friends, one of the most important was Jimmy Hines, political leader of Ben's district, and a power in Tammany Hall. I had heard of him, of course, before I met Ben; I had agreed to appear at one of Jimmy's benefits just before we were married. Later I read in the newspapers charges that he was the "Tam-

many Swagman," but even after District Attorney
Thomas Dewey sent him to jail for dealings with the
notorious Dutch Schultz, I couldn't believe him guilty.
I had always found him kind and decent: he and his wife
Geneva took part in my charity affairs, and Jimmy could
rarely say no to anyone.

Once I went to him with word that the Charlanna
League had voted to appropriate money to be divided
among the needy who couldn't be helped by the city or
were too proud to accept relief. Could he give me a list
of those in his district? Or take the money and see that
it was properly distributed?

"You'll have to find them for yourself, Lillian," he said.
"If I gave you a list or took the money, I might be accused of using your group for my own political purposes,
and you'd be accused of abetting corruption!" He
laughed, but he did not give me a list.

The first time I actually heard Jimmy linked with
Schultz was one bad morning when I was struggling with
an agonizing hangover. The house phone rang. There
were police reporters in the lobby, and could they be sent
up?

For a moment I was more stunned than befuddled.
Police reporters? Had the doorman said "police reporters"
or "police and reporters?" What had I to do with the
police? Was this a hoax—someone trying to gain admittance? Were they kidnappers who knew I had money?
Or holdup men? How could I escape, I thought frantically. They would come up the front elevator—I might
flee down the service elevator . . . if it happened to be
there when I dashed through the kitchen—

On the other hand, if they were reporters, I had better let them up and treat them nicely. The press was powerful.

My knees trembled, but I said with bravado, "Send them up." I'll give them a drink, I thought. Newspapermen like to drink. And I gulped down a few, for courage.

The doorbell buzzed. My maid opened it, and suddenly nearly a dozen reporters and photographers, waving flashbulbs and cameras, were dashing into the room.

"Where is he?" one demanded excitedly.

"Who, the judge?" I stammered. I stood in the reception hall, one arm braced against the door jamb, barring them from the living room, like Jeanne Eagels in "The Letter."

"Look, Mrs. Shalleck," one reporter snapped. "We know he's here. Where's Dutch?"

For a moment the word didn't register. "Dutch? Dutch who?" I pulled away from him, drawing the collar of my dressing gown tight around my throat, tossing my head defiantly, like Lenore Ulric in "Kiki."

Another reporter said in a quieter voice, "Dutch Schultz, Mrs. Shalleck. Didn't you read Winchell this morning?"

He showed me the clipping. Walter had asked: "What two brothers, legalites, and the show girl spouse of one of them are hiding Dutch Schultz in their penthouse apartment on 86th Street?"

I became panicky. Two brothers? Legalites? 86th Street penthouse apartment? It all added up. Joe, a criminal lawyer, might defend people like Schultz. But Ben—how was he involved? And would he hide anyone like Dutch Schultz in our home?

I telephoned the judge while the reporters rummaged through the apartment. Ben talked to some of them on the phone. He told me later that he threatened libel suits if they connected the Shallecks any way with Schultz in print.

After they left I was a bundle of nerves. I could picture all New York and Hollywood talking about Lillian Roth hiding a gangster in her apartment.

The afternoon papers cleared it up. The showgirl whose picture appeared on page one wasn't Lillian Roth, but Hope Dare, who lived in a penthouse on *East* 86th Street. Ours was *West* 86th Street. One of the lawyers Winchell had in mind was Dixie Davis, Hope Dare's boy friend. The Shallecks were innocent.

Ben got home as early as he could. "What better reason could a woman in my position have to take a drink or two?" I cried. "I had to take it for my nerves."

Rabbi and Mrs. Stephen Wise, whom I had met through the Charlanna League, knew how much I wanted a baby. They called to tell us about a beautiful five-month-old baby girl, now in England, whose parents had died in Hitler's concentration camps. Mrs. Wise later showed me a photograph, and I fell in love with the little girl. "If I could only adopt her," I said. "I'd give her so much love—"

Mrs. Wise put her arm around my shoulder. "We'll try," she said. "Perhaps we can make arrangements to bring the child over for you."

I was ecstatic. This was the answer: this would solve everything.

In gratitude I threw an enormous "Drop In" party,

with proceeds to go to the Wises' favorite project, the Mrs. Stephen Wise Guest House for Refugee Doctors. To give the party a proper institutional air, I sent out invitations reading, "The Regina League invites you to a Charity Cocktail Party." There was no such league, but Regina was the name we were going to give our little adopted girl.

The party was a brilliant success. Food came from Reuben's and Lindy's and Dave's Blue Room; liquor from the White Horse and King's Ransom people and Jack and Charlie of "21." We received millinery, bags, shoes and gowns from Milgrim's and other stores, and raffled them off. Sherman Billingsley brought some Stork Club regulars, and the guests were a rollcall of Broadway's best-known personalities. I raised more than $5,000.

Mrs. Wise kissed me. "I never dreamed that a little girl like you would be able to do all this in one afternoon!"

Late that night Charlotte and Harry Ritz, who were leaving next morning for California to fill a picture contract, sat up with us far into the small hours, helping us celebrate. I had made the Wises happy, Katie was happy, Ben was happy. Regina was on her way.

"There's only one thing that I'm concerned about," I said to Charlotte, as we sat about our little dinette. "Mrs. Wise tells me it may be four or five months before the baby comes over. What will I do with myself until then?"

Charlotte was describing the house they had rented in California. "What time does your train leave?" I asked idly.

Harry looked at his wristwatch. "Nine a.m.—five hours from now."

"You know," I said dreamily, "I have a yen to get on that train with you. Everytime I hear a train whistle, I get an eerie, empty feeling—I want to go someplace, I don't know where—"

"Well, why don't you?" Harry spoke up. "Come along with us."

"Yes, why don't you?" Ben echoed. "You've been working hard. Katie and I will join you out there when my vacation begins. And if Regina arrives before then, we'll send for you."

Without any great certainty as to what I felt in my heart, I began packing. Dawn was breaking. To be sure of whatever it was I wanted to be sure of, I tucked away five bottles of rye whiskey among my clothes.

I did not know it, but my six unfulfilled years with Ben were coming to an end—empty witness to what might have been.

CHAPTER XIV

ALL MY HOPES lay in Regina. I marked time, and marking time was intolerable without drinking. And I told myself that I could always stop when Regina came.

A letter arrived from Ben. Something had gone wrong. Our little orphan wasn't coming to America after all. But he and Katie would be with me in six weeks.

The news was like a physical blow. I had counted so much on the baby! That night the Ritzes, knowing my dejection, took me to a club party. Brought to our table by mutual friends was a man, perhaps ten years older than I, who was introduced to me as Art. Art looked a little like Bing Crosby, and a little like my father—blue-eyed, light brown hair, an engaging grin. He had a dry sense of humor.

"Do we have to stay at this party?" he asked after a while. "Let's take a little drive around."

Harry and Charlotte didn't mind. Perhaps they understood better than I knew at what loose ends I was. "We're just a bunch of old married couples," Harry said. "You go ahead and have some fun."

We drove to an all-night bar, where Art quietly matched my bourbon and water with ginger ales. "Don't you drink?" I asked. "Once in a while," he said. "But when I do, I get bad. Nobody's safe around me then, because I go wild."

"I know what you mean," I said. Here was a kindred soul. I grew to know him better in the days that followed. We spoke the same language. He seemed to enjoy my company, and I—I found it easy to relax with him. Thus I rationalized the fact that I enjoyed parties, nightclubs, prize fights and long drives with him. He was morose more often than not, but I could cheer him up: he leaned on me, and that gave me strength.

Things began to look up a bit. I got an offer to appear at the Trocadero, one of Hollywood's smartest nightclubs, and Art helped me pull myself together.

I took a lovely suite nearby. The morning after my opening M-G-M phoned me. They wanted to test me for a part. Perhaps I would be launched on another picture career and forget the loss of Regina.

Ben wired me the night before he and Katie arrived. I telephoned Art. "It will have to be goodbye," I said. "You were wonderful to me when I needed a friend— but I'm awfully fond of you, and that isn't good. It would be better if I don't see you again."

He took it philosophically. "Anything you say," he said. "But I'll be around town."

That night I went to Lita Chaplin's home and began to drink. At midnight I drove to my apartment. Once inside, I felt utterly dejected. There was no Regina, no Art. And I had to face the judge and Mother in a few hours.

When Katie and Ben arrived at three a.m., they found me on the couch. They shook me. I managed to say blearily, "Hello, Ben. Hello, Mom." In my stupor I heard them.

"There's just nothing that can be done with this girl," the judge was saying. "What *are* we going to do, Katie?"

And my mother's despairing voice: "I don't know what's gotten into Lilly. She's such a good girl, Ben; she must be sick."

Miserable days followed. As usual Ben wanted to do nothing. He refused to play golf; neither did he wish to go swimming, or play tennis, or go nightclubbing, or do anything but join Katie in gin-rummy—and read his newspapers.

I found myself turning again to Art for comfort. I could face him being myself, without a sense of guilt or incompetence. Art was anything but suave and dapper: I discovered now that he belonged to the betting world, about which I knew little. He can't quote Gladstone, and Roosevelt never congratulated him, I thought, but he can cheer me up.

Finally I spoke to Ben, "I can't go back to New York with you. My future is here. M-G-M wants to test me. I must try my career again. I just can't go back to New York and that empty life. . . . Ben, without the child there's nothing. Let's face it."

"Maybe you're right, Lillian," he said. "But you've been drinking. Sleep on it, and we'll talk it over tomorrow."

Next morning I felt the same. I tripled my pre-breakfast drink to give me courage to tell Ben I had to go through with my plans. We had words and at one point Ben, pale with anger, approached me. I stumbled and fell down a flight of stairs just as my mother appeared.

It was the Katie of old who raged at Ben. "That's no way to treat my daughter, drinking or not drinking," she shouted. "You know she hasn't any balance when she's like that. She could have killed herself."

Ben apologized. "It was an accident," he protested. I was in a red haze of fury as I got to my feet.

"Last night you agreed with me. I'm not so drunk I don't remember. Now you can get out. You haven't supported me, you haven't done one thing for me. I loaned you money, when you needed it, I don't owe you anything. You can get out—and get out this afternoon!"

After he left I paced the room. What had I done now? It helped matters little that Art met me an hour later at a bar. I expected him to comment on the news of my breakup, but he was silent.

In the next few weeks we drank together and Art began to show a different side. "You've got to control your liquor," he said unexpectedly one night, and there was a flicker of disgust in his eyes. For a moment I had a sinking feeling in my stomach.

"All right, I'll try," I promised. And since he was so interested, would he tell me what all this led to? We were seeing a great deal of each other. Was he going to marry me?

"Look, kid," he said, "you're not even divorced yet."

"If I knew we were going to be married, I'd go to New York and make arrangements."

He thought that over for a moment. "If you don't know what you want, why don't you traipse back to the judge?"

That shocked me into two days of sobriety. Then Katie

had to return to New York: Ann was not well. I was alone and started to drink again. I was not accountable to anyone now.

Art walked in one night, his mood sullen. "Still drinking, eh? If you want to see what drinking is, I'll show you." He brought out three bottles of bourbon and began to drink steadily. "You know what you are," he said suddenly. "You're a no-good bum!" He began to slap me. I broke away, only to have him put out his foot and trip me. I scrambled to my feet and managed to make the door. "I'll show you what liquor is—" he flung after me.

I was frightened. Never had a man treated me like this before. I tried to explain away the episode. Hadn't he warned me how liquor affected him? I wasn't so charming when I drank, either. When he met me again, one night, at the Clover Club bar, I attempted a middle course. "Just one bourbon, Art," I said, as I slid onto a stool next to him. "That's my limit tonight."

He guffawed, and I knew he had been drinking. "Set up ten in a row here," he ordered the bartender, then turned to me. "Show the customers, Lillian. Drink 'em all. You know you can do it."

Rather than create a scene, I downed five in succession. Later, at the bar, as I clung to him glassy-eyed, he suddenly shoved me away. "You're a bum," he said thickly. "Why don't you go back to New York? I'm sick of looking at your face." He reeled away.

Next day I called the William Morris agency. Could they book me in the East? At once? The answer was yes —Billy Rose's Casa Manana, in New York.

Something of my old gaiety returned with my name in

lights. Everett Marshall and I co-starred in the revue, and the critics were cordial. The week was also brightened by a visitor, Mr. Mark Harris, who sent his card in first, and then came backstage with orchids for me. He was a powerfully built six-footer, in his late thirties, distinguished in appearance, with an easy smile and a smooth continental manner.

"Do you recall meeting me, Miss Roth?"

Vaguely I remembered him. I had met him once with the judge, hadn't I? That was right. Was I busy this evening? If not, would I like to go places and have fun, all around town?

Why not? I thought. We made the rounds: the Stork Club, "21," El Morocco, Toots Shor, the Plaza. He telephoned me every day. He called for me every evening. The New York World's Fair of 1939 was in full swing at Flushing Meadows, and Mark was engaged in public relations there. He was delightful company. He knew how to order correctly at the best restaurants, insisted upon the proper wine with each course, and never failed to send orchids. He was solicitous: gallantly he opened doors, pulled out chairs, made sure I wasn't sitting in a draft, saw to it that I received the best of everything. He was ardent and masterful; and at the end of a week, he told me he was madly in love with me.

As I considered this, my dressing room telephone rang. It was the judge. He invited me to go to dinner, one evening, and I accepted. Later, in my apartment, he told me he was glad to see that I had calmed down. Hollywood, he went on, was no place for me. I belonged here, in New York. So saying, he became amorous.

"If that's the way you feel," I said, repentant, "perhaps we should go back together again. The decree won't be final for a year, you know."

But Ben wasn't prepared to make it official again. He suggested that we could, however, see each other often, as if nothing had happened. He was ready to take a little house for me in Long Island. . . .

I exploded. "I was your wife! Do you think I'd become your mistress?" I screamed, and pushed him away. I downed a drink of bourbon, and then another . . . I blacked out. When I woke, it was morning. The aroma of Ben's cigar was still in the room.

The days that followed were chaotic. Art began to call me from the coast. Would I accept his abject apologies? He'd warned me he was ugly when he drank. He missed me terribly: I must come back to him.

Now it became impossible for me to cope with the situation. Mark telephoned me at all hours trying to persuade me to marry him. The judge upbraided me for ruining our marriage, yet refused to take me back as his wife. Art telephoned from the coast, pleading with me to return. I was confused, my life upset and bewildering. There was only liquor to help me escape trying to think at all. Finally, in my fourth and last week at the Casa Manana, although I pulled myself together for my act, I was in agony in the finale, because the alcohol had worn off and I needed more. My jaws stiffened, perspiration dripped from me, my voice faded to a whisper.

"I don't understand it," Billy Rose said. "Something must have happened, Lillian. You've been doing such a swell job—"

I barely made it through the last days, and when the show closed, I collapsed.

Katie was frightened as never before, and watched apprehensively as the doctor examined me. He gave his verdict. "Young lady, you need at least a six months' rest."

"You mean a ranch?" I asked, weakly.

"No. I mean a quiet sanitarium where you won't drink."

"Me, away for six months?" I cried out. Katie held my hand. "I won't make you go, Lilly. Don't worry, baby, I'll take care of you myself."

But I wouldn't let her. She had suffered enough. Instead, I hired a nurse and rented a cottage in the country. My nurse gave me the salt-water cure, which causes a revulsion toward alcohol. She dosed me with salt-water at every meal: it made me so ill I retched constantly. "I'm carrying out the doctor's orders, dear," she said. "I'm not taking any liquor away from you." She left a fifth of rye near my bed. When I tried to take a drink to halt my shakes, the nausea and cramps were excruciating. It was unbearable.

"Call Mr. Harris," I begged her. "I want to go back to town. Tell him we're flying back."

The Newark Airport was a sea of fire when Mark and my nurse helped me off the plane. I was a sight. I was bloated. I bore the marks of the mental anguish of the last few weeks, and I shook uncontrollably. "Good Lord!" exclaimed Mark. "You look awful—what happened to you?"

The nurse smiled thinly. "She doesn't like to drink any more, do you, Lillian?"

I could only glare weakly at her.

"Don't worry," said Mark. "Everything will be all

right." He took me to a hotel. Had I any money? "I have a few hundred dollars in my purse," I moaned. He explained that he had no money with him. "I'll take it down and pay your rent in advance." He left.

A few minutes later the desk clerk called up. "If you're taking the room by the month, you'll have to pay in advance."

"Didn't a man just come down and pay you?" I asked, bewildered.

No one had paid the bill.

I was distraught. I dismissed my nurse and telephoned Evie Jabon, a girl friend, to come over. By the time she arrived I was in a state of collapse. "Kiddo, you need a drink," she said, and ordered a bottle of rye. A few drinks calmed me down, and we managed to get into a cab and move to the Hotel Delmonico, where I was known.

Mark telephoned an hour later.

"I just thought of something I had to do when I left you," he said. "Then I went back and you were gone. I'll be right over."

I was confused. He didn't offer to return the money. In the next week I wrote checks constantly. I was under medical care, given vitamin injections, fruit juices, bromides, sleeping pills.

A new doctor came on the case. The dope and medication had taken their toll: I lay in a half-stupor. We were alone. He approached my bed and bent over me: I felt his warm hands on my body. I tried to protest, but the words would not come. He began caressing me, and suddenly my arms were pinned. It was a nightmare, in which I struggled wildly but my limbs were powerless: I seemed to be in a straitjacket, awake and yet not awake, paralyzed in a coma.

When Mark arrived later, I had come out of my stupor, but I knew what had happened. The doctor was gone. For the first time in my life I had been completely incapable of taking care of myself. I stammered out the story.

Mark looked at me incredulously. "Are you trying to tell me that he attacked you?"

"Yes," I moaned. "Yes."

Mark did not believe me.

"Ask him," I wept. "See what he says."

Mark returned later. "Lillian, you must have had a hallucination from the drugs," he said, soothingly. "I spoke to him in his office, face to face. He was stunned when I told him."

What can I do, I sobbed to myself. Nobody will believe me.

Two days later the doctor entered my room. I shrieked, "What are you doing here? Get out—"

"You're ill, Miss Roth," he said blandly.

"Get out!" I screamed at the top of my voice.

He got out.

Six months passed in a blur. Mark helped me prepare a statement to the press about my divorce from Ben. It read well:

I've been on the stage since I was a child. It's part of me and all my friends are stage people. I love parties—the kind that last until the small hours. However, it's different with my husband. He has to have sleep and a clear mind for his work in court. We had a long talk the other day and decided things just wouldn't work out. I still think he's a wonderful man.

For the rest, it was like a bad dream with vaguely familiar characters: Mark, my mother, myself. I remember day-long vigils in bars, driving a car eighty miles an hour through Long Island, plowing speedboats through Hell's Gate at fearful speeds on stormy nights, my mother crying as I drank and Mark drank with me.

In my lucid moments Katie warned me. "He's borrowing twenties and fifties from you. It will be thousands later. I know his type."

What difference did it make? I thought. Mark and I had something in common. We suffered the same weakness, the same agony: he could drink with me. We inhabited our private universe which others might not understand. I didn't love him, but who knew what love was, anymore? And who cared?

I had missed the newspaper stories about Mark—about his habitual drunkenness, his criminal record. He'd had several federal indictments, usually on confidence matters. At the time I met him he was out on bail on a charge for which he had been arrested a few months before. No one volunteered to tell me, but there was plenty to be learned about Mark's past.

He did tell me that he had a nine-year-old son by a previous marriage. The child was in boarding school. I saw Sonny once—blue-eyed, blond-haired, helpless and lonely.

I fell in love with the idea of caring for him. I thought, this is what I need. At last, a child to mother!

CHAPTER XV

I T STARTED in the Glass Hat on Lexington Avenue, where we ordered dinner. The date was January 22, 1940. The world outside was in turmoil. Hitler's armies were rolling across Europe, and violence raged over thousands of miles of earth. But Mark and I were working out, in our own tiny way, our salvation. We had been on the wagon for two weeks, each sustaining the other. For the first time in a long time tomorrow was beginning to promise a little more than yesterday.

Mark leaned across the table and said, "Mommy"—his pet name for me—"we've been so good, let's just have one little martini before dinner."

One couldn't hurt. Neither could a second, particularly since we firmly stopped at that. We smiled at each other over our glasses. We were proud of ourselves. Alcohol was our worst enemy, and at last we were doing something about it. And we got along well. "Why don't we get married?" Mark asked. "Maybe we will," I replied. "Let's start a brand new life together," he said—"you and I and Sonny."

"Maybe we will," I repeated. It was an attractive picture. My divorce from the judge, obtained on grounds of mental cruelty, had become final months earlier. I put one condition to Mark first and above all else: "Let's see if we can keep on the wagon," I said. "That's the key to everything."

Mark was carrying out his part. He was to leave early tomorrow for Detroit where, he said, he had an important war contract on tap. He was short of money, he remarked as we strolled to my apartment after dinner. Could I spare a little cash? I gave him $90 for his fare, and a check for $500 for expenses. Then we relaxed with a quiet game of Klabyash.

About nine o'clock, feeling hot and tired, I decided I'd take a shower. Then we would play one more hand, and he would go home and get a good night's sleep in preparation for his journey.

I came out of my room to find him slumped on the couch with a silly grin on his face. A quick glance into the kitchenette told me what had happened. He had consumed a fifth of gin in twenty minutes!

I stood over him, almost beside myself with disappointment and anger. How could I stay sober if I couldn't count on him? What a mockery the picture he had painted—Mark and me and Sonny! Anger rose in me. "Get out!" I suddenly screamed. "You can't be trusted—get out of here. I don't want a drunken bum staying in my apartment all night. Get out! My mother was right—" I pulled at him.

He rose swayingly and took a step forward. Suddenly his fist exploded in my face. My head rocked and I felt a sharp stab of pain; a pinwheel of flame whirled in my eyes.

Next thing I knew I was lying on the bed. There was blood over me and the bed, and the wall was splashed with it. "My face," I moaned. "My face." My lower jaw was hanging, swinging back and forth.

The telephone rang. I looked about, dazed. Mark answered, his voice smooth as butter. "Hello, Linda. She's fine, thanks. Yes, we'll try to make it."

I was half conscious, my face numb. "Your jaw is broken," the doctor was saying. I sat in his office for hours until he completed wiring my jaw. "You won't be able to open your mouth for six weeks," he said. "You'll have to live on liquids."

The next days were an unreal phantasmagoria. Ruth Bernstein and her husband, Bernie, found me in my apartment, passed out. I had been drinking steadily for five days. She took me to the hospital, where I was fed through a tube. The doctor had had to give me whiskey: "If you take that from me I'll go stark raving mad!" He said, "Let her have it. She must have something for the pain—either dope or liquor. The liquor won't kill her."

It was ten days before Winchell had the scoop, just a line—"What playboy broke Lillian Roth's jaw?" It was sufficient. My name was splashed over all the newspapers. Lillian Roth, the playgirl, beaten up at a wild party. With my wired jaw I got on the phone and painfully tried to reach Walter in Florida, to tell him this was no playboy-playgirl episode.

Katie was with me now, heartbroken. "Lilly, what are you doing with your life!" My father flew in from Boston. "Baby, you're messing yourself all up! If I get my hands on that bastard—" My sister Ann lamented, "Oh, Lillian, you're getting to be a girl people talk about."

I returned to my hotel and waited. Orchids arrived—

from Mark. Then a telephone call from him. He had gone to Washington, D. C., on urgent business. A few days later, another call: against a background of Hawaiian music, he wept tears of self-reproach over the telephone. I hung up and hired detectives to find him. They searched for several days. Then I remembered the Hawaiian music. Mark's attorney lived at the Belmont Plaza hotel, which featured a Hawaiian band in its bar.

Accompanied by two detectives, I waited in the lobby of the hotel, on the chance that Mark would come there. I was right. He walked in and I pointed: "That's him," I said. The detectives arrested him. Jailed on a charge of assault, Mark was out next day on $1500 bail. That afternoon his attorney pleaded with me. If Mark's disgrace became known, Sonny would be expelled from school. Mark himself was prostrate: if I would only see him so he could ask my forgiveness. . . .

"All right," I said, wearily. "I'll see him."

Carrying a box of roses, his eyes red-rimmed, Mark visited me. "I didn't mean it, Mommy, I swear to God I didn't." He began to cry. "You know I wouldn't hurt you intentionally. I don't know what comes over me when I'm drinking. My God, how many fighters have been hit, over and over again, and never a broken jaw! I didn't know what I was doing. I blacked out. . . ."

So he went on. Why would he do it when he adored me, when his son wanted me for his mother?

I wished desperately to believe him. Was it impossible for me to get along with anyone? And why should Mark set out to harm me? I *had* been good to him. Thus I reasoned. And having pleaded his case well, he disappeared again.

My lawyer asked for a closed court session when the assault case came up, on the theory that it had embarrassing boudoir overtones. I was assured that his request had been granted. But when I arrived the day of the trial, I learned that it was to be an open hearing before three justices.

I was furious, and the bourbon I had taken to fortify me for my ordeal did little to help. "You're not going to disgrace me!" I shouted at the judges. "I refuse to testify in front of all these people."

I began to walk out. A court attendant seized my arm and deftly brought me around until I was in front of the bench again. "You're supposed to protect innocent women," I stormed. "Is this the way you do it? I know what goes on behind those black robes!"

The presiding justice snapped:

"That's insolence. You say any more and I'll hold you in contempt. Sit down."

I sat down. My attorney pleaded for a private hearing. The court refused. Instead, the case was postponed. The presiding justice gave me a parting lecture:

"I would probably send you to jail for your unwarranted outburst, Miss Roth, if I did not take into consideration that you are a very nervous, high-strung person and temporarily out of your mind."

I thought, it's as good a diagnosis as any.

The case dragged on for months. I stubbornly persisted in my inability, brought on by fear of newspaper headlines, to remember that Mark came to my apartment and broke my jaw. If it had happened on a street corner, there would have been no difficulties.

Ultimately the charges were dropped, and I went to

Chicago to work. The club wasn't as nice as other places I had known, but I felt I had to keep going, if only to forget everything that had to do with Mark. I couldn't forget, however, because the publicity preceded me, and brought out the curiosity seekers. Some nightclub reviewers described me as "Lillian Roth, formerly of 'The Vagabond King,' now of the drama, 'She Who Got Socked.'"

I was going downgrade. I had gained weight. I acted like a lush, and I looked like a drunk, and my comings and goings in public places were marked by nudgings and whisperings.

Mark came on from New York, ostensibly to see Sonny, who during the trial had been sent to live with an uncle in Chicago. He dropped in to see me at the club one night. Again, he was the persuasive wooer. Could I never forget one unfortunate, drunken blow? "Can you throw away the rest of your life, and my life, because of one blow? I love you, Mommy," he said. "I adore you. You know it."

I was sick, I was heartbroken, I was ashamed, I was alone. Who offered me more? "All right, Mark," I said. "Let's try."

He was insanely jealous. One evening when he found me chatting and laughing with a patron of the club, he threatened my life. He made an ugly scene. On another occasion he lunged at me. "Don't you fool around with anyone else," he roared.

On closing night I called my personal maid, Elizabeth. "I'm afraid of him," I told her. "I want to get out of town without his knowledge. Will you help me?"

"Yes, ma'am. I'll go home and pack for you."

"We can't go to a hotel. He'll find us."

"Don't you worry, Miss Lillian," she said. "Safest place is with my family. My father's a preacher and my mother's a school teacher. You come with me tonight." She took me to spend the night in her home in Chicago's Harlem. To think this was my only haven: thank God, I thought, for these sweet colored people. He'd never dream of looking for me here. For the first time in years I felt like a child cared for by tender parents. The apartment boasted two large beds, one in the kitchen, the other in the bedroom. Her father said, "You'll feel better in the kitchen bed because it's more homelike." And there I slept.

In the morning I had to have my drink, and they managed to make me eat some breakfast. What now? Where could I hide? We devised our plan. Lita Gray Chaplin, my good friend, lived in Balboa, California. Elizabeth and her husband would drive me there, and take care of me until I got hold of myself. I wired Lita, and sent Elizabeth to my hotel to gather up my things.

She had packed half my clothes when Mark, who apparently had been searching for me, strode through the open door. He ripped one bag out of her hands and began pummeling her. "You get nothing from me," she shouted, holding grimly to my overnight bag and striking back with her other hand. "Miss Lillian's afraid to call the police but I got nothing to lose."

When she arrived, she reported: "He begged me to tell you he loves you, but, ma'am, I wouldn't believe his sweet talk."

We left the next day. I lay in the back of my car, a

big Cadillac, and guzzled liquor. The 2,000-mile trip itself is a blurred memory in which the dominant recollection is that of constant nausea and illness. Once I insisted upon driving: I drove the car into a ditch. By the time police arrived, Elizabeth's husband had put me in the back seat and was at the wheel. "Lie quiet," he warned me. "I'll tell them I was driving." Another time I became so violent in my self-disgust that I pushed open the back door and was almost sucked out before Elizabeth managed to pull me, screaming, back to safety. They placed me between them in the front seat and never left me out of their sight until we reached Balboa.

Lita paled when she saw me. "Lillian!" she exclaimed, horrified, "we've got to put you to bed!" They carried me into her house and her physician cared for me. I collapsed completely. Years later she told me she was almost shocked dumb by my appearance. My face was purple, my eyes all but lost in the midst of two ghastly white circles, my cheeks were networks of broken blood vessels, I was more than twenty pounds overweight, my stomach was swollen from lack of food. I suffered something akin to beri-beri. After all, I had lived on liquor during the entire trip.

When I began to recuperate, Lita rented a little house for me on the island, and Elizabeth and her husband remained to take care of me.

Ten days later I was brooding over a scotch in my living room when a sound made me look up. My heart almost stopped.

There was Mark walking soberly in the doorway, and there was Sonny, running to me, throwing his arms around me and crying, "Mommy!"

"How are you, Mommy?" said Mark gently, bending down and kissing me on the cheek.

My mind formed the words, "Oh God, what's the use!" I could not fight it anymore. I had been buffeted about too much. Sonny sat on my lap, prattling away, and Mark was on his knees, his arms around me, saying brokenly, "I don't know, Mommy, I don't know, believe me when we're married it will be different. We need you, darling, we both need you more than we know ourselves."

He had found me simply enough. I hadn't packed the brace I had worn on my teeth at night after Mark broke my jaw. He found it, concluded rightly that I would wire my dentist to forward another, and so learned where I had fled.

Whether because of my weakened condition, or my liquor-fogged brain, or the conviction that it was fated to be, I do not know—but Mark and I went before a judge, and we were married.

The reporters and photographers came en masse to the apartment we rented in Beverly Hills. Pictures were taken: Mark, sweet and protective, sitting with his arm around me, Sonny playing happily at our feet. The head-line writers made a day of it. "LOVE LAUGHS AT BROKEN JAW;" "LILLIAN ROTH SOCK LEADS TO ALTAR;" "LILLIAN ROTH WEDS JAW-BUSTER."

That afternoon several men came to talk business with Mark. He took me aside. "Mommy, have you about $20,000 that we can get right away?"

I said no. All I had now were my policies and bonds.

"Well, Mommy, you want us to start off right, don't you? These men have a terrific deal." He explained that he could buy into Joan Blondell Cosmetics, a legitimate business to which Miss Blondell had loaned her name, if he could raise $20,000.

Next day I went out and borrowed the money on my policies.

Sonny became the focus of my life. He came to me one day and spoke with an earnestness that tore at my heart. "Was my mother a bad mother like my daddy says?" I put my arms around him and kissed him. "Your daddy must have made a mistake," I said. "He wasn't feeling good when he told you that. I saw pictures of your mother. She had blonde hair and blue eyes like you, and she's watching you now and she's so glad you have someone to take care of you." I added: "She's really your mother. I'm just Mommy. But let's not tell daddy anything about this."

We had wonderful afternoons together. It was great fun to bring him games and books, and to take him to the movies. Perhaps, I thought, this little boy will make something of my life. Maybe through him I will become a different woman, and Mark a different man.

My only solace was Sonny—and liquor. There was always a bottle in my medicine cabinet and under my mattress. I tried not to let Sonny see me drink. But I had to have liquor to stop my screaming nerves, my exploding brain, to dull the knifelike certainty that I was going nowhere, doing nothing, living as a shadow in an empty world.

I never fooled Sonny. For when he would find me in one of my nervous fits, or weeping, he would say. "Don't you need some of Daddy's medicine?"

Nothing changed. Mark was charming one moment,

brutal the next. When he was drunk, he beat me, often in Sonny's presence. The humiliation of being whipped in front of the child caused almost as much pain as the actual beating. He would pour a drink for himself, then one for me. "Want it?" he'd say. When I put out my hand, he would fling the contents in my face.

He asked for money. "Mommy," he would say, "we need $5,000 more." "But, Mark, I just cashed in a bond last week," I would protest. "I thought that was all you needed. I'm going into my life insurance now."

"All right, baby, let's forget it," he would say. "How about a couple of drinks?" We began to drink—drinks I didn't need. When I was all but passed out, he would say, "Oh, Mommy, there's something I forgot. Here's some papers to sign."

Even in my blurred state I knew what was happening. I thought, he's quiet now, and easy, but if I say no . . . You better sign it, I would tell myself, or you'll get what you got last time when he went into one of those maniacal rages and took Sonny from you.

He had grabbed Sonny and vanished with him for two days. When he returned, the child was trembling with fear.

I thought, "Oh, God, all right," and signed. Later I learned I had signed away my insurance policies to strangers whom Mark had made my beneficiaries in return for cash.

One night we had a ringside table with Lita Chaplin and her husband, Arthur Day, at Grace Hayes' Lodge. The floor show started just as the waiter was serving our dinner. The entertainers were Peter Lind Hayes and his wife, Mary Healy. In show business it's customary to refrain from eating while a fellow performer is on.

"Eat," said Mark, when I made no move toward my food. He grabbed my wrist.

"Sh-sh-sh—I want to hear them," I said. "Professional courtesy." He'll be all right, I thought. He won't dare cause a scene, not with Lita and Arthur sitting there. "I'll eat in a little while," I said.

"Listen, Bum," he shouted, "if you don't have that plate empty by the time I count ten it's going into your face!"

I laughed nervously and took one bite, and turned my face to the stage again. Suddenly I felt the blow of the plate in my face—food splattered over me and slid into my lap. The plate had hit me on the bridge of the nose. Blood gushed forth. Waiters came running and the table overturned as Lita's husband rose and grabbed Mark. I found myself running outside, and then I was in a cab, headed for home, the blood thudding at my temples.

I had no key. There was nothing to do but wait in the hallway until Mark came home. He found me sitting on the floor, propped against the door of the apartment.

He jerked me to my feet. "Come on," he said roughly. "We're going nightclubbing."

I stared dazedly at him. "The way I look?" I faltered.

"The way you look," he said. "Let 'm all see what a bum I've got to live with."

With my blood-spattered dress, my lacerated face, my dishevelled hair, he forced me to accompany him to one club, then another. People saw me, and gasped. I was like an automaton, without will, without hope. Here you are, I thought dully, once famous, now infamous, living with a paranoiac. You can't go lower.

The day came when he beat Sonny in my presence. What I could not do for myself, I found courage to do for Sonny. I packed a bag and took him with me to a neighboring hotel. "Please," I begged the night clerk, slipping a $10 bill into his hand, "don't let Mr. Harris know we are here. We must get some sleep. My little boy is a nervous wreck."

During the night a bellboy rang. "Your husband is coming up the service stairs." Mark had found me by bribing the night clerk who had taken my money and, as I learned later, considered me a hopeless drunk.

I raced with Sonny down another flight of stairs and took a cab to a second hotel. There at eleven a.m. Mark's lawyer reached me. "I'm afraid you'll have to bring the boy back. Otherwise, your husband will swear out a warrant for kidnapping."

"Promise you'll be there so he won't touch us," I begged. I need not worry, he said. Twenty minutes later I entered my apartment, Sonny clutching my hand. A case of liquor had been opened and bottles were strewn about. Mark, waiting for me, had been entertaining two men. The lawyer wasn't there.

He jumped up, swept Sonny off the floor and all but tossed him into the bedroom. Then he began shaking me, roaring at the others, "Get out, I'll take care of this bitch, stealing my son!" I screamed at the men, "Don't go—" but the door was already closing behind them. In the bedroom Sonny whimpered, "Don't hurt her, Daddy, she was only taking care of me."

I tried to make the door but Mark was quicker. He kicked it shut and began punching me, slapping my face with his open hand, muttering hoarsely, "Make a fool out of me, will you—" I pulled loose and rushed into the bathroom, cowering against the stall shower. He leaped at me, pulled me back, then hurled me against the shower. I slid into it. He loomed over me, grabbed me by both shoulders and jerked me up sharply—the shower handle split open the top of my head.

Then I was running screaming through the streets, blood blinding my eyes. Next thing I knew I was in St. Vincent's Hospital. Dr. Francis Thomas, a surgeon, was stitching my scalp.

I signed a warrant for Mark's arrest, Dr. Thomas giving his testimony to the police. Amy Ford, a friend, rented a room for me in her hotel. For two days I was afraid to show myself on the streets. I hid behind drawn blinds, drinking, afraid to think, drinking to blot out what had happened to me. On the third morning there was the sound of a huge body hurled against the door, a thunderous crash as it broke down—and Mark was in the same room with me.

He was cold fury. "You're sitting down and writing the District Attorney that you were dead drunk when you signed that warrant. You want to withdraw the charges and tear up the warrant."

I sat, transfixed with fear. Suddenly he grabbed my arm, and with all his 210 pounds bearing down on me, twisted me to my knees. I couldn't scream because his free hand was clasped over my mouth.

"I'll kill you," he said between his teeth. He increased the pressure on my arm. "Will you write the letter?"

In agony I tried to gasp "yes." I managed to nod, and slowly, he let me up.

The District Attorney called us both in, together and

then separately. I repeated the letter's assertion. I wanted to withdraw the complaint because it wasn't true. I was jealous of Mark, I said: I had accused him of the beatings in hope the police would make him quit philandering.

"Mrs. Harris," the District Attorney said to me, slowly. "I must warn you. I hope what you are now stating to me is the truth. Because if you keep withdrawing these charges, when the day comes that you really need help, you'll not be safe in any state in this country. The record you have made will count against you."

I clung to my story. I was telling the truth. How did I explain the bruises? I fell down. My balance, as they well knew, was sometimes precarious. And the weird, patched hair-do, the result of Dr. Thomas' stitches? A beauty operator had burned me with a permanent wave machine, I said.

What does it all matter, I thought. I deserve no better than Mark. He is the measure of what I have become.

CHAPTER XVI

I was too helpless to think of a way out immediately for myself. But something had to be done about Sonny. One day he proudly began to show how he had been taught as a Boy Scout to make his bunk. Unpredictably, this infuriated Mark. He pulled the boy away from the bed so violently that the child fell. "You don't make it that way, Sonny," he snarled. "You make it this way. And you know why? Because *I* say you make it this way."

Again, when I took the child to a movie and returned twenty minutes late, Mark, drunk as usual, grabbed me by the hair and pulled me down to my knees.

"Ever see a bum, Sonny?" he sneered. "This is what a bum looks like." Sonny stood paralyzed with fright.

I waited until Mark was mellow with brandy one afternoon. Then I suggested, "Let's send Sonny to a boarding school where he'll get the training he needs. You want him to have that big physique you have, don't you? He'll get it there."

Mark agreed. I enrolled Sonny in a nearby military school. It was lonely without him, but at least I would see him week ends. But soon I was deprived even of that. Mark started meeting his son Friday afternoons and taking him to a friend's home. I was a bad influence—that was the only answer I could elicit when I asked where Sonny was.

When I persisted in my questions, Mark grew ugly. He had been drinking a great deal. One night I awoke screaming. He was beating me. A vise of excruciating pain gripped my chest, and I blacked out. Sometime during the morning I was speaking weakly on the telephone to Dr. Thomas, begging him to come over. Every breath seared my lungs: I was breathing fire.

"You have five broken ribs," he said, after he examined me. "I wasn't drunk, Doctor," I moaned. "He started it while I was asleep. He beat me unconscious while I was sleeping."

"Lillian," Dr. Thomas said quietly. "You must do something or sooner or later this maniac will kill you."

When he left, I thought, as well as I could think: what was there to do? I was not even safe with the police. Hadn't I signed a warrant, hadn't a doctor given evidence—and look what had happened. There was no way out. Or I was too confused to think of one.

I realized that I was slowly disintegrating as a human being. I was paralyzed, without will or direction—paralyzed by my drinking, my misery, by the frightening combination of events that seemed conspiring with almost human intelligence to destroy me.

It had to come to an end.

One Friday night Mark vanished with Sonny. He was seen at a Hollywood nightspot and reportedly Sonny was sleeping at the home of a blonde nightclub hostess with whom Mark stayed.

Acting on a hunch, I gathered enough courage to go to

[173]

an address I found written on a slip of paper in Mark's bureau. A buxom blonde greeted me. Sonny was there. After the first few icy moments, she explained that Mark told her I was constantly in a stupor, and Sonny was not safe with me. "I'm surprised to see you up and about," she added.

"I've been having a terrible time," I told her. "It's true I've been drinking, but it's Mark who has the drinking problem. Along with that, he seems to be a paranoiac. He's calm one moment and mad the next. Look what he did to me." I opened my dress and showed her my bandaged ribs.

"Mrs. Harris!" She was horrified. "I wouldn't have believed—"

As in a third-rate thriller, the door opened and Mark walked in. He bore down on me. "You drunken slut," he rasped, "I'm taking you to the corner of Hollywood and Vine and I'll teach you how to show yourself. I'm going to strip every inch of clothing from you."

The blonde screamed. "Mark, you're crazy!" He pushed her roughly aside, pulled me out of the house and forced me into his car. As we drove, he began ripping at my clothes. At Vine Street I managed to open the door, almost tumbled out, and ran sobbing to the nearest taxi. "Hurry, please, for God's sake," I gasped. "My husband is going to kill me."

We had not yet begun to move when Mark laid his hand on the driver's arm.

"Look, Mac," he said, lowering his voice confidentially, "my wife is very drunk and she doesn't know what she's doing. You can see what she's done to her clothes. She's just come out of an insane asylum and it looks as though

[174]

she'll have to go back."

The driver looked at me, frantic and shaking, and then at Mark, calm and self-possessed.

"Excuse me, Buddy," he said to Mark. "I thought you were going to harm her." He put his hand back and opened the door. He looked at me through the rear-window mirror. "You better go with your husband, lady."

Our landlady was bending over me next morning in the apartment house, shaking me and shouting that it was a shame to have people like me on the premises. She had heard the racket the night before, but hadn't inter-fered because she thought it was a husband-and-wife spat. "But just an hour ago your husband phoned me from out of town and asked me to look in on you," she said. "I didn't tell him you had another man here last night, but all I have to say is, it would have served you right if I did!"

My eyes were black, my lips were swollen, I was one mass of pain, but the landlady wouldn't believe my ex-planation that Mark drove me home, sneaked out the back way after beating me, and then telephoned her.

I could not argue with her. A refrain drummed in my brain: *I've got to get out, I've got to get out.* I managed to pack an overnight bag, and went to Amy's apartment. I threw all caution to the winds. What could he do that he hadn't done before? I telephoned a lawyer to start di-vorce proceedings and to hire a bodyguard for me. Then, accompanied by a policeman, I returned to our apart-ment.

Ringing the bell, even pounding on the door, was of no avail. "We'll have to break it down, then," the policeman said.

He stepped back a few paces, when the landlady joined us.

"She's no good, officer," she snapped, flinging a look of utter contempt at me. "She has the sweetest husband in the world but she's always passed out in there. This woman is no good. I'm telling you."

"All right, lady, you've told me, now you go about your business," the policeman said.

He broke down the door, with the help of the handyman in the building. We walked into the kitchen, then the living room. Mark appeared from the bedroom, a puzzled expression on his face. "I've been asleep," he said, as if collecting his thoughts. "What seems to be the trouble, officer?"

"Asleep with all that noise?" the policeman demanded. Mark nodded.

"You're awake now. Pack your things and get out."

My husband took on an injured air. "You're not listening to her, are you, officer? This is an awfully sick woman. She is out of her mind."

"Tell that to the court. You've got to leave these premises and keep your hands off her—"

Mark's face was beginning to show storm signals, and I hid behind the policeman, who turned to me. "Now, lady, don't you be afraid—"

Mark lunged at me.

Without a word the cop jabbed him in the side with his stick. "Get out of here before I take you in!" he roared. Mark threw a venomous glance at me and left.

For the next week I ventured out only with my bodyguard, although most of the time I tried to blot out everything with alcohol. Then I had a recollection of my lawyer calling to say that I could dismiss my bodyguard, because Mark had gone to Chicago. A few days later the doorbell rang while I was talking with Johnny Ford, Amy's 22-year-old brother. I opened the door.

Mark walked in. He hadn't gone to Chicago after all! "Get out, Johnny," he said. "I want to talk to Lillian. I'll be downstairs in a few minutes."

"Don't go, Johnny," I cried.

"Get out of this room or you will be killed," Mark said quietly.

"Johnny—" I pleaded.

Mark turned to me. "What's the matter, you sleeping with him?" I thought desperately, was he going to involve this boy in our divorce suit? "You better go," I said, and Johnny, white-faced, left.

Mark sat down on the lounge, crossed his legs comfortably, and smiled. "You think you're going to have everything your way, don't you?"

"No, I didn't think I was going to have everything my way."

"Come here, I want to talk to you."

"What for?"

"Just come here, I want to talk to you."

Perhaps I can humor him, I thought fleetingly, as I approached him. As I came near him, he suddenly drew his right knee back, and viciously plunged his shoe into my stomach, driving me backward across the room into another chair.

I lay there, retching, gasping for breath. For a timeless moment we stared at each other.

The telephone on the stand next to me rang. Slowly, like a sleepwalker, I answered it. "Yes," I managed to say.

[177]

"Lillian, it's Amy. Everything all right?"

"Amy, would you please—" I began. I wanted to complete the sentence with "come over right away." But Mark grabbed the phone and before I realized what happened, he was using it to club me savagely on my arm, on my elbow, beating me again and again, from wrist up to shoulder, from shoulder down to wrist, methodically, steadily. In a daze of agony I heard Amy's voice, thin and anxious, emanating weirdly from the rising and falling instrument. "Lillian! Lillian!"

Mark stopped beating me. "Everything's fine," he said casually into the mouthpiece. "She's just so drunk she passed out." He replaced the telephone.

I was slumped in the chair, more unconscious than conscious, my right arm dangling. I heard Mark in the bedroom. Was he searching for liquor? Then, no sound for minutes. Perhaps he had blacked out. Perhaps I could telephone for help—

Laboriously I lifted the receiver with my left hand. There was a noise. Mark had rushed back into the room. He grabbed a long black address book off the stand and whipped me across the face with it. Pain tore at my right eye: warm blood gushed over my cheek. The wire edging of the back of the book had ripped open the right eyelid.

"You think you're going to get help," Mark said clearly. "I'm not through with you yet."

I ran wildly toward the window to scream for help, perhaps to hurl myself through it. He seized me from behind, dragged me into the bedroom, and threw me to the floor. As I lay there, he opened the closet, pulled out my clothes, and began ripping them. In a frenzy he tore and pulled until everything was in shreds. He looked

[178]

about him like a madman for a moment. Then he grabbed
a suitcase, dumped its contents on the floor, and swept
into it my perfumes, my jewels and my furs. He ripped
out the drawers of my vanity, found an envelope con-
taining several hundred dollars, and pocketed that. Then,
methodically, he tore into tiny bits everything he knew I
treasured—David's photographs and letters, photographs
of Katie, Ann and myself as a child star, postcards and
mementos I had kept through the years. He began kick-
ing me. Mercifully I blacked out.

I woke to agonizing consciousness. It was dark. My
right arm lay useless at my side. I crawled to the telephone and called an ambulance. At St. Vincent's Hospital, Dr. Thomas took over—for the third time. He only
shook his head as he worked, giving me opiates for the
pain, treating my eyelid and the livid contusions on my
arm, breast and stomach. The police interviewed me,
photographed my bruises for use in prosecuting Mark,
and advised the hospital they wanted the X-rays for
evidence.

The District Attorney visited me.

He spoke briskly. "This girl began divorce proceedings.
She thought she was perfectly safe. Now look at her. I
want her husband brought in."

This time Mark really had flown to Chicago, taking
Sonny with him. Extradition would take time and money,
and my funds had dwindled shockingly. "I know this
man," I told the D. A. "We will get him with his own
help. He'll call me sooner or later."

He called me from Chicago. The old charm came gush-

ing over two thousand miles. It was an incredible conversation. "Mommy, what can I say? Liquor made me do
what I did. Besides, we're in trouble. Sonny came down
with diphtheria. I should never have taken him away from
you."

"That's all right, Mark. You put Sonny into a hospital
and come out here and we'll see what we can do."

"Fine, I'll be right out. You know I love you?"

"Of course."

"Will you tell the police to lay off extradition? I'll come
in myself."

"All right, Mark."

A week passed. No Mark. Two weeks later—another
call from him. He had been in the hospital with Sonny
all this time, he said. Not until another month had
elapsed did he arrive. Sonny, of course, was not ill and
had never been. Mark had waited so that by the time
the trial was held, my bruises would have healed. When
he landed at Los Angeles Airport, he was arrested and
charged with felonious assault with intent to kill. Conviction meant three to ten years in jail.

Next day, he was out on bail and telephoning me. He
was only human, he had the frailties of a man who was
in love and mad about me and sick about himself . . . I
must see him.

"O. K., Mark," I said. "Come over." It happened to be
the night before the case came up.

If I had it in my heart to pay him back in full, I would
have prepared more fully than I did. To touch him now
would be unclean, even to revenge myself on him was to
humiliate myself. But I bought a monkey wrench just

[180]

large enough to fit into my handbag, and asked three friends—Peter Burke, a song writer, Lewis Williams, a pianist, and Johnny, to be at my apartment earlier in the evening.

"There's only one way to handle a guy like that," Johnny said. "Take him out in the alley and give him the beating of his life."

I shook my head. I wanted no more scandals. This was between Mark and me.

Presently the bell rang. "Hello, Mommy." It was the old Mark. He appeared a little startled to find a welcoming committee, but his self-possession returned immediately. "How do you do, gentlemen?"

"I thought we might go for a ride, Mommy," Mark began.

"Oh, we can do that later," I said. "Sit down and relax."

He took a chair. Peter stood a little to his left, Lewis a little to his right. Johnny stood behind him.

"I'd like a drink," I said. "Wouldn't you, Mark?"

He nodded. "Sure," he said. "Sure, Mommy."

I poured myself a drink in the kitchenette, mixed a tall highball for Mark, and returned to the living room.

"I remember, Mark, how you gave me a drink in Chicago once," I said. "It was scotch and soda. It was like this."

I threw the contents into his face.

He looked at me uncertainly, pulled out a handkerchief, and laughed. "Mommy, darling, are you drunk?"

"No, darling, I'm not drunk. I just have a good memory." With all my might I gave him a backhand across his face, my ring gashing his cheek. He began to bleed.

[181]

Sputtering and howling, he made a grab for me. Peter and Lewis pinned his arms, while Johnny got his head in a hammerlock.

"You remember the kicks on the shins—do you know how it feels? It feels like this—" I kicked him on the shins, and kicked him again.

He howled. "You bitch—"

"You remember how you beat me black and blue with the telephone, and how you split the top of my head open in the shower? Remember how you laughed because I always carried a drink for us in my bag? Well, I've got something for you in my bag now, too." I lifted my bag with the wrench in it and brought it down hard on his head.

The blow dazed him for a moment: he was crying and begging. "Boys, this is a sick woman. I love her. She's crazy, why are you letting her do this to me? She's crazy."

"Now, boys," I said, and I was amazed at my own audacity. "I'm going out for a ride with this man. And he is going to do everything I say. He's going to be a little lamb, because the case comes up tomorrow. Aren't you going to be a little lamb, Mark?"

"You poor, sick, little Mommy," he said, dabbing at his cuts with a handkerchief.

"He's going to be a little lamb," I went on, "because if he makes any bruises on me he knows he'll rot in jail. Isn't that right, Mark?"

He shook his head. "Boys, you should do something for her. She's real sick!"

"You don't know how right you are!" I yelled. "I'm sick—sick to death. I don't care what happens to me. Come on!"

The three men escorted us downstairs and watched silently as he got into the car and I after him. "Now," I said, "you take me everywhere I want to go. First, Hollywood and Vine."

When we got there, I said, "Do you remember how you tried to rip off my clothes here?" I slammed my bag against his head.

"Oh, Mommy!" he groaned. "Why do you want to talk like that!"

"That was one place. Now, drive up Hollywood Hills." When we got there, I said, "Remember how you scared me, threatening you'd make me jump out of the car here? Well, move over in that seat. I'm going to drive down this hill. I'm not afraid to die, you lousy son of a bitch, and you're going straight to hell with me. I'm not jumping out of this car, but you're going with me straight to hell!"

I jammed the accelerator against the floorboard, and we began to roar down the hill. Mark pulled the brake sharply. The car skidded to a violent stop.

"I knew you didn't have the guts!" I screamed. "Now, get out! Get out! I'll see you in court tomorrow."

I was crying—tears of rage and self-pity and hatred for this man who had degraded me. I cried for all that could have been, loathing myself for what I was, and what had brought me to this. When I reached home, I drank myself into oblivion.

On the witness stand I told my story. Mark testified in his own behalf. "Judge, how can you believe her?" he asked, as a man bewildered because the truth is not self-evident. "Everyone knows she is a drunk. Why, she almost killed me last night." And he exhibited his scars.

The court commented on the incongruity of a man like Mark having to defend himself against me. My hospital X-rays and photographs did the rest. Mark was sentenced to six months.

The judge summed it up: "You ought to get down on your knees to this lady because she permitted the charge to be reduced to simple assault, so that all I can give you is six months. You deserve the maximum of ten years. I can't express my contempt for a man who beats a woman."

Mark looked over at me and laughed. "Mommy, I won't be in there six months. I'll still get you. Watch."

My marriage to Mark Harris was annulled on the ground that when I married him I had no cognizance of his criminal activities.

CHAPTER XVII

THE YEAR I had known Mark seemed one long nightmare. Now it was over. Where did I stand? How was I going to pick up the pieces? Katie pleaded with me to live with her. She was in Long Island, at the home of my sister Ann—little Ann who used to lament that she "never got anywhere in show business." But Ann was married, her husband was loving and attentive, a baby was on the way, and life had taken on a sane, recognizable pattern for her. The other half of "The Roth Kids" was a drunken, thrice-married has-been.

I didn't want Katie to see what was happening to me. And Dad had remarried and was living quietly in Boston. I didn't fit in there, either.

There was nothing to do but remain alone. When I tried to cast up my accounts, I found that I still had some money left of my fortune—a few thousand dollars. I could still sing, but nobody was particularly eager to hear me. The bad dream was over. Now what?

I cared for nothing, yet I had to go on. I was constantly ill. It was impossible to face daylight without sunglasses: light seared my eyes. I walked hurriedly on the street, peering fearfully over my shoulder in expectation that Mark would suddenly materialize from nowhere and bear down on me. If a friend waved at me, I ducked:

I had no wish to see anyone, and took to slipping down sidestreets. I rarely went out before nightfall. Then I bought sufficient liquor to carry me through the night and following day. My bottle became my only friend. I talked to it at night. "What are people, what are friends?" I asked. "Only you console me."

But if I wanted to be able to continue to buy liquor, I had to continue to work. I managed to obtain bookings in Chicago, Oakland, and then Vancouver. After the tour I wired fare to Katie to join me in California.

She came to live with me—a little more tired, a little more apprehensive, the same questioning look in her eyes, but still with the same saving grace of humor.

My thirty-first birthday was a month away when Dot Pondell, my make-up girl so many years ago, invited me to a party at her home and introduced me to Victor Engel. "You two ought to know each other," she said. Victor seemed familiar from the first. There was a gaiety about him which I found attractive. I had not known such an outgoing personality since Fred Keating. And, like Fred he could make me laugh, and I needed laughter.

When he took me to dinner, he watched silently while I drank. He never lectured me. In my high moments he thought me charming, and when I impersonated people for our friends, he applauded louder than the rest. "You're wonderful," he would say. No one had said anything like that to me for a long time.

Often I passed out when we returned from dinner, but there was no reproach. Instead, while I slept off my drunkenness—Victor was sure I would stop drinking sooner or later—he played gin rummy with Katie.

I liked his solicitude for her. He treated her as if he were her son. It helped make up a little for me.

They were engrossed in a card game one night when I stumbled out of my bedroom. I had suddenly become wide awake. "Daddy's in trouble," I said. "I know it."

My mother looked at me, compassion and despair struggling in her face. "Are you having another of your nightmares?"

"No. It's a premonition, Mom. I'm going to call him."

Although it was past midnight, I put through a call to Boston. It was refused by Arthur's cousin, who undoubtedly conjectured that I was drunk. For a moment I was stopped: then I sent a wire. "Lillian needs operation, must contact Arthur." I signed it "Katie."

A few hours later a reply came: my father was in Boston Hospital with a blood clot in his leg. Surgeons planned an amputation.

I had to go to Boston, although I was in no physical condition to make the trip across the continent. Wearing dark glasses, and with two bottles of bourbon in my bag, I got aboard a plane and managed to get to Boston Hospital. Half a dozen relatives were there: without an exception, they turned away when I appeared. My father was a pitiable shadow of himself when I found him in a public ward.

"Hello, sweetheart," he said, but there was panic in his eyes. "Lillian, baby, for God's sake, don't let them cut off my leg."

But there was no other course.

I made arrangements for a private room and private nurses. When Arthur came out of the ether, I was at his bedside. He grinned weakly. "You know I'm tough," he whispered. "I'll have myself a wooden leg and bounce out of here in no time." Later in the day he begged huskily, "Do me a favor, Lillian. They've given me so much morphine my eyes are popping. Please get me a good bottle of brandy. It will be good for my heart—the doctor said so."

I bought him a fifth, and we drank together.

I took a room in a small hotel. It was impossible for me to hold any food. I drank small amounts of liquor through the day, but it would not take effect. I sat by Arthur's bed, sober-drunk. On the fourth day he woke from a drugged sleep and, apparently for the first time, saw me as I was. "For God's sake, Lillian," he exclaimed in despair, "Lillian, you could be a beautiful girl again, you could be on top of the world. For God's sake, when are you going to leave that bottle alone! You're dying—you need a bed next to me." He groaned. "If I were only up! I can't stand to see what you're doing to yourself."

That afternoon the doctor informed me they must amputate again. When Dad was told later, he said, "Don't worry, kiddie. I'll be all right." He was silent for a moment. "I wish you'd try to get yourself booked at some club—maybe you'd go easier on that bottle."

Ann arrived, and we took turns keeping vigil at his bedside. We visited his shabby little apartment, and talked to his wife. The story of his life during the past few years was written on the walls of those dark, half-furnished rooms.

He had refused, his wife said, to let me know about his financial reverses. They had had a few happy, prosperous years, but Arthur still had visions of making that last big killing, and was unable to keep a job long enough to learn the names of his co-workers. His big deals never materialized—and all this during the period just preceding the wartime boom.

They had lived in a large apartment at the beginning, later moving to smaller quarters, storing all but bare essentials. They had been unable to meet the small payments and the warehouse had taken possession of their furniture.

I gave his wife several hundred dollars before I left Boston. "When you're ready for that artificial leg, Daddy, I'll take care of it," I promised him. I paid his medical and hospital bills, prepaid his rent for several months, and took an upper berth back to California.

At least, I had done one decent thing for my father.

On the train I suffered acute abdominal pains. In Los Angeles Dr. Thomas once more examined me. I must have an operation. Mark's blows, my drinking, internal inflammations dating back to the baby I had lost, all played a part.

"Oh, my poor Lilly," my mother said, trying not to cry, "everything happens to you—you're not spared anything."

She still believed that my difficulties were due to others, not to me. "You were always used, used by everybody," she wept.

I signed a waiver absolving the hospital of responsibility, if the operation proved fatal, for my drinking, as Dr. Thomas told me, made me a bad surgical risk. When I awoke, he held my hand. "You're tough, Lillian," he said. "I never thought I'd pull you out of this one."

Next day he sat by my bed and talked earnestly to me.

"I've told you often before that you must not drink. Now, you *can't* drink. Do you understand? If you do, you may die."

I thought, suppose I did? I have nothing behind me but shame, nothing before me but the gutter.

"Vic," I said, when he visited me, "the doctor says I need a tonic. Buy me some cherry brandy." When friends called I made the same request. Some days I consumed more than a fifth of brandy. Dr. Thomas came into my room one night to find my callers playing cards while I lay tipsily in bed.

His lips compressed. "Take her home," he ordered. "We can't handle her here." *Even he is giving me up*, I thought. A day later I was wandering about my apartment hugging a bottle.

Ann came out for a brief visit. There was a moment when Victor and I were alone. "Let's fly to Nevada and get married," he said. In my drunken state it seemed an excellent idea. Although I recall Victor's proposal, and remember the flight, the wedding ceremony is a blank. I recall whimpering to myself while Victor lay beside me, *I've done it again. I've done it again.*

We walked in on my mother. She was playing cards with a group of women. "Mother," I announced, "I'm married." The cards fell from her hands, and she stared at me, her eyes beginning to brim with tears. "Oh, Lillian," she whispered. A lifetime of anguish was in those two words.

Next day she and Ann were gone. The note my mother left read:

"You're married, and Ann and I are going back to New York. I have to do it this way, darling. I can't stand to stay here and watch you kill yourself."

With Pearl Harbor, Victor was drafted. I wired an agent, who booked me into the Hurricane, a Broadway nightclub. Victor and I drove to New York, and there he bid me adieu in his soldier's uniform.

My opening night brought excellent reviews. Well, I thought, I can still make it. I must still be good. This deserves a celebration—just a drink or two. And wasn't I alone, my husband gone off to the wars? More reason to try to forget. Waves of self-pity engulfed me. I made a far from pleasant record at the Hurricane the remainder of the week. The management spoke to me—the orchestra leader complained that I reeked of liquor. All I could think of was, why are they picking on me? Don't they know I may never see my husband again?

I was requested to leave the show after the first week. Now I drank heavily to console myself. One morning before dawn I awoke and looked at the wall. In the half-gloom of my room I saw a tremendous spider, big as a rat. I froze. I thought, that is a black-widow spider, and if it comes near me and bites me, I'll die. I felt a gurgling in my throat and I passed out. When I woke a little later, the spider was gone. I thought, I must have had a bad dream. But the next morning it was there again . . .

Since Victor was taking his basic training at Camp Belvoir, Virginia, I got an engagement in nearby Washington, then arranged with the help of the camp's morale officer to bring the troupe to Victor and his fellow-trainees. But at Belvoir I became violently ill, wracked by sharp, stabbing pains. The army doctors diagnosed it as colitis and a liver ailment—a polite way of saying that I suffered from acute alcoholism.

I had to return to New York. I took a room by myself.

Then I learned that Dad, too, was living alone, in Boston. He had separated from his wife. It was a strange thing, my father alone in a room, and I alone in a room. Suddenly I felt I had to talk to him.

I telephoned him at midnight. There was no answer. I rang repeatedly, but not until 3 a.m. was I able to reach him. "Daddy," I said, "I just can't get you off my mind. Are you all right?"

His voice came back: "Of course I am. You know, I've been thinking of you, too. How are you, baby? Have you given up that lousy booze?"

"I'm all right, Daddy. I've got a little sore throat at the moment, but as soon as I can, I'm coming up to see you. You sure you're all right?"

"I'm fine."

"Well, where were you just a little while ago?"

"I was right here, baby."

"I bet you're drinking," I said.

"I bet *you're* drinking," he said.

"No, I'm not."

"Well, I'm not—I swear I'm not."

I felt better when I hung up. At six o'clock in the morning the telephone rang. It was a man's voice. "You don't know me, Miss Roth. I have something to tell you. Your father is dead."

The hotel maid had found him slumped across a card table. He had been playing solitaire when he suffered the heart attack.

I sat with a bottle. What else was there?

CHAPTER XVIII

I SPOKE DISTINCTLY.

"I'm warning you. I know you're broadcasting everything I'm thinking. Now, you stop it!"

"Who is this?" demanded the bewildered voice at the other end of the line. I had dialed the radio station located atop our hotel.

"You know very well who it is. I don't have to tell you. You better stop, that's all. Goodbye."

I had been aware of it my first day in Niagara Falls, for everything I touched vibrated. I exuded radio waves.

"You're silly," Victor laughed. "That's the vibration from the Falls. Everyone knows that."

He couldn't convince me. We had been in Niagara Falls since his discharge from the army a week earlier. I wanted no one to see or recognize me: Niagara Falls seemed as good a hideout as any.

Victor had a job, selling dry goods, at $70 a week. Except for a few savings bonds, my funds—everything I had—were gone. I spent the days walking a German shepherd dog Victor had bought me, and testing my unusual ability to pick up and transmit electrical waves. Everywhere I felt the trembling. Everywhere I saw military men guarding the enormous power installations, watching me suspiciously as I passed. Suddenly I realized why. *My dog is a German dog. They think I'm a Nazi spy.*

"Vic," I said a few nights later, "I'm electrified. Foreign agents think I know our defense secrets and they've wired our room to get my vibrations."

"Oh, Lil, will you lay off that stuff? I told you the Falls make everything shake. The only thing wrong with you is you drink too much."

I feared to look into our bureau mirror, because it might well be a diabolical machine planted there by Canadian Nazis to telecast my face to Berlin, where the secrets could be read through my eyes. I could not sleep. "Vic, the mattresses are wired. I'll be electrocuted."

"Don't be silly," he said wearily. "Come over on my side."

"They'll electrocute me on that side, too, Vic. Wherever I lie, my body will contact the electricity in the bed."

He sat up and looked at me.

"Lil, you're sick, you know that?"

"How can you be so ridiculous? How can I be sick? I have no fever. What are you talking about?"

"O. K. So you're not sick. But if you ask me, I think you ought to go back to your mother in New York and I'll go back to California."

"Oh, no. You're not getting rid of me like that. The marriage service says in sickness and in health, but I'm not sick," I repeated. "And how can she take care of me? I have no money for either of us. I can't go back."

Victor punched his pillow and lay down again.

The radio commentators described our soldiers trapped

in the Pusan bridgehead. I knew it all a moment before they told me: I mapped it out on the floor for their benefit. Here was Asia: I indicated it with my left toe. I took a step. Here was Germany, under my right foot. Did they see it clearly? I asked, doing a grotesque hop-scotch to indicate the swift march of events. For I understood it all, and with my vibrations I was in tune with top secret information.

The commentators spoke even when my radio was turned off. Sometimes, in their eagerness, their faces materialized from the cloth mesh covering the loudspeaker, and, mouths working and eyes glistening, they advanced toward me. I backed up, frightened, but not too surprised. This was understandable to anyone who had read about the extra-sensory perception experiments at Duke University. I had always had premonitions, and what were premonitions but extra-sensory perception?

That the enemy could draw my knowledge away telepathically weighed heavily on me. Perhaps drinking would be considered patriotic under such special circumstances, I reasoned. If I became muddled with liquor, I'd confuse enemy agents: they'd tap my brain and get nothing but mental static. I liked the idea.

Fortunately, it seemed that I was vulnerable to the enemy only on cloudy days, for everyone knows the sun weakens radio waves. On cloudy days I hid in my darkened room, drinking patriotically and avoiding the mirror. On sunny days, I ventured out.

One afternoon, strolling serenely with my dog, I passed a church. Near the door a neat printed sign read: YOU ARE WELCOME. ENTER AND REST. On impulse I walked into the dark, cool interior and slipped softly into a pew near the altar. *Oh God*, I thought fleetingly, *if You are in this church, help me: I cannot understand what is happening to me.* I looked to one side. There was a large, life-size statue of Christ on the cross, the face marked with pain. I felt very humble. It occurred to me, with surprise, that I was sitting in a church with a dog. But wasn't a dog God's creature, too?

A bell tinkled. A priest, genuflecting as he passed in front of the altar, glanced at me. For a moment our eyes met, and held. Then he disappeared through a door at the side of the altar.

I walked dreamily out of the church, into the warm, terribly bright sunshine. Was not the meaning of the glance between the priest and myself clear: *Do not hide any more. You are in God's world and you are welcome. You do not have to hide any more.*

"Vic," I said that night. "Let's leave this town. I'm sure my nerves will straighten out if we go back to California. And I might get a few bookings there." Victor, who was bored with the Falls, thought that a good idea. We could live with his married sister in Los Angeles—she had an eight-room house—until I earned enough money to rent an apartment for us. But where would we get money for fare to the coast? What with our hotel bills, and my two quarts of liquor a day, we hadn't been able to save anything from Victor's salary.

I phoned Katie collect and she sent me a money order for $600, every cent she could scrape together. She had obtained it by pawning what she had left of the jewelry Ann and I had given her through the years.

Once in Los Angeles, Victor got more money by selling my silver fox cape for $50—the last fur I had, which

Mark had overlooked.

At his sister's house I tried to taper off on a quart of wine a day, the cheapest drink I could buy. Victor obtained a job in a credit jewelry store. I had little to do with his sister, her husband, or their three children, aged twelve to seventeen. Instead, I spent my time in our second-floor guest room, sipping wine and poring over the Bible.

If God wanted me to hide no longer, I must read His book. Marie Stoddard wasn't here to help explain the difficult passages, but certainly the Bible should partially insulate me from the vibrations, the radio waves, the spectral faces, the enemy agents trying to siphon away my secrets.

Victor and his sister had words about me. Her voice was shrill and carried to our room. "I've got children in this house! I won't have her here. Not another day."

I opened the door and came to the head of the stairs. "You needn't shout," I said clearly. "I understand." I heard her voice again. "I'm going out to shop. All I say to you is, be sure she's out of here by the time I get back."

I approached her later. I asked carefully, "Does Vic want to get rid of me, too?"

She said, "Yes. You'll have to leave today."

I packed a bag and left. I ventured to ask some friends if they would put me up overnight until I decided what to do. They politely declined. I stood on a street corner, bag in hand, bewildered. I could not wire Katie that Victor had put me out. I walked aimlessly. How would I get into a hotel? They were crowded because of the war. From some dim recess of my memory, Christian

Science came into my mind. A few minutes later I was in a Christian Science reading room. The words trembled before my eyes: "In my Father's house are many mansions." I walked out of the reading room into a drug store and fumbled through a telephone directory.

Hotels . . . hotels . . . My fingers stopped shakily at Hotel Christo. That was enough. The name was a sign. I telephoned the clerk: a man had checked out a few minutes earlier—a room was available if I came over at once.

It was among the cheapest one-night hotels. "I must be humble," I said to myself. "Didn't Mary Baker Eddy say that Jesus Christ was humble?" The curtains in my room were filthy, the furniture ancient. A Gideon Bible lay on the table which was pockmarked with the butts of a thousand cigarettes held in the vanished hands of a thousand lonely souls. . . .

I undressed, got into bed, and fell asleep with the Bible under my pillow.

I awoke suddenly, light-headed. I was alone, the first time in my life I was absolutely alone. God, I thought, will take care of me. He will provide. The morning sun streamed in, a bright pathway of dancing dust motes in the murky gloom of my room. I turned my eyes away: the bright light burned. . . .

I was lying in bed, looking up. The curtains fluttered, as if teased by a gentle wind. They parted slowly, and a white figure appeared with two men on either side. The figure was Christ, dressed in white, a gold band about His forehead. I could not recognize the others. They wore dark skull caps and dark clothes. The Figure approached me. His hand seemed to float forth and with infinite tenderness passed over my hair. My eyes closed, and I slept.

The shrilling of the telephone awakened me. "I've been looking everywhere for you." It was Victor. "Lil, I did the wrong thing. We'd better get together. We'll work something out."

He took me to an apartment, but he was away most of the day and night, returning only to supply me with yellow pills. I took the pills to sleep, and the liquor to bring me out of the lethargy of dope. The combination tore at my nerves. When I tried to walk, or do anything at all, I went into raging tantrums at my inability to function.

Then Victor left me. He never said a word. He had had enough.

Everything became confused. An elderly man from the film colony who had known me since "The Roth Kids," unaccountably appeared in the room and tried to make violent love to me. Now I was in the street, clutching the arm of a soldier, begging him to come to my room and "get that ugly old man out of there." Now I awakened from a heavy sleep. It was daylight. The old man and my landlady were chatting at my door. "I knew her mother and father," the old man said. "I'm a good friend of the family." "Well, I'm glad, poor thing," said my landlady as she left. "Do take good care of her." The door shut behind her, and the old man turned toward me with an odd smile on his lips. I tried to cry out, and then I was asleep again.

Was it an hour later, or twelve hours later? I opened my eyes. A thin, effeminate young man was in my room, drunkenly trying on my dresses. It was unreal as a dream. Was I back in Chicago, at "Artists and Models?" Were we preparing for the party in the barn. . . .

"Get out of here!" I moaned.

"Hi, Lillian," he said. "My name's Lionel. Vic sent me to watch over you. I won't bother you." He giggled.

I began to wail.

"All right, all right," he said. "I'll go."

Then it was night again, and I lay half conscious on the sofa. I heard a whisper, as from far off: "Lillian, Lillian, Lillian." It came from the ventilator. There was no one in the room. Am I going mad? I looked at the clock: it showed three o'clock, and it was dark outside. "Lillian!" the voice whispered urgently, and the ventilator rattled. I stumbled out of bed and found the landlady. "My God, see if I'm going crazy. Is there somebody in that ventilator?"

In her bedclothes she rushed to my room. She opened the grate and looked down. Lionel was there, in the basement, drunk. He had been watching to see if any men visited me. Later I realized Victor had brought me to the room in hope men would call on me so that he would have grounds for divorce.

I slept, and woke again. Now everything was gone. My radio, my records, my clothes.

In one awful, lucid moment, I paced back and forth in front of the jewelry store where Victor worked. I grabbed his arm when he emerged for lunch. "Vic, I need money. You've taken everything. I got to have a little money—enough to get by. I have to pay the rent. I have to eat."

He pushed me away, and walked on. I struggled after

him, clutching at his clothes. "Get away from me," he
said hoarsely, under his breath. "You're just a drunken
bum. Get away from me!"

"I'm not drinking, Vic," I gasped, laboring after him.
"I promise you. For God's sake, let me have a few
dollars."

He turned on me, his face white. "Get away from me,
you—". Words failed him. "Get—or I'll call a cop, you
miserable, no-good bum!"

Days later I sat dully in a lawyer's office. Victor had
sued me, and on his terms. "Let him get the divorce,"
the attorney advised me. "Or he'll drag you through the
courts with your drinking, and that old man, and all the
rest."

"I tried to keep the old man out," I faltered. "He had
a key and the landlady let him in. Half the time I didn't
know he was there."

The attorney sighed. "And throw away those pills your
husband left you. They keep you all doped up. You're
passed out most of the time."

I sat numbly. The door opened and the lawyer's secretary came in. She had a stunned look on her face. "President Roosevelt is dead," she said in a hushed voice.

Why annoy the lawyer further? The entire country
had suffered a great loss. "Do what you think best," I
told him. On the way to the elevator I stopped in the
ladies' room and took a long, comforting drink from the
bottle in my bag.

No one offered to help me in the days that followed,
save a poor woman who lived in two rooms above a
Chinese laundry. I do not remember how I met her. I

[201]

remember visiting her, laboriously toiling up the steps to the hovel in which she lived, playing with her children, trying to ignore the roaches scurrying across the floor. She alone offered me food, which I could not eat.

And then—a long, blank period.

I did not know it, but I was not altogether forgotten. There was still my mother, in New York.

Katie, with hardly a penny to her name, was living with Ann's mother-in-law, for Ann's baby had arrived, and there was no room for Katie there.

Among the few people my mother saw were two friends, Estelle and Phyllis Demarest. At their apartment she met Edna Berger, who lived next door. Edna, a warm, outgoing and extremely resourceful girl, was international representative of the American Newspaper Guild, a job which took her out of town much of the time. She liked Katie, and often talked to her about me.

One evening my mother visited the Demarests, and Edna dropped in. Katie was obviously under great tension. Finally she brought out a letter she had received that day. It was from the lawyer I had seen about Victor's suit for divorce. He had written that I was practically on the streets. Victor had left me. "She's without funds, Mrs. Roth," he wrote, "and seems to be a chronic alcoholic. She seems to be taking drugs of some kind. She's not rational. I advise you to come out and get her."

There was an embarrassed silence. Katie began to cry. "She's my child," she wept, "and drunk or sober, she's been a good daughter. I must help her."

"Katie, how much money will it take to bring Lillian here?" Edna asked.

"If I could send her $150 for fare—"

"All right," said Edna. "You have it. We can't let that girl die. We'll send her the money to come here so you can take care of her."

Katie sent me a money order for $150.

Ten days passed without word from me. Edna called the West Coast, checking with everyone who might know my whereabouts. They found me living in a small hotel. I had spent the money for liquor, pills and toys for the children of the woman who lived over the Chinese laundry.

"Since we've gone this far," Edna said to Katie, "let's go through with it. Here's money to buy a ticket. Go out there and bring her back yourself."

With great effort I managed to be at the station. My mother, her face pale and strained, came off the train and walked by me. She had not recognized her own daughter! When she did, she wept like a child. "What's happened to my baby?" she cried. "What have you done to yourself!"

In the cab I lay against her shoulder. "I can't help it, Mom," I wept. "I can't live without liquor. And I just couldn't make the trip back home alone."

"What will we do, Lilly?" my mother asked in despair. "Oh, my God, what will we do!"

She rented an inexpensive room for us and obtained a job for $20 a week in a five-and-ten-cent store so that she could care for me until the divorce came through, and provide me—even though she loathed it—with at least a pint of liquor daily so that I would not go completely out of my mind.

This. I thought—my mother working in a five-and-ten—

was bottom. My pride, my dignity—both were gone. This was the state to which I had brought the mother of Lillian Roth, whose name had been in lights from Hollywood to New York, who had ridden in gold-plated Hudsons and had earned over a million dollars before she was thirty! My mother, whom I wanted to give everything in the world.

On the lowest morning of all, I went to the California State Employment Office and filled out the necessary blanks. What kind of job, they asked? I could think of nothing I was fitted to do. Finally I wrote, "receptionist." My tears blotted out the word.

BOOK
TWO

CHAPTER XIX

ALL RIGHT, *Lillian, let's have a little heart-to-heart talk with yourself. Let's admit it: you're a hopeless drunk. It's not easy to become a hopeless drunk. You must work at it—and you certainly did. You thought a drunk was someone who falls in love with liquor at first sight, and drowns himself in it. You know better now. You know that alcohol creeps insidiously into your life, so insidiously you aren't aware of it until it's too late. Now and then someone will say, "Aren't you drinking too much, Lillian?" You smile at that. You think, "Well, maybe I have been taking a little bit too much to drink, but heavens—I never feel anything the next day. I have wonderful recuperative powers. I still do my shows, and I manage all right. Good Lord, I would never be like that person, I mean, that famous singer who died of liquor—I mean, that's so silly, well, I just couldn't be that way. . . ."*

Well, you could, Lillian. Trace it back yourself. In the Vanities, after that European trip, remember? It was four or five whiskey sours a night. Hangover the next day, but you managed until the next night. Soon the four or five became a pint, and then a fifth. And you couldn't start the morning without a drink. First it was beer; then bourbon in orange juice. (What had that Hollywood star suggested: half gin, half lemon juice?) Then, the two-ounce bottles in your bag grew to six ounces, and finally fifths. . . . Odd, no one ever commented (except Mark) that you were rarely seen without those big handbags. Well, good reason, reason enough.

Soon you were on a fifth a day, taking the stuff slowly, a drink or two every four or five hours. Then, every three hours. Then two hours. Finally, every hour. Then a quart through the day, and a quart through the night; and if you weren't drinking too swiftly you reached a kind of sober-drunk, where you weren't hung over.

"Well," you thought, "at last! I can finally hold my liquor." What a laugh! You didn't realize you were pouring it into yourself so steadily that you couldn't have a hangover because you were always drunk.

As the years went on, something terrifying happened. You couldn't hold as much. You began to throw it up. One part of you cried, "I want it!" The other part cried, "I can't take it!" Your body reached a point of revolt: you simply could not hold it. You drank, and you threw up. You were sick all the time. Sometimes you vomited all morning before your stomach retained an ounce of it —the drink your body needed so desperately.

The next stage was worse. You lay in bed and drank around the clock: drank, passed out, waked, drank, vomited, drank, vomited, drank, passed out. . . .

Then, still worse, the shakes. Your system demanded more liquor but your system refused to accept it. The punishment was the shakes; and with the shakes, agony. Eyes, nose, sinuses, head, throat, chest, stomach, legs. . . . Only liquor could relieve it, but your body rejected liquor. And after the shakes, the horrors, the

*delirium tremens, when you heard sounds that were not
there and saw things that did not exist, your being was
one gigantic, inflamed, tortured mass of mental and physical anguish. . . . Then the hours of pacing your room,
and tearing your hair, and you have reached the worst
stage of all: your medicine is your poison is your medicine is your poison and there is no end but madness.*

Edna told me later:

"Katie brought you back with her from the coast in
December, 1945. I was about to go off on a Guild assignment. Now, you must remember [said Edna] I had never
met you. I remembered you as a child star, and I had
always admired you tremendously. We were the same age,
but when I was a 20-year-old college student, you were
already a Hollywood star.

"Katie walked in with you. I was horrified. I had never
seen a human being in such a state of helpless drunkenness. You seemed less than human, like a whipped animal,
completely submissive, scared to death. And your appearance! Your hair was wispy and straggly: your face
and body were bloated, but your arms and legs were thin
as pipe-stems. I cried when I saw you.

" 'What will I do?' Katie said. 'Where will I take her?'
I said, 'You'll stay here and take care of her. You might
as well use my apartment while I'm away.' "

Edna went on her assignment. Minna came in from
her home in the Bronx to stay with Katie and me. I drank.
I had to drink. Sometimes, when Katie, completely exhausted, went to bed, Minna sat up until dawn with me.
She went through the DT's with me. I clung to her: deep
in my alcohol-soaked brain, she represented a subtle kind

[209]

of comfort. She was one person (not from the confused, nebulous world in which I had lived, but from the solid world of everyday people), who remained my lifelong friend. I clung to her and to this one tie with normalcy which I had been able to maintain despite everything, this one sound, healthy relationship I had built through the years which alone had not crashed.

The bottle was on the table next to my bed. From it came delirium, but from it, too, sometimes came oblivion.

Minna said, later: "You suffered hallucinations. You thought you were battling tigers and lions. 'They're trying to destroy me and I won't let them,' you moaned.

"Once you imagined I was a mummy. 'Minna!' you shouted, 'You're frightening me. You've turned into a mummy in front of my eyes! I see you as you were 10,000 years ago! How can that be? Why do I see you that way?'

"I tried to comfort you by saying it was your over-worked imagination stimulated by alcohol, but I was frightened myself.

"Then you said, 'I've got to finish the bottle. I don't care what happens. I've got to finish the bottle. I want death.'"

I was in agony. The blinds had to remain drawn in the room; daylight seared my eyes. My sinuses were inflamed, my nose congested. I found it hard to breathe. My arms and legs ached with neuritis.

Mother and Edna called Judge Shalleck. Shocked at my condition, he sent me to his doctor. The verdict was impending blindness, the onset of cirrhosis of the liver, advanced colitis, and a form of alcoholic insanity. The reports from a nose-and-throat specialist, an ophthalmologist and an internist confirmed these. I had drunk myself into gibbering helplessness. Death was not far away.

Edna pleaded with me. "I know," I said dully. "I'm trying to stop. I've cut to a pint a day but it isn't enough. I have to have more to stop the pain and what I'm hearing and seeing. I'll never pull out of this." I became maudlin, gay and maniacal in turn.

A neighbor, alarmed, took Katie aside. "Mrs. Roth, you can't live with your daughter, as much as you love her. She might murder you in your sleep in one of those drunken rages."

I could not keep food down. I vomited all morning. At night my colitis was so agonizing I could not remain in bed. "I don't even know how to kill myself," I wept to Edna. "I'm not even good enough for that."

Each day I begged for more liquor. "What can I do?" I cried. "I've got to have more." I could not bear the pity in her eyes as she gave me a couple of dollars.

The moment I crossed the threshold of a liquor store, I began to shake uncontrollably. The thought of the drink I would soon have completely unnerved me. With two dollars I could buy only a pint, but I was ashamed, for it was a dead give-away: only drunks bought so small a quantity. I improvised. "I just want enough gin to make a couple of martinis—do you think a pint is enough?" I asked the clerk, who had only to look at me to know the truth. Or I said, "I'll take a fifth of gin," opened my purse and exclaimed, chagrined, "Oh, dear, you'll have to make it only a pint. I didn't take enough money."

Finally Edna sat down with me. Was there no one, no one in the world, who could help me? No one I trusted to help me? And suddenly, out of the limbo of sixteen years, there flashed into my distraught mind the name of Dr. A. A. Brill, the psychiatrist to whom I had gone so long ago.

Edna took me to see him the following day.

Dr. Brill had my medical history before him when I entered. His eyes were kind and his smile understanding as he rose to greet me. "You are a little late for our appointment, aren't you, Lillian?"

The flood gates opened. "Oh, Doctor!" I cried. I paced wildly back and forth, trying to find the words to tell him in a few minutes all I had suffered during those sixteen incredible years. "I'm in such pain; I'm so sick! The things I see and know I see! The things I hear and know I hear! The people coming at me who think I know something about saving the world, and I can't think what it is. When I walk I think I'm falling in space, that buildings are crashing down on me, that bridges collapse when I cross them. I can't eat, I can't breathe, I can't see, I suffocate, I vomit, my hands are stiff, I can't hold anything, I'm so ashamed of myself, I've sunk so low . . . I'm hopeless! I'm hopeless! Nobody can help me!" I fell into a chair, sobbing.

Dr. Brill talked to me, quietly, and examined me. He sent me into an anteroom and spoke to Edna.

"She is at a breaking point physically and mentally. I don't give her three months to live unless she's hospitalized immediately."

Would that help? Edna asked. Would it stop the drinking?

He shook his head. "I can promise nothing. I can only

tell you, if you want to prevent her death, she must be taken to a hospital at once."

"Will you tell that to her?" Edna asked. Dr. Brill smiled sadly, as if to say, what difference could that make? "Very well," he said. "Bring her in." Edna led me back to his office.

"Lillian, I have just told Miss Berger what I am going to tell you. You haven't more than three months to live."

I stiffened, but remained silent. The blood slowly drained from my face.

"There is a chance to save your life. You must be put in a hospital at once."

I broke down. "I'll do anything," I wept, "anything. I don't want to be a burden. I want to be a human being again. I'll do anything you say."

Dr. Brill told Edna he would arrange for my admittance into the Westchester Division of New York Hospital—a mental institution.

Later he telephoned her to say they would accept me in ten days. I must commit myself and remain six months to a year. I waited.

One night Ann, who had no idea how ill I was, took me to see "The Lost Weekend," a film about an alcoholic. She hoped it might shock me into sobriety. Instead, when Ray Milland, the star of the film, watching a drinking scene on the screen, yearned for the bottle he had left in his coat in the checkroom, the effect upon me was startling. I wanted a drink so desperately I had to restrain myself from rushing out of the theatre to a bar. I suffered like a person on the rack until the picture ended: then, at the first chance, I drank myself into insensibility.

The morning came when I was to enter the hospital.

"I'm worried," I said nervously to Minna. "I think it's really Bloomingdale's I'm going to, and that's for insane people."

Minna denied it. So did Edna.

Whatever place it was, I made sure I would not go unprepared. I bought six two-ounce medicine bottles, filled them with gin, and put them in my bag. The usual fifth might be too conspicuous.

Edna and Minna drove me to the hospital: Mother remained behind. Dr. Brill had warned that if she came along, at the last moment I might change my mind and refuse to commit myself. I sat quietly in back with Minna, drinking to keep up my courage.

We stopped once, when Edna asked a gas station attendant:

"Which way to the Westchester Division of New York Hospital?"

"Straight ahead, ma'am," he said briskly. "You can't miss it—Bloomingdale's."

I began to babble. "Listen, I heard about a woman who went to Bloomingdale's. They gave her needle baths and put her in straitjackets and beat her with rubber hoses. Please, I beg of you, don't take me there!"

They soothed me. "Oh, no, dear, it used to be Bloomingdale's. Now it's only for people who are a little upset."

There was nothing I could do. When finally we drove through the huge iron gates and along a winding driveway and came to the great formidable red brick building, I said to myself: "When I was a little girl, I thought someday I might want to be a nun. Maybe this is my way of being a nun. This is my convent. Maybe God has sent

[214]

me to this place. I'll just go in and give myself up. I have no other place to go."

Estelle Demarest had given me a small pocket Bible. I clutched it tightly in my hand as we walked into the building.

The receiving doctor wrote down my name.

I made a last attempt to remain in the world. "I wonder, Doctor, whether I'm not making a mistake coming to a place like this. I have extra-sensory perception. In Niagara Falls I felt things other people didn't. Just last night I told Edna that we'd contact the moon and this morning's newspaper says we had contacted the moon by radar. Doesn't that prove I don't belong here?"

"Now isn't that interesting?" the doctor said. "You just sign right here, please."

Then I knew it was no use. What good was my intuition, if people refused to believe. Perhaps if I had gone to college I might have been able to explain what I meant. All right, I'll sign and go in. But I forgot my pocketbook. Might I return to the car and get it?

The physician nodded. "Of course. But come right back, please."

My bag was in the car, but the bottles were gone. "Edna!" I cried, "you took the bottles!" She shook her head. "Minna! Then you've taken them!" She swore she hadn't.

I was crushed. How could they do this to me, refuse me one last drink? I returned to the reception desk and stood there, shaking uncontrollably. If only I could have had that last drink and gone in like a lady!

CHAPTER XX

For the first time in my life I fell on my knees and prayed. "Dear God, I thank You for giving me sanctuary and keeping me from destroying myself."

I rose trembling and sat on my bed. I was in a small room, with a bureau, a gray metal clotheslocker, a straight-backed chair, and a single window covered with vertical iron bars. There was no door.

A few minutes before a nurse had led me down a long red carpeted corridor to this room. I had a bobby pin in my hair; deftly she detached it and put it in the pocket of her uniform. She took away my necklace; my wrist watch; my garters. She searched me for other objects with which I might harm myself. She placed my clothes in the locker, and used one of the many keys on her belt to lock it. Then she helped me into a nightgown buttoned up the back, and left me a long beltless robe and slippers.

I had just begun to absorb my surroundings when three men entered. It developed that since I had committed myself, I was a ward of the State, and these were physicians to interview me. This will be a breeze, I thought: I've been interviewed before. I realized how I must have appeared, in my shapeless hospital nightgown, my hair in strings, my robe flapping about my ankles, but I bowed graciously. "Come in, gentlemen, please." I sat on the bed and they took chairs. One rose courteously: "Wouldn't you like to sit here? It's more comfortable."

"Oh, no," I said, sitting up stiffly. "I prefer to sit in straight-backed chairs." They exchanged glances. There, I've done it, I thought. Of course I know I'm sitting on a bed. What I meant is that I like to sit up straight. But let it go.

One physician took up the interview.

"You signed several statements when you entered, Miss Roth. We want to see if they are correct, because we must take care of you. We represent the State of New York."

"But I'm not a State case," I said. "I've come to a private hospital."

"Yes, my dear, but you're under our jurisdiction and we must protect your interests. Now, is it true that you feel you're going blind?"

That was right. I had signed that. "Yes," I said, "your faces aren't very clear to me. Sometimes everything floats in a gray mist before my eyes and I can barely make out vague figures moving about."

"Do you have dryness of the throat, pain and inflammation of the sinus?"

Yes. Yes again, yes. Item by item they proceeded through the long catalogue of my suffering.

"And you have had various thoughts of suicide?"

I had to tell the truth. I had signed that statement. "Yes."

"Do you hear voices?"

"Yes. Sometimes I think the radio is on when it isn't." I paused. "But I do feel psychic—as though people are trying to get messages to me."

"What kind of messages?"

"Telepathic messages."

One doctor asked:

"Why do you think you have such a strange power?"

"There's nothing strange about it," I retorted. "Don't they do things like that at Duke University? I've read that university professors in London have communicated telepathically, too."

"Yes," said the first doctor. He looked at his notebook. "Do you see things?"

I wouldn't tell the truth. "When I'm upset, I see spots before my eyes, but don't you see spots when you over-eat?" I thought, I must show them I'm not as insane as they probably think I am. "Right now I can see the tie you're wearing, and it's a very nice one."

"Do you like the pattern?" he asked, politely.

"Yes, and the color, too. I always chose the judge's ties for him, and I can tell a good Sulka tie when I see it."

There was a moment's silence.

"Did you make a statement that you would write a book here?"

"That's right."

"What about?"

"I was going to clear a man named Jimmy Hines."

The notebook closed. "Thank you, Miss Roth. That's all. Thank you very much." They left.

I was alone. A few minutes passed. While I had been questioned, I had heard sounds of people moving in the corridor, the jingle of keys on the belts of the nurses.

Now everything was silent. Some of my confidence began to melt.

I ventured out of my room. The corridor was empty, and I strolled down it. Small rooms like mine lined it on either side. I peered into them. Each was empty. Where was everyone?

I turned at the end of the corridor and found myself in a large, library-like room. It, too, was deserted. I wandered over and tried to pick up a book, but my fingers were too stiff.

Suddenly there were butterflies in my stomach: my hands shook. *I was all alone.* "Oh, Mom," I cried soundlessly, "Where are you!"

Then, a slight stir. I turned. A handsome, black-haired, ruddy-faced young man was at my side. "How do you do, Miss Roth," he said cheerfully. "I am Dr. Head, your psychiatrist. How do you feel? Are you nervous?"

"Oh, no," I said hurriedly. "I'm a little worried about what will happen to me. I really don't know why I signed in here, Doctor." I thought, he's cute. I wish the nurse had left me a comb or lipstick.

"We want to take a few simple tests," he said. He looked at me. "Don't you think you'd like a pill first to quiet your nerves?"

"No, thank you." I was firm. I was not asking them for anything. "I'm just fine, Doctor, just fine."

He told me to sit down, and gave me a complete physical examination. He had me walk forward; then backward; then sideways; then on my haunches. "My goodness, Doctor," I protested. "I'm a singer, not a contortionist. Please!"

He laughed. "Miss Roth, I'm just trying to judge your

sense of balance. Now, will you please get on your knees and walk across the room that way?"

I gave him an arch glance. "Shall I sing a chorus of 'Mammy' enroute?" Katie would have liked that.

Dr. Head laughed again. "We're going to get along fine, Lillian," he said. "We're finished for a while now." A nurse silently appeared, and led me down the corridor to a huge living room in which about fifty women sat at their ease in lounging chairs and sofas. They were all well dressed: they might have been guests at one of my charity affairs.

For a moment I was the judge's wife again. "Hello, everybody," I said gaily. They all stared straight ahead. Each remained lost in her own private world. I sank into an empty chair, to find myself next to a pretty girl, about 23, who was in an animated conversation with someone who wasn't there. She talked so swiftly as to be almost unintelligible: her lips moved, she nodded, simpered, raised her eyebrows in astonishment, then listened intently.

As I watched her, the enormity of it struck home. These were mad women! What was I doing among them? I could not catch my breath: I felt my heart leap in my throat: I began to shake. Oh, God, I'm getting the horrors. Don't let them get too bad or they'll put me in a straightjacket.

A bell rang. The women rose like automatons, formed a line, and began to file out. "You go with them, Miss Roth," a nurse called. "It's lunch time."

"But I'm not hungry," I protested.

Her voice took on the tone of authority. "You go ahead. You'll eat." I followed the others into a large dining room and sat down. I fumbled for a knife and fork: they fell out of my hands onto my plate with a loud clatter. An attendant tried to feed me with a spoon, but I gagged: my throat was too constricted. The shakes came on me with renewed fury. Sweat poured from me. The room began to spin, and slowly I started to slide off the chair.

Strong arms half carried, half helped me to my bed. I lay shaking so violently the springs creaked. I thought in panic, *now I'm getting it. I've got to control this, or they'll lock me up and I'll go mad. I can't let them know.* Screaming inwardly, I struggled out of bed and asked the nurse on duty in the corridor: "Isn't the doctor coming?"

"Yes, there'll be a doctor here soon."

I tried to wait in my room, but the nurse sent me back to the living room. I paced back and forth; my legs were getting stiff, I could scarcely bend my knees. My jaw began to tighten, my teeth seemed to loosen in my gums. A strangling sensation crept over me. *I'm going stark, raving mad. A knife, a knife to plunge into my stomach and twist up to my heart, like the Japanese, tear myself wide open to end the agony . . .*

I had never known such torture. In the world outside I was always confident that I could find a drink to ease the pain. Here I was utterly helpless, and if I betrayed any sign of the hell I was going through, they would put me in the mad ward . . .

I walked the infinite distance to my room, step by step. When, ten minutes later, a doctor entered, I was sitting on the bed, soundlessly pounding the mattress with my fist. I looked at him, unable to speak.

"Give her an ounce of paraldehyde," he told the nurse.

Minutes passed. "Where's what he ordered," I implored her. "For God's sake, where is it?"

It came, a colorless liquid in a whiskey glass, and I gulped it. I had molten fire in my mouth, exploding through my nose. I choked, but got most of it down. Then the nurse helped me into bed. I lay there, tossing. *I'll go out of my mind, this time I will!*

I tried to keep my voice steady when Dr. Head arrived on his night rounds. "I don't think I can stand it here, Doctor. But please, don't lock me up, no matter what I do! I'm trying so hard to control myself."

"I'll give you more paraldehyde," he said. I shook my head and sobbed, "It's ghastly."

"You'll be crying for it if this thing keeps up," he said, and shuddering, I took it down. Before he left he gave me two pills. "We don't like medicine here, but I'll give you these for the first few nights. They'll help you."

They helped: but that night was one of the loneliest, most wretched, I had ever known. It was impossible to sleep: every 15 minutes a blinding light flashed in my face. A nurse with a flashlight made her rounds four times an hour. Almost as frequently an embarrassing weakness came over me, dating back to the lecherous old man who had painted me as a child, an urge to run to the bathroom like a little girl. Each time my nurse noted my visit in her book. The fifth time she asked, "What is the matter with you, Miss Roth?"

"I can't help it," I said miserably.

I lay on my cot, staring at the ceiling. The moon was out: the cold-blue white moonlight streamed in through the barred window. I counted the bars, over and over again: six of them. They made a sharply defined pattern on the floor, and as the long night went on, the six-barred moon-made shadow slowly crept across the floor. I turned to the wall and wept.

Finally morning came, and it was the second day. Bells rang, people emerged from their rooms, and a nurse appeared, carrying a tray of orange juice and tea. I lay exhausted in sheets damp with perspiration. My mouth was swollen: I tried to run my tongue across my blistered lips.

"You had a rough time of it last night," the nurse said, "but this orange juice will help that burning throat. Paraldehyde always does that to your mouth."

As I was to learn later, all an alcoholic receives in a hospital, or even in jail, is a cursory sobering up treatment. However in an institution like Bloomingdale's, which rarely takes alcoholics, the chronic drinker receives psychiatric and medical treatment similar to that afforded regular mental patients.

Dr. Head gave me additional tests. I was asked to name the Presidents of the United States. I took ink-blot tests, interblocking tests, maze tests, association of ideas tests.

I thought, he *is* handsome. Looks a little like the judge, only younger. Undoubtedly they assigned a handsome doctor to me because they expected me to fall in love with him. Everyone knows you fall in love with your psychiatrist. I could make myself half-way presentable if I had a brush and comb . . .

Somehow I got through the second day. I was left alone to wander about. I learned I was on an observation floor: virtually every move I had made from the moment

I entered had been under scrutiny.

On the third day my nurse said, "You may dress your-self this morning." I was allowed slippers, underclothes, and a simple cotton dress. She combed my tangled hair, but kept the comb. She allowed me to put on a dab of lipstick, but kept the lipstick. I have no cold cream, my skin is dry, I've bitten my nails down to the quick; and then, a sudden lift: there must be a tiny spark of self respect left in me if I want to look better.

The nurse said, "Make your bed."

"Make my bed?" I echoed. "You don't make beds here, do you?"

"You certainly do. That's part of your therapy."

I had been without alcohol since my arrival. The paral-dehyde, vitamin injections and other medication helped tide me over what otherwise would have been an unbear-able period. For 16 years I had been drinking; for at least 12 years I had taken at least a quart of liquor almost every day and nearly that much each night; for much of that time I had never gone more than three or four hours without a drink. Now I had been dry for more than 50 hours.

But that night my alcoholic dreams, which I had warded off for so many years, returned. Sometime after midnight it seemed that I was awake. I had escaped from the hospital. I had hidden a bottle in my room, and become drunk on it. I ran out the doors and through the bolted gate, and the doctors, their white coats floating after them in the wind, pursued me down a dark, lonely street, now hiding behind trees and bushes to pounce on me, now looming wild and gigantic before me. They caught me, they forced me into scalding hot and freezing cold baths, and tied me in a straightjacket. Or it seemed to me that just as I stealthily put out my hand for the bottle I'd hidden far back on the closet shelf, behind the school books with the questions I had to answer—just then the bottle rolled toward me of its own accord, slipped out of my paralyzed hands, and crashed thunderously to the floor. The nurses rushed in, their outstretched hands pawing at me, their eyes accusing, converging upon me from all directions—or was it the judge's wrathful face which slowly came into focus?—and I stood transfixed, utterly abject, shamed, humiliated . . .

I awoke with a start. The dream had been so vivid I could have sworn I smelled the fumes from the broken bottle. My nurse entered, I choked down an ounce of paraldehyde, and the long night went on.

On the fifth day, Dr. Head came in with a smile. "Good morning, Lillian. I've got a surprise for you. You're going to be moved today."

I had a moment of fright. "For better or worse?"

"For better, naturally. You're going to the convalescent floor. That's pretty good. Most patients aren't moved off this floor for two or three weeks."

I perked up. "Oh, I *am* getting better. Does that mean that I won't have to stay a year or even six months?"

"Now, don't start counting your days. You'd better adjust yourself to the idea that you're going to be here with me a long time. You'll get used to it. You don't get well over night."

Now I had a room with a door, although regulations required that it be half open at all times. The window was barred, but on the dresser lay my lipstick, my comb, my brushes and bobby pins. There was even a mirror on the wall.

A new routine began. I rose, made my bed when the morning bell rang, washed, went into breakfast. A community therapeutic shower followed breakfast, to relax us. We sat in a line, naked but for a sheet, while nurses sprayed us with hot water, then tepid, then icewater needles. Gym and dancing followed. After showers and a rest period, another bell was the signal to put on hats and coats, wait in line for an attendant to unlock the door and lead us out, perhaps fifty in a group with a nurse shepherding us like schoolgirls in ribbons with a nun in charge, into the lovely grounds surrounding the buildings. After a little fresh air, we were taken to mental therapy rooms.

Some painted, some sanded boxes, some made leather goods. I worked in leather, making cigarette cases for my mother, for Ann, for Minna and Edna. My special project was a large leather wallet—my "hope wallet"—and as I explained in a letter to Minna, I hoped someday to fill it so I could repay those who were taking care of my bills at Bloomingdale's.

"Why don't you try painting?" the nurse in charge asked one day, as she admired my leather designs.

"Did you ever see me paint?" I demanded. "I still draw the same face I drew when I was four years old."

She smiled. "Keep up that good humor, Lillian. It means you're getting better."

After therapy, we were lined up again, the door was unlocked, and we were led out.

In the afternoons we were taken on long walks. As we

[226]

trudged along, I saw buildings in the gray distance. I thought: there, far away, is an apartment house. There is an elevator in it. Men and women are going home, or going out to dinner, or to the theatre. People are living warm, complete lives. A sense of loneliness so shattering as to be unbearable, tore at my heart, and I wept.

It was usually a silent walk. Each of my companions was alone. One girl, a lovely, fragile blonde, keeping step with me, suddenly spoke. "Do you know why I'm here?"

"No, why?" I asked.

"I'll tell you," she said, and lapsed into silence.

The following day she asked: "Do you know why I'm in here?"

I shook my head. "Why?"

"I'll tell you," she said, and became silent again.

The next day she came up to me and uttered one word: "Horses."

"What about horses?" I asked.

"I'll tell you," she said, and was silent.

The following day she began, "I told you I'd tell you about horses."

"That's right," I said. "There's nothing wrong in liking horses, you know. Everybody has a weakness. You like to gamble. I used to like to drink."

"No," she said. "I don't gamble, but my husband is divorcing me on account of horses."

As we walked we passed several truck horses used on the farm attached to the institution. "Well, if you like horses," I said, "there are some over there—"

She looked up, and turned away in disdain. "Oh, not those kind—I mean beautiful, handsome horses, the kind

[227]

I ride—big, gleaming horses." She began to blush. "I can hardly wait until morning to be with them again. I'm just afraid I can't be faithful to my husband."

I cudgelled my brain. A strange perversion? Hadn't Catherine the Great developed a sex problem concerning horses? My companion went on blithely. "It's amazing, my control over them. Tremendous as they are, I can take a horse and balance his four hoofs right in the palm of my hand." She trotted the fingers of her right hand around the palm of her left hand.

My table mate was another pretty young girl. At lunch one day she whispered, "Do you know what I am?"

"A very nice girl," I said encouragingly.

She leaned closer and whispered. "No one's supposed to know what they're in here for, but I know what I am, I'm a manic depressive!" She said it proudly.

Involuntarily I pulled back. I was sick, for I was in here, but I was not that sick.

After dinner I smoked the one cigarette allowed, and played a few hands of bridge. Four of us sat at a table. I thought to myself: a dementia praecox, a manic depressive, a schizophrenic and an alcoholic. But women are women everywhere, even in an institution like Bloomingdale's. They discuss the doctors, the nurses, the food, and the inevitable subject—men.

I turned to my partner: "Do you play Blackwood?"

She simpered. "Backward?"

I said, "Oh, no. That's all right."

The schizoid said, "Well, I play the common sense system."

In our games it was not unusual to bid three hearts,

hear your partner bid two spades—and let it pass.

In the middle of one hectic hand, the oldest woman at the table, about sixty, said, "Sh-sh . . . Keep it down. I have something to tell you girls." We all bent close, lest the nurses hear. "This morning, when I went up for my shock treatment, my doctor raped me in the very middle of it."

I said, "Oh, he didn't!"

She said, "Yes! And that wasn't the first time." She blushed.

I knew how incredible this was, because at least half a dozen attendants are required to carry out shock treatment.

After bridge, bedtime came swiftly enough. At eight o'clock, a bell rang—preparation for bath—and at nine o'clock, another, signalling lights out. In the darkness I lay sobbing to myself. Now my sorrow was in search of a target. This time I cried for my father as bitterly as if he had died that day. How much I had to atone for. . . .

I was fifteen, and he and Katie had had a violent quarrel, and he had gone back to Boston, where many of his friends still lived. Through the years my parents' fallings out had been interrupted when we left town, patched up when we returned; but as time went on, Arthur became more jealous, more uncontrollable when he drank. Now there was great bitterness between them.

"Mom," I asked, "do you really love Dad?"

Tears came into her eyes, and she shook her head. "He's killed any love I've had for him by his temper and his drinking. I just can't take it any more."

Well, then, I said, from now on, I would take care of us. I packed my father's trunk and sent it to him with a

[229]

letter. "Daddy, I love you very much," I wrote, "but it just seems we all can't get along together." I thought, maybe he is happier in Boston, and what I am doing, I am doing for both their sakes.

Although he and Katie were together again at intervals, particularly when I returned to New York from Hollywood or from long tours, their real separation dated from that day. And the breakup of their marriage.

Why had I taken things into my own hands so determinedly that day? If only I had understood my father and his alcoholic problem I would have been so much better a daughter to him! Why had he to die, forsaken and alone, in a hotel room? Why hadn't I listened to his warnings against liquor? He was a weak man, but he knew his weakness and wanted me to be strong. Why had his last years to be filled with poverty, pain and failure? And with it all, my bottomless disgrace?

Then my tears were shed for my mother. She and I had worked all our lives. I had reached the stage at which I should have been able to brighten her declining years by giving her everything she wanted . . . and what had she now? My heart broke for her.

In those long nights relief came in the early morning, an hour before we were allowed to rise. At 7 a.m. I was able to turn on a small portable radio Edna had sent me to a station which featured the rough, rumbling voice of Arthur Godfrey, then a disk jockey.

Sometimes he seemed to be in the room with me, talking in his easy, friendly manner. Perhaps I am getting better, I thought: here is one voice I'm surely not imagining. Often my nurse entered and chided me. "Don't you know other patients are still asleep?"

I pleaded with her. "It's very soft and my friend's talking—and it's so nice to have a man around."

"Oh, Lillian, you're incorrigible," she would say, but she would permit me to keep the program tuned in softly.

I had many interviews with Dr. Head, meeting with him two and three times a week. Together we went back through the years. As he saw it, I had an abnormal, unstable childhood. My mother had been overprotective, my relationship with my father unsatisfactory because it was incomplete. Even now my thinking was that of an adolescent. I had no sense of security: my constant anxiety about my parents, their quarrels, their separation; the lack of normal association with children my own age; the absence of a normal home life; the traumatic sex experience I had had as a child—all these played their part.

My physical relationships with men had been unhappy. Disappointment became a pattern in my life: the death of David, the children that never were, the home that never materialized, the dramatic success that never came. I had not helped myself by driving myself before large audiences: I had always tried to be someone I was not. My sense of inferiority was intense; somehow I had the conviction that I was never good enough, even in my own work; I felt I never pleased my mother; my inferiority was even greater because I had not had a complete education. Whatever success came to me was always an empty victory.

"You were afraid of the world, and you always sought a buffer against it," Dr. Head explained. "You married each time with a subconscious hope that your husband would protect you. Invariably you chose the wrong man."

Yes. I had married Willie because of loneliness, hoping he would help me forget David. Willie represented not love, but lightheartedness, gaiety, simplicity, a happy soul with whom I might fly to the other end of the Milky Way.

But it hadn't worked out. I married the judge, then, for the respectability and normalcy other women possessed. That failed, too.

Then I turned to Mark, thinking a strong, even brutal man, who lived hard and daringly, would provide the ballast I needed. And he proved to be a drunken sadist.

And Victor? I had not intended to marry him, and I had married him. There it was, period.

Dr. Head observed: "You were attached to your father, but you grew up virtually without him. You wished desperately to look up to him, yet you were forced to protect him. And you haven't forgiven yourself for what you think was your part in separating your parents.

And my mother? Why did I feel such enormous guilt? I beseeched him. "When I think of her, I could cry my heart out. She wanted so much for me and I disintegrated before her eyes. Even a stranger couldn't have endured seeing that happen to another human being. I blame myself and blame myself."

Dr. Head summed it up: "I think you've had this breakdown because you've reached the age of 34 and nobody loves you. In the back of your mind you're not even sure your mother still loves you. You feel you can turn to no one. You have no children; you have no husband; you feel you've disappointed and utterly shamed

[232]

your mother; you've lost your father; you've alienated yourself from your sister; finally, your pride is crushed by strangers giving you charity."

He went on slowly, choosing his words: "And you are tearing yourself apart, Lillian, because you try to hold your mother responsible for your being here."

He made absolutely no sense to me.

"Whatever it is, I must see my mother," I burst out. "I've been here almost a month without seeing her. I must see her."

"You'll become upset," he warned.

"Please, Doctor—I must see her."

Katie and Edna were my first visitors. Although it was wonderful to be with them for the short hour permitted me, the loneliness after they left was all but unbearable. Dr. Head spoke sternly: "No more visitors if you get like this, Lillian."

"Oh, Doctor, I'm from an emotional family," I cried. "Please don't say that to me—you make me feel awful."

"All right," he said. "Don't excite yourself. Minna can visit you next week and your mother the week after."

I no longer felt charged with electricity, but I developed a passion for oranges. I stole them from tables and from the rooms of other inmates. I begged Katie to bring them. I traded cookies, candy, gifts, for oranges, and I lay in bed, with oranges tucked under my pillow, peeling and eating them slowly, relishing each succulent section, piling the rinds neatly under my bed.

The orange phase passed: in its stead, I lusted for gum. I was insatiable, and five sticks at a time in my mouth only whetted my hunger for them. Yet I was beginning to relish the taste of food, something I had almost forgotten.

One Sunday rest period I was allowed for the first time, to look through the *New York Times,* one of the few newspapers permitted in the institution. A story related the experiences of Mrs. Marty Mann, Director of the National Foundation for Research on Alcoholism. An alcoholic, she had been in and out of hospitals. Many doctors tried futilely to aid her. She attempted suicide once, and actually jumped—living to tell the story of how she achieved sobriety through Alcoholics Anonymous, a group of ex-drinkers who had their own methods for keeping themselves from liquor.

Panic seized me. I had been tricked! If doctors hadn't helped Marty Mann, if institutions hadn't helped her, what was the good of me being locked up here? I felt like a caged animal. My heart beat so wildly I thought my chest would burst. Four more months to go—maybe more?

Next morning I showed the paper to Dr. Head. "Read this!"

"Lillian," he said, after glancing at it, "we know about this. Alcoholics Anonymous is not for you—at present. You are a sick girl mentally and physically. You would be unable to understand their therapy at this time; you would fight it. Our principle job right now is to build you up physically and to teach you how to live for a long time without alcohol."

My liver was permanently damaged, he went on. I could be healed to a considerable degree. "But you cannot be impatient," he said. "You are not ready for the world, and the world at the moment does not want you. But—" he smiled, and took my hand, "they will, believe me, they will."

That night I searched among my possessions until I found the small leather Bible Estelle Demarest had given me. Dr. Head had kept it the first two weeks. "We had to be sure you weren't suffering from a religious mania," he had said. I fell asleep reading it.

The day came when Katie was permitted to visit me alone. A long hill led from the bus stop to the hospital gates. I waited outside for her. She could not afford a cab, and I watched her laboring up the hill. She arrived, panting and out of breath. I wanted to cry. Yet, before she left, some perverse impulse made me fling at her, "It's your fault I'm here. God damn it, you ruined my life! If it hadn't been for you, I wouldn't be here, because nobody wanted me, that's why I'm here!"

She stared at me, fighting hard not to cry; and after a little while, she turned and left.

I sobbed to Dr. Head: "Why did I treat her that way?"

Sometime in the night, time became telescoped. I was six years old. . . .

"Lilly, baby," my mother said, warmth and expectation in her voice, "we're going over to Uncle Jack's and you can pick out a little coat for yourself. You're going to be the best-dressed little girl in the neighborhood."

Uncle Jack had a drygoods store under the 2nd Avenue El. When we walked into his apartment above the store, he was hugging and kissing his wife. "They've just been married," my mother whispered. I had never seen her and daddy hugging and kissing. I felt strange.

[235]

Uncle Jack turned to me gaily, picked me up and threw me into the air. "What can we do for you, sweetheart?" he asked.

"I want Lillian to pick out a coat all by herself," Katie said.

"Righto!" he said. He turned to his wife. "Pearl, do you want to come along? Lillian is going to pick out her own coat." We went downstairs and he placed two velvet coats before me, one blue, one purple.

"Let her have whichever one she wants," said my mother. "She's the boss."

I liked the blue coat. But I thought, no, I better not take it. I said, "I'll take the purple coat."

"You sure that's the one you like?" Katie asked.

"Do you like it, Mommy?"

"Whichever one you like, I like."

"Well, I'll take the purple one," I told my uncle. As he wrapped it, I felt wretched. It wasn't the color I really wanted. I took it because I felt that my mother would not like the one I chose, if I chose the one I liked.

What was my fear? That her face might reveal fleeting disapproval? Was it that I would rather endure anything than surprise a look of pain on her face? Why did her pain, however small, strike into my very being?

And then I was awake, in a bed in Bloomingdale's, an institution for the mentally sick, weeping for my mother . . .

I tried to explain to Dr. Head.

"We're so close," I said. "Maybe it's our sense of humor, but in our most tragic moments, it seems we can laugh together. Maybe we're near tears when we laugh, but

. . . It's hard to put into words. We'll be at a party, and something will strike us simultaneously as roaringly funny, and we'll grow hysterical laughing together. Then we'll be ruined for the evening, because each time our eyes meet we begin laughing all over again. It's this laughter we have, this closeness between us, as if we were one person—no matter how bad a thing becomes, it's never too awful if we have each other."

"Yes," he said. "Your mother is your real love."

Perhaps it might help if I saw Ann, I suggested. We had had little to do with each other in recent years, and Katie had kept from her as long as possible the serious nature of my illness.

She came up with Katie. I had asked Ann to bring me paper tissues, because I cried so much that I never had a sufficient supply. "Did you bring the tissues, Ann?" I asked the very moment she came into the room. Yes, she had: she had left them downstairs at the receptionist's desk, as directed.

I exploded. "Why? Why? It will take them three days down there before they examine them and send them up to me! I need them now! How could you do that to me!" Savagely I berated her.

Dr. Head said later: "My dear girl, when you leave here, I advise you not to live with your family because you react badly after you see them."

Finally I was allowed off grounds accompanied by Edna and Minna for a brief visit into nearby White Plains. It was a strange experience. The streets and traffic frightened me. The faces on the street—how intense and contorted they were! I realized why. I had become so accustomed to the apathetic faces about me in Bloomingdale's.

"Let's have some coffee," Minna suggested. We entered a restaurant. As though in a dream, a tray of martinis materialized and floated by me: a waitress, threading through the crowd, held it high, balanced on one hand. My eyes fixed on the martinis and followed them as though I had been hypnotized. The tray was lowered and placed on a table before three women. They lifted the glasses to their lips, and drank: and I drank with them. I felt the dry tart taste going through my nose, I tasted the acrid bitterness of the olive, and I gagged. That was how it had been in the old days: even when I was hungover, my hand would not lift the drink before me, nor could I swallow: anticipation paralyzed me, and I gagged.

I fought off a choking attack until hot, black coffee came, and I forced it down, scalding my mouth and throat. Then I looked up again, at the women with their martinis. I sipped my coffee, and glanced at Edna and Minna. Did they know I still wanted a drink?

CHAPTER XXI

I WAS getting better. Proof: I was allowed to make a trip to New York by myself. It would be a test. No one was to pick me up. I would do it all by myself—buy the tickets, board the train, hire a cab, go to my mother's apartment.

The hot sun shone, and I walked slowly, wanting to cover my face, my ears, from the noises of the street, the voices of the newsstand dealers, the swirl and confusion of traffic in New York this April day, this bright sunlit Spring day.

I clutched my Bible in my hand and recited the verse to myself:

"Thou shalt not be afraid for the arrow that flyeth by day nor for the destruction that wasteth at noonday . . ."

I turned a corner. There before me was a liquor store —the first I had seen, or been conscious of, since I had been in Bloomingdale's. I turned my head sharply away, and stared across the street until I was well past it.

A few stores further, a huge sign over the sidewalk: BAR. I shut my eyes tight and counted to 30 as I walked —time enough to pass it.

Then BAR & GRILL & RESTAURANT loomed ahead of me. Through the large window I saw men drinking beer. I jerked my head away, rushed into a drug store and ordered coffee at the counter. I drank it swiftly, because the walls were beginning to spin, and my throat to constrict.

What would happen if I take a drink? I'm an alcoholic, Dr. Head says. If I drink, it means death. What does he mean by death? Not that I will drop dead if I take one drink. Of course not. He means cirrhosis of the liver. But he had warned me—to drink again would cause insanity. That was absurd. Certainly, if I've been sober for four months, how can one drink drive me crazy? What had he said: "You are an alcoholic. If you drink, you will go insane. If you continue to drink, you will die. Lillian, for you to drink is to die."

"You're trying to scare me." Panicky. "You mean I'll get sick and die eventually."

He shook his head. "No, not eventually. Soon."

His words were still in my mind as I rang my mother's bell.

"Lilly! You made it. And all by yourself!"

The experience was unreal. She led me into the single studio room that was now her home. She had cooked lunch for me, dishes I had always enjoyed as a child. "You look wonderful, baby," she said. "Yes, Mom," I said, but long before train time I glanced repeatedly at the clock. "I better go back," ran through my head. "I haven't anything to say to her."

We took the train to Bloomingdale's, slowly walked the hill to the gate, and waited silently for the nurse to unbolt the door. "I've brought my daughter," said my mother, and kissed me, and held me close for a long moment, and went back alone in the dark.

Then, a weekend in New York, we visited some of mother's friends, and later, she and I returned to her room. I thought, "When I do get out, what have we got to look forward to? We have no money. What will we do?"

We sat opposite each other, silent. I burst out crying. I ran to her and sat in her lap and put my arms around her and sobbed, and as I sobbed I played with her neck and her hair, as I had done so many years ago. I was 34 years old and my mother rocked me back and forth like a little child.

I returned alone to the hospital that night. I was frightened on the way to the train. The dark began to take on shape. Again the Bible's words ran through my brain. *"Thou shalt not be afraid for the terror by night . . ."*

I walked hurriedly. "Good evening." A man was beside me, matching his step with mine, tipping his hat, smiling at me, murmuring words. I shut my ears. *"Because Thou hast made the law which is my refuge . . . therefore shall no evil befall thee."* The man had dropped back. I was alone again. *"He shall cover thee with His feathers and under His wings shall thou trust. His truth shall be thy shield and buckler."*

I thought, in the train: perhaps when God made mothers, their hearts were the shield and the buckler, and their love the wings placed over you to protect you. Had I not sat in my mother's lap like a little girl?

Again and again, the past, the distant past, came back to me. How old was I? Two? Two and a half? Three years old? I lay, half asleep, in a back bedroom, in a house in Boston. There was a living room, and the bedroom

[241]

beyond, separated by a draw curtain. In the bedroom lit by a yellow gas jet on the wall, my mother stood before the mirror, putting on a great hat with big yellow feathers. She wore a tight black skirt, but such a pretty skirt, with a large white blouse. What a small waist my mother has, what a tiny little waist, I thought.

I watched the shadow of my mother on the wall, and then she was bending over and kissing me, and then she was not there and the shadow was gone and the gas jet burned alone and I did not like the feeling in the room at all. . . .

"Don't you think you might go back to show business?" Dr. Head asked.

"Why would anyone want to hear a drunk like me?"

Dr. Head looked at me rebukingly. "I think you ought to stop thinking of yourself like that," he said. "You haven't had a drink for more than five months. Isn't that true?"

I nodded. Nobody could take that from me.

He thought for a moment. "Are you jealous of anyone in your profession?" he asked suddenly.

It was a chance shot, but it struck home. Jealous? Not exactly jealous, but I—well—I envied Ethel Merman. All at once I was aware how deeply it had rankled in me. "When I was in lights," I said, "she was a stenographer and she often came to the Paramount to watch me work. A friend once took me to hear her sing. She was singing professionally then, and soon became well known. She did numbers I did, and made shorts, too." I was silent. Then the words burst from me. "Why, Dr. Head, when I watched her do songs like 'Sing, You Sinners!' I thought

[242]

I was watching myself."

Dr. Head nodded. "Go on."

"I wondered why she sang that number so often. She had every right, but, well—I didn't like it. She had a wonderful way of putting a number across, and she had a magnificent brassy quality. I admired her. One year she did a Broadway musical. I was cast to play the same role in the film. The director said, 'My, Lillian, you're using a lot of Merman's mannerisms.' I said, 'Well, if you look up a picture called "Honey," in which I sang "Sing, You Sinners!", you'll find that I always used those mannerisms.' "

I remembered more. There had been the summer of 1935 when I was married to the judge, drinking too much, unhappy and seeking ways to keep busy. Paramount screen-tested me for a musical, liked the test, and went so far as to draw up contracts for me. This was to be my great chance. And suddenly Ethel, who had been busy on another picture, was free, and Paramount signed her instead.

"I remembered thinking then, 'This girl has taken my place. We're so alike in our delivery.' I lost my desire to make a comeback. I was miserable in my marriage, and when I turned to escape in the one thing I knew—my profession—people would think me an imitator. I was trapped. All I wanted then, when my marriage broke up, was to earn a little money . . ."

And Ethel haunted me. Every engagement I played on that long road which took me to this room in which I now sat, people said, "You know, you sound so much like Ethel Merman!" It had become too difficult, too embarrassing to explain. "Ethel was now one of our great stars, as she deserved to be," I said.

"Then you were jealous of her?"

Jealous? No. That wasn't the right word. "But as I saw her success, I saw what I had thrown away. Looking up from the depths of my alcoholic shame, she represented what I might have been."

"Don't you know that you can be a headliner again?" Dr. Head asked gently. "And in your own way, so you won't be compared to her?"

"No. People will always say I'm a carbon copy of someone else. If I can't be me, what can I be?"

Dr. Head sat back thoughtfully. "When you go to the city on your next visit, why not look up an accompanist and rehearse a few new songs? You can practice your lyrics here. Maybe that will be an outlet for you. I'm sure it will make your mother happy, too."

Katie made the arrangements. She told my former accompanist, Helen Stevens, that I was "coming in from the country, and wanted to learn a few numbers."

Helen was kindness itself when I came to her the following weekend. The first song she gave me, however, was "They Say Falling in Love is Wonderful." It had been made famous by Ethel Merman. "Helen," I said, "That's Ethel Merman's number and I just can't do it. They'll say I'm copying her."

"Nonsense," Helen snorted. "You'll have your own interpretation. You ought to learn it—it's the popular number of the day."

I rehearsed it, and "J'attendrai," and "If This Is But A Dream, I Hope I Never Wake Up."

When our session was over, I offered Helen a ten dollar bill which Katie had put into my purse for the purpose. Helen pushed the money aside. "Don't be silly," she said. "You've overpaid me in the past. I'm not taking money from you."

For a moment I flushed. How much did Helen know? How much could Katie have divulged? But Helen was an old friend. I could trust her.

"See you next Saturday," she said, and kissed me.

I hummed "J'attendrai" on the train back to Bloomingdale's. Would I ever face an audience again?

Then, suddenly, six months had passed, and almost before I knew it, Dr. Head was bidding me goodbye.

He had a few words of caution. I should get to work as quickly as possible. Avoid people and situations likely to upset me. "Your first six months outside will be tougher than the six months here," he said. "Remember when you told me that the people you saw on the streets outside seemed tense and anxious, and those here calm and placid? That's because our people here have security and protection. They're kept from shocks and hard knocks. Outside you'll be thrown into noise and confusion, you'll be jostled, people won't treat you with kid gloves because they won't know what you've gone through. You'll be upset emotionally and you'll want to drink. You'll meet people who will offer you liquor. It will be only an arm's length away from you all the time. You should know all this, and be prepared."

He paused. "Remember, for you to drink is to die."

He gave me a box of seconal sleeping pills for my first

few nights. "Don't make a habit of these," he warned me. "And keep in touch with me, Lillian. I'll be able to give you support if the going gets too hard. But try to stand on your own two feet as long as possible. You can do it."

I was free.

CHAPTER XXII

THERE HAD BEEN nothing in the newspapers when I
had been incarcerated in Bloomingdale's, and there was
no mention of my release in June, 1946. Katie was living
in Long Island with Ann. Edna was out of town: I went
to live in the two-room kitchenette apartment to which
she had moved on the 11th floor of London Terrace, at
Ninth Avenue and 23rd Street. I had a place to stay, but
the old anxieties crashed down on me. I needed money,
and I had my pride. I had to pay my debts. My bills at
Bloomingdale's had run between $600 and $700 a month.
They had been taken care of by Edna, Minna, and Milton
Merkin, Ann's husband, who appointed themselves a
committee to raise money from other friends for my expenses.

I was 34 years old. I had earned over a million dollars
in my career. Now, one day out of Bloomingdale's, all I
owned in the world were my Bible, the sleeping tablets
Dr. Head gave me, and $2.50 in cash. So far as clothes, I
had a pair of worn white golf shoes, a couple of skirts
and blouses, and a $17 coat Katie had brought up to
Bloomingdale's for me.

What first? I telephoned Katie, and she managed to
come into town for the day. She suggested that I call

Milton Berle, but I was too ashamed. Instead, we telephoned his mother and Sandra immediately took me backstage at the Carnival, the Broadway nightclub where Milton was breaking all records. Milton was one of the very few who knew where I had been, for Katie had confided in Sandra.

"Look, kid," he said encouragingly. "A star is always a star, no matter what happens to her. You'll be back on top again. Keep rehearsing with Helen Stevens and drop over and see Bobby Kroll. He's a good song arranger. Tell him I said to whip up a few numbers for you."

I could not bring myself to ask Milton for money. It was a hard decision, but I turned to the judge. On the telephone he was cool. He was busy—but, oh, all right. He'd see me next day in Lindy's.

My heart sank. I knew how I looked. I put on a skirt and blouse, my little coat, borrowed a hat from Edna's closet, and in my white golf shoes, set off for Lindy's. When I glanced into a mirror on the way, I saw a grotesque caricature of myself.

I sidled into the restaurant. A few minutes later Ben strolled in. He stared at me—and laughed. "You look like a peasant," were his first words. "You certainly got fat." He took the cigar out of his mouth and looked me over. "You'll have to get some dresses, that's for sure."

His words completely undermined the calm I thought I had achieved. "Ben," I said, my pride utterly deflated, "I must have $25 a week until I find some work."

He thought for a moment. "Well, I'll give you $25 now and we'll see what you need later. I've got a lot of expenses right now."

He counted two tens and a five into my hand. I felt

the perspiration trickle down my back. I had never asked anyone for anything: now I was taking handouts.

My first stop was the Brill Building, the song writer's mecca, to pick up sheet music. I saw two familiar faces. One turned away. The other said, "Getting music? You going to work again? Are you kidding?" I turned on my heel, picked up my music and, on the way out, bought a newspaper. There was an item in a Broadway column and it read: "An ex-singing star, a drunk, is being backed by Milton Berle on the comeback trail."

Oh, my God, I thought. Now everyone will know!

How could I walk up Broadway again and meet the faces I had to meet? How was I to go on living?

I took a bus home. Opposite my apartment building was a liquor store. I went in and bought a pint of brandy.

In the apartment I poured myself a drink. I let it stand for a moment, watching it. The brandy was mahogany colored. I put the glass to my mouth and let the brandy go down my throat—my first drink in six months.

It flowed, warm nectar, warm life itself, down my throat, into my stomach, spreading warmth throughout my body. No pain, no choking—only a lovely, warm, reassuring glow.

I was not alone any more.

I sat, savoring it.

Slowly, my hands firm, my fingers sure as a surgeon's, I poured a second drink. My body tingled all over, as though I'd bathed in champagne.

I rose to my feet, and waved my hands gracefully, and began to dance in time to the great warm beating heart of the universe. I sang, "La-de-da-de-da." Oh, this is wonderful! I don't really feel the effects at all, not the slightest. To drink is to die? He was trying to frighten me. I feel no ill effects. I danced slowly about the room, from window to window, at each one pulling down a shade, all in time to the music in my soul. In the half-dark, I sank into a chair. I took a slow, leisurely third drink, and let it steal its way through the wondrous universe that was myself.

Suddenly, an imp of fear tugged sharply at my brain. The bottle is almost empty. What will I do? Will the old thing happen? Will I get panicky if there is no more? Will I get the horrors after these few drinks wear off?

Feverishly I rushed downstairs and bought a second bottle. All during the night, as I drank, I poured water into it, lest panic overtake me if I saw an empty bottle. I knew I was deceiving myself. I knew this was the beginning of the end.

I awoke in panic next morning. I would need alcohol. I had failed. But I *must* fight it. Perhaps I could manage on light wine and beer. But fits of anxiety seized me; with darkness, I knew, stark terror would assail me.

I thought of Katie. Why should we be separated? How bad could a mother be for a daughter, or a daughter for a mother? I telephoned her. Could I come to see her? "Baby," she said happily, "our thoughts must have crossed. I was just going to call you to come up here because Ann and Milton have gone away for the weekend."

Ann's home was an hour and a half distant. I thought of the strange faces at Pennsylvania Station, the train ride, the ordeal of seeing Katie . . . Would she know I had been drinking? I grew nervous. A couple of straight shots of bourbon would soothe my nerves, and a package of mints would camouflage my breath. But the couple of drinks became three, and four, and five, and finally I had finished an entire fifth of bourbon; and when I descended the steps to the train, I had another pint concealed in my suitcase.

I stared at the tracks. Ought I jump in front of the incoming train? Why am I going to Long Island? To show my mother how utterly rotten I am? But I knew she'd want me even this way, rather than dead. . . . The train roared into the station, and I was still on the platform.

I could not find a seat in the hot, crowded car. The combination of July heat and alcohol drenched me in perspiration: my clothes stuck to me; I reeked so strongly of liquor that people turned their faces away from me. In shame I tried to hold my head down so that my breath would not offend, but I felt I was smothering. I suffered, and the ride was interminable.

I was drunk when I arrived. I walked down a long street. Katie was on the porch, waving as I came near. "Lilly, Lilly!" she called out. I began reeling up the steps. Then she understood. The blood drained from her face. She put out her hand against the porch pillar for support. "Oh, my God—" she began. She guided me into the house.

Later, after the words and after the tears, she found a bathing suit for me and took me onto the beach and I lay there, as in the long ago in Havana, in a drunken stupor on the hot sand. Through my paralyzed mind, like an endless record with the needle caught, the words droned relentlessly: *you've only a pint, a pint, a pint, for the whole weekend, you've only a pint, a pint . . .*

Back in the house, I passed out, after several hours. I awoke in the middle of the night. Katie was asleep. I searched for liquor. There must be some in the house. Katie had undoubtedly hidden it. I came upon several cans of warm beer hidden on a top shelf in the kitchen cupboard. I drank them on the spot. Then I waited for daylight and the liquor stores to open, walked into town, bought several small bottles, and hid them about my room. I remained in the room all weekend. From time to time Katie ventured in, trying to conceal the fact that she had been weeping. "Why don't you try to come out and eat something?" she begged. "Please, baby."

I could not.

Monday morning Ann returned. White-faced with anger and helplessness, she gave me $20. "Here's some money for your purse," she said. "Now you better go. We're sending you back to New York. You know Sam and Stell Krepps—they'll drive you right to your door."

In the car I no longer felt shame. Panic and desperation had taken over. I told Sam, "If you don't want me to kill myself tonight, you'll stop at the first liquor store and let me buy a quart of gin." I knew I would have the horrors—I was caught in the terrible chain reaction. My body demanded liquor now. Each small drink only triggered an irresistible need for more.

Reluctantly, out of pity, Sam stopped the car and I got the gin. During the drive to New York I held it on my lap like a baby until I was left off in front of my apartment building.

Next day, carefully and logically I planned a drunk

to end all drunks. With Ann's $20 I bought all the liquor I could—bourbon, brandy, Scotch and gin. This drunk would be all out, full-circle, complete: and in my own good time. I would kill myself at last. I wanted to saturate my body with alcohol. It was my life to take, if I wanted to take it; and all by myself I yearned to feel this indescribable luxury, this beautiful, orgiastic, perfect crescendo ending in my suicide. All by myself—I the star, I the victim, I the audience, I the critic.

I undressed. I got into fresh pajamas and a bathrobe. I drew the blinds so that daylight would not hurt my eyes. How cozy you could make it for yourself when you were bidding the whole wretched, indifferent, bewildering world goodbye!

I dug into my trunk and brought out my scrapbooks: the records of my life insurance and annuity policies which strangers would collect when my death became known; my bank-books, cancelled, but still proof of what had been; my photographs and family snapshots and letters, all that remained after Mark's rampage. I threw everything on the floor. "There's my life," I said aloud.

I sat down in the midst of it, arranging myself gracefully as though I were posing for Paramount publicity. A bottle was beside me, and a full glass of liquor in my hand. I began looking through the records of the life of Lillian Roth.

What had I been, and what was I now? Who were the men who loved me so, and where were they now? The men who had taken my body, my spirit, my dignity, who had stripped me of all security? I drank: "Here's to my past loves." I flipped through the pages of my scrapbook. A review caught my eye: LILLIAN ROTH STEALS

VAGABOND KING. *Oh, Lillian, weren't you wonderful! Wonderful!* A scene-stealer! If they could only see you in this scene, now! . . . *How would you like to go to Hollywood, Lillian?* . . . Don't you think, Mr. Lubitsch, this is a super-production? Oh, I beg your pardon, I mean Mr. DeMille. I drank, filled my glass again, and drank. *You must be careful those eyes don't get you into trouble, Miss Roth.* . . . I thought, I can hardly see out of them now. My drink tastes salty . . . Am I crying? Yes, cry, Lillian. Be maudlin. I wept.

No, I could not blame anyone. I—I was the one to blame. I had it—I threw it away.

I thought of Minna. But I could not call her. What could she do? What could anyone do? And was there anybody I knew to whom I had not given pain?

All through the day I drank, keeping to my room. But when twilight came, the liquor had not done its work. Instead of exhilaration, I felt dragged out and depressed. Perhaps a sleep, and I'll start over again. I swallowed a couple of yellow jackets, and presently I floated out into time and space. . . .

I was on the couch and someone was shaking me, shouting into my ear. "What is it?" I moaned. "Oh," she cried, her voice high and shrill, as if from a great distance. "You gave me such a scare. I thought you were dead!" It was Bernice Janney, a friend of Katie's, who had dropped by.

"Oh, please let me be," I wanted to beg her. "I've taken sleeping pills. I can't come out of it." But the words caught in my throat. I was paralyzed. She managed to shake me into consciousness and got me up finally, and helped me dress, and like a sleepwalker, I was led into a restaurant. I could hardly keep my head up. "You must get some food in you," she insisted. I ordered two martinis. "Lillian, don't," Bernice pleaded. "If you don't want to drink yours, I will," I said. I drank her martini, and mine, and ordered two more. I refused to eat. Bernice sat opposite me, repeating helplessly under her breath, "Lillian, what are you doing to yourself!"

I said, "Look, Bernice, let me alone. I'm no good. Don't you understand? I'm just no good." She tried to comfort me. "You get a decent night's sleep and you'll be all right." I humored her. "O. K. Bernice, I'll sleep."

She took me back to my door and kissed me. "Try to take care of yourself, dear," she urged me. I bolted the door, struggled back into pajamas and bathrobe, and began to drink. I knew how to die—like Helen Morgan, that beautiful, talented, tragic woman. What a great she was! Watch the greats, Daddy always used to say. I watched her through her short life. Now, watch me . . . Too bad no audience would see me at my best. I drank whiskey and water, rye and water, gin and water, because everybody knows that water makes liquor hit your blood stream quicker. I blacked out, and came to again, and blacked out, and came to again.

David was suddenly in my mind, and I wept. You can't blame this on him, Lillian. You weren't such a good girl, you know. Actually, you cheated on David. You took a chance when you went out with Robin Hood. You took plenty of chances.

Each time I came to, it was in fear and terror, awakening to awful reality. *You were in a hospital. You were treated by doctors and psychiatrists. You were discharged. And now you're drunk again. Lillian, you're*

[255]

*nothing. You're less than nothing. There's nothing to you,
or about you, worth saving.*

I blacked out.

I came shudderingly to my senses.

I had no idea how much time had elapsed. A fit of
trembling seized me. I curled up tightly on the floor,
tensing every muscle in a mighty effort to stop my shaking. Something fluttered—I saw it out of the corner of
my eye. There was *something* on the wall. I felt my hair
raise. O God, help me! There was that spider as big as
a rat. *This is imagination, Lillian. Hold on to yourself.
It will go away. It did before. It's a hallucination. You
know it. Hold tight* . . . I squeezed my eyes shut. My
stomach turned, for it was in my eyes, imprinted in the
red haze behind my eyelids. Then the spider slowly faded
away, and I stared incredulously as three faces slowly
came into focus—inhuman faces with sticky hair, with
fangs for teeth, with scraggly black beards, with obscene-
ly white eye sockets. Bloody and wraithlike, they materialized themselves like visions from a shroud. They
floated nearer—and in their center, the grinning, moon-
faced man from the Admiration Cigar ad.

I shrieked and scrambled madly to my feet. I rushed
into the bathroom and slammed the door, resting against
it as I gasped for breath. My heart hammered in my ears.
I shut my eyes into a lurid red fog. Slowly I opened
them: the faces were gone. I turned to open the door—
and the faces were oozing like smoke out of the tile wall!
I whirled one way, then the other—where I turned, they
were. I reeled out of the bathroom and threw myself
under the bed, to hide.

Oh, God! Bugs—were these the bugs my mother brushed off us in that hotel room in that long ago? It was beyond endurance. I scratched wildly. Bugs were crawling over me—no, not bugs, spiders! Million-legged insects swarmed over me. I slapped, and tore at my skin. I rolled closer to the wall, but they spilled over the edge of the bed, down my neck, over my arms and legs. I lashed out at them, kicked at them. I crawled out from under the bed into the closet, and pulled the door shut and clung in the blessed darkness to the clothing that hung there. But the spiders came scurrying under the door after me, a black writhing swarm that covered the floor and began climbing upon me. I banged the door open and pushed past the spiders, screaming.

Only liquor would stop it. I managed to gulp a drink down, then retched; tried another, and finally kept it down. One minute, two, three—I grew calm. Then, absolute silence, save for the frantic pounding in my ears. I was all alone. I was a tiny pinpoint of intense throbbing light rushing away into vast distances, growing smaller like a star dwindling away to nothing, a tiny throb in the vast quietude, a void in the heart of a vacuum.

All sound had vanished, save only a soft, infinitely gentle tolling of bells far away.

Sometime in the night, pawing about the floor, I found my Bible. The 91st Psalm went through my brain. *His truth shall be thy shield and buckler* . . . But where *is* He now, I thought. Oh, God, help me! Oh, God, what shall I do? I waited, but there was no sign—no answer. *For He shall give His angels charge over thee, to keep thee in all thy ways.* Where *is* He? Where are the angels? There isn't anybody here. I looked around carefully.

Absolutely no one here.

Perhaps it means *real* angels. Perhaps I must jump out of the window and die and through death meet the angels.

Oh, God, I said. It says, *He shall call upon Me and I will answer him: I will be with him in trouble: I will deliver him.* But God, I *am* calling on You, I don't blame You if You don't answer. If I could spend six months in an institution and still wind up a drunk, what good am I even to You? You gave me every chance. I'm rotten. I've disappointed what God there is, if there is a God. Doesn't the Bible say, *no evil shall befall you?* But evil has befallen me, and pestilence is all around me, and I am in darkness. Oh God, where are You?

I cried for myself, and went off into a strange half-world, awake and yet not awake. I lay like a somnambulist. Far off thousands of violins were playing, "I've got the world on a string," over and over. "Got the world on the string, world on a string." The same few bars, over and over. I used to sing that song. The violins faded away and as if by signal, the radio commentators took over, speaking frantically, their words running together in their eagerness to warn us, "The Japs are invading! They're coming across!" I lurched to my radio. It was off. I pulled out the plug, but the babel of voices continued, in all accents, cultured British, and twangy American, and guttural German. . . .

Dear God, this is what put me in Bloomingdale's! I tore my hair, I banged at my ears, I put my head under the cold water tap in the bathroom, but the voices, now soft as a babble, were like an endless undertone. I wrapped a towel about my head, and staggered back to the bed, and fell across it.

I awoke in darkness. Were they branded on my eyes, or in the walls again?—gigantic spider bat-faces with cigars in their mouths. They came nearer. The burning ash of the cigars would put out my eyes. I rolled out of bed to the floor, crawled to a bottle. I screamed, and the scream echoed down the dark corridors of my brain and vanished in a thin white trickle of sound.

The voices came back, soft, submerged, babbling: "She's low she's awfully low do you think she'll make it she's done terrible things to herself her mother never raised her girl to end like this she's no good maybe she will get out of it do you think she will do you think she won't." They rose, and died away.

The faces, as if on cue, took their place, the glowing cigar tips whirling like pinwheels. The spiders came, they dropped from the ceiling onto me, they crawled over me. I dug frantically into my skin. I knew I saw all this, felt all this, heard all this, yet all this was not real.

"It's in my head," I thought wildly, beating my head against the wall. I tore at my hair. "It's only in my head. If I get it out of my head it'll be gone." I could endure it no longer. I threw open the window. I'll jump, my head will crash against the pavement, my brains will spew out—and I'll be rid of it. All of it, all that accumulated horror will pour out of my skull and I'll have peace.

I stood up, arms outstretched, against the open window. The wind blew on me, hot and cold, a burst of heat like a terrible desert blast. I shuddered, started back, stumbled, and fell backward to the floor. I blacked out.

I do not know how many times I must have blacked

out during the days and nights I remained alone in my room. Toward the end I remember slowly getting to my feet, and working my way to the bathroom. I peered at my image in the mirror. My eyes had difficulty focusing, but slowly I saw myself. Was that ghastly human being me? My hair was matted and filthy. My face was a purple blotch, my cheeks lacerated, my lips black, split and caked with blood. My fingernails were ripped and bleeding. My pajamas were soiled and in shreds. My eyes were almost swollen shut.

Look at yourself objectively, Lillian. What would you do if you met yourself on the street, knowing what you know about yourself? She's better off dead, you'd say in horror, lifting your dress lest you contaminate yourself, turning your face away lest you become sick at the sight of her. God assuage the grief and shame of the mother who bore her, of the father who once said in joy, "Look at her, Katie! Isn't she beautiful!"

I began to pace back and forth, faster and faster, banging the wall with my palm at each turn, raging at myself. You won't take another drink. You won't. You stop right here . . .

I could not. I drank, and again I was calm. I was sober drunk. Think clearly, try to concentrate. You have several outs. What are they?

One. If Katie learns about this, she will be forced to put you away for your own protection. She certainly won't let you wander about sick. Now, you can swallow the rest of these sleeping pills. I counted them laboriously. An even dozen. Well, yellow jackets are powerful. Maybe 12 of them would do the job. But if they failed and you wake up—you'll find yourself in a state institution just the same. So that's one—try to commit suicide by an overdose of sleeping pills.

Two. You can still jump out that window.

Two isn't half bad.

Wait—isn't there a three? Dr. Head? When the going got too tough, call him, he said.

Carefully I walked to the telephone, and rang Bloomingdale's, and waited for the familiar voice to come on the wire. When I heard it, I broke down.

"For God's sake, Doctor," I sobbed hysterically. "I've got the horrors. I've tried to come out of it for days and I can't. I don't know what to do. I've no place to go, no place to turn. Please, Dr. Head, come and see me right away. I'm going out of my mind!"

He heard me out. "Now Lillian, don't get excited. This is Sunday. It's impossible for me to get away. Take a few sleeping pills, go to bed, and I'll come to see you Tuesday morning."

"Tuesday? Well, then, you'll find me in the Morgue!" I screamed, and slammed the receiver. I reeled again to the window and looked down. I stood there, the 12 seconals in one hand, arguing the question . . . Eleven stories. That's final, for sure. But a ledge protruded only three stories below. Icy fear gripped me. Suppose I land on it? A three-story fall might not kill me, but only smash my face. I'd live with a grotesque face and broken bones all my life. I'd be even worse off, then.

I thought desperately. Is there no sure, painless way out of this? Can't I even kill myself without botching the job?

Suppose I miss the ledge and go all the way. I won't be a pretty sight, either, after I strike that pavement. What will they say about me? Will they say, "Isn't it terrible, what happened to Lillian Roth? She was such a talented girl." Oh, no, they'll say, "She deserved it. What was she but a no-good, drunken bum?"

That's what Art called you. And Mark. And Victor. The judge never said it to your face, but he would say it now. David's folks would say it. They would all say it. And suddenly, standing there, I knew, knew beyond all question or doubt, that I was not a no-good bum. My mother knew I was not. Had she sacrificed so much, had she suffered so many years watching me go down, down, down into the gutter, only to have me end as a no-good bum, a drunken suicide with a smashed face buried in a pauper's grave?

I won't let them say it. I won't let them see me that way. I won't jump—

Marty Mann. The name leaped into my brain. What had the *Times* said? She lived to tell her story to Alcoholics Anonymous.

I clutched at the straw. I wasn't ready then, said Dr. Head? I'd have to be ready now. Now, *now!* With great difficulty I managed to get into the tub. Later, with shaking hands, I tried to dress: but perspiration rolled from me; alcohol seemed to ooze from my pores: no sooner was I into my underclothes and dress than they were soaking wet. I borrowed a dress from Edna's closet and put it on, finally. I must be halfway presentable when I go to Alcoholics Anonymous. They mustn't think I'm too much of a drunk.

It was nearing 12 and the noonday sun was creeping lazily into the bedroom when I dragged myself out of there.

CHAPTER XXIII

I FOUND MYSELF standing before the headquarters of
Alcoholics Anonymous. The building was a former church
on 41st St., near 10th Avenue, in Hell's Kitchen, only a
few blocks from where I'd lived as a child. Hadn't I once
told Estelle Milgrim that I would be back on 10th
Avenue someday—penniless and alone?

I hesitated. Was this an evangelist society? Would
people pray over me? But, maybe they would teach me
how to drink normally. Laboriously I climbed the steps.

"Where do you get information, please?" I asked a man
walking out.

"In that office down the hall," he said, pointing.

In a small cubby-hole sat a fat, jovial man about 60,
wearing a cap. Ah, I better be careful. Guards at mental
institutions wear caps like that. Bet he'll want to test me
to see if I belong here or in an institution. "Hello," he
said. "What can I do for you?"

"A girl friend of mine is very drunk and almost jumped
out a window. She needs help. What can I do for her?"

"My, my!" he said, as he stood up. "Well, now, don't
you worry. Let us take care of it. But first things first.
Aren't you having a little trouble, too, Miss?"

I grew indignant. "Me? Oh, no. I just came over to

get information for this girl." Later I learned that alcoholics invariably begin with the story of another person's troubles, real or fancied.

"O. K." he said. "What's your name?"

Again I hesitated. "Aren't you supposed to be anonymous here?"

"You don't *have* to give your name, Miss," he said. "But we're all friends here."

"Oh, well. It's Lillian Roth." It doesn't mean anything, anyway, I thought to myself.

"Well, Lillian, why don't you come upstairs and have some coffee with us?"

As if by common consent we both forgot my fictitious girl friend. He helped me up the stairs. We entered an enormous room in which many persons sat at long wooden tables, picnic style, drinking coffee, nibbling at cake, some playing solitaire, others talking. In the rear I saw a cafeteria.

"What is this place?" I demanded. "Who are these people?" I was confused. The voices were back whispering in my ear. *She's going in there. That's a laugh! They won't even want her. They'll probably send her away. They'll know she's mad. She's taking an awful chance, the fool. Boy, what a mess! Look at her shake!*

"These are all alcoholics," the jovial man said, his voice gratingly loud over the chorus with me. He waved his hand expansively. "They've all solved their alcoholic problem and they're happy now. Someday you'll be happy, too."

Isn't that ridiculous! I thought. Me happy! These people haven't gone through my hell. Silly my being here. And do I really want to get sober? I have nothing to look forward to. I started to turn away.

The jovial man gently wheeled me around and led me to a table. Someone else was at my elbow, guiding me into a chair. There were blurred faces about me, and suddenly I was pouring out my woes, trying in a few minutes to tell the tragedy of my life—how I had been all alone in my room . . . "Well, I know you won't believe it, but I almost committed suicide!"

One of the faces said, "I almost did, too."

"You did!" I was shocked. "My story isn't unusual?"

A cup of steaming black coffee was pushed in front of me.

"No," a man said. "Drinking follows the same pattern in all alcoholics."

I seized on the word. Alcoholic? I don't like that. I drink a little too much but no wonder, with my problems. I better get out of here. They don't understand me.

A woman said, "Don't run away yet, Lillian. We've just met."

How did she know I was going, I wondered? Maybe she has the gift of mental telepathy, too. . . . Her voice continued: "You don't have to be ashamed to tell us what bothers you. In fact we already know. We're all completely honest with each other. And that's why we can help each other."

O. K., I thought. Be honest. "I'll show you something," I said fiercely. I fumbled in my purse and my shaking hands managed to extract a pint of gin and the box of sleeping pills. "See these? I came in here and deceived you. I had these with me all the time. Now I'm giving them to you." I held them out dramatically, and a hand appeared and took them.

"Good," a man's voice said. "You've made your first move to sobriety—giving yourself up."

I talked ceaselessly. People came, sat with me, drifted away. A long time had passed without a drink: I had to get out of there. And after all, I had some bringing up. You mustn't overstay your welcome. The courteous thing now is to leave.

I rose shakily to my feet. Two men approached me. "Where are you going?"

"I'm going home, but I want to thank you for your hospitality."

"We'd like to take you home," one man said. His spectacles glinted in the light. "May we?"

"Oh, thank you but I can make it alone."

"It's a pretty long walk," he went on, conversationally. "One of us has a car. In fact, we have a lady who would love to go along. She lives in your neighborhood, too."

I couldn't lack graciousness. "Well, then, of course," I said formally. "Whatever you wish." I thought, I must get rid of them, quick. I've got to have a drink.

Outside I was introduced to a plump woman, her face round and smiling, her dark hair short and curly. "This is Julia," said the bespectacled man. "I'm John—and this is Larry." Larry helped me into the car, and as he did so, he pressed a small cold object into my hand. I looked at it. It was a crucifix. Oh, I thought, he thinks I'm Christian, but I'll take it. I wouldn't want to hurt his feelings.

As we drove off, John remarked, "Julia works for Bellevue."

"Bellevue!" I exclaimed.

"Yes, she's in the receiving office."

Receiving office! They had tricked me! They were taking me to the alcoholic ward. But my panic subsided when it became apparent we were driving down 10th avenue, to my apartment house. When we arrived, I stepped out with dignity and extended my hand. "Thank you very much, Julia. And thank you very much, gentlemen. It was most pleasant."

"Would it be all right if we came up for a minute?" John asked. "I'd like to make a telephone call."

Good God, I thought, don't these people know when a person wants to be alone? But how could I refuse? "Of course," I said.

Once upstairs, they seemed in no haste to leave. I sat, outwardly calm, but I felt rivulets of sweat running down my back. My nose was becoming congested. I had difficulty getting air: my jaws were growing stiff; my heart began to pound with the effort to breathe. My fingers were clenched. I had not had a drink in six or seven hours now, and . . . I don't know what way to turn I thought in panic. I can't make a scene or they'll take me to Bellevue.

"I don't want to frighten you," came John's voice, suddenly. "I've been watching you. You need alcohol or a hospital. You ought to go to Knickerbocker Hospital for five days. Have you any money?"

I shook my head. He knew the next stages, as I did not: first, your nose grew more congested, then it bled, then you went into a paroxysm of coughing and choking, and then into violent convulsions. "Hospitalization costs a little money," he was saying. He paused. "Do you really want this program?"

"Yes," I said. Yes,yes,yes. "I want help. What do you

mean, program?"

"We'll come to that later. Easy does it. Have you any liquor in the house?" I had to be honest with him. "Yes,— about a quarter of a bottle of gin."

"Well," he said, "if you can't afford a hospital, maybe we can help you here. Right now, I think you need a drink."

Oh, I thought, these people *could* be trusted! They *do* understand. This man's from heaven!

I led him to the bottle in the kitchen. He poured a drink for me, and held it to my mouth for I could grip nothing in my hands. It went down, and I grew a little calmer. I could swallow again, I breathed more easily, my jaws relaxed, my fingers released.

Julia said, "Honey, I must leave now, but I'll pick you up tomorrow if you want me. Meantime I'm going to send over another little lady to stay with you a little while this evening."

Then she was gone, leaving John and Larry.

They talked. I thought, I can't stand this. I began to feel the insects crawling under my clothes again. But John and Larry were involved in a long, never-ending story of their alcoholism: the money they had once been worth, the agony and shame they had suffered. There was no continuity to their story. They droned away, first one, then the other. What had all this to do with helping me get sober? I dared not tell them the torture I suffered this very moment. They might be psychiatrists trying to determine if I was sane or insane. *It's impossible for people to sit this many hours with me unless they are psychoanalyzing me.*

Someone knocked on the door. A man and a woman

entered, and then there were four of them, talking, talking, talking, while I thought frantically *how am I going to get them out?*

They went into my kitchen and brewed coffee. "Here, drink this," they said. "It will be good for you." Isn't this ridiculous, I thought. Can't I drink coffee by myself? I drank coffee. Sometimes it seemed I dozed off, then awakened. They were always there, talking.

John glanced at his wrist watch. "It's three o'clock," he said, and the four rose. The liquor stores were closed, the bars shut down now. The only liquor I could have now was the gin remaining in the bottle in the kitchen—and there wasn't enough there to help me.

"You're exhausted now, aren't you?" John asked. "You'll be able to sleep."

"Yes, yes, everything's fine. I couldn't expect you to stay another minute. Thanks very much. It was so good of you to take this interest in me. See you again some time. Goodbye."

They left. The door closed on them, and I sighed. I raced into the kitchen—and stopped short. I dared not finish the gin now. I would probably need it terribly before this long night was over. It had to last.

I slipped into bed, and the voices began. *They're going to get you, they're coming to get you, they know all about you.* Julia's face appeared; it dissolved into many faces, then dwindled into a spinning blob, then expanded into another face. What do you expect, I asked myself. You've only had that one drink John gave you since two in the afternoon.

The faces—Julia's, John's, the moon-faced Admiration Cigar man, the old man with the silver paint brush, came at me. I pulled the covers over my head and stuffed the corner of the pillow into my mouth to smother my screams.

After a little while, I passed out into a nightmarish coma.

I came to before dawn, laboriously dressed, and watched the clock, waiting for 9 a.m. when the liquor stores opened. I dared not drink the gin. A fit might come upon me and I must save it for that.

At 8:30 the telephone rang. "Well," said John's voice, "feeling a bit rough today? Can I come up?" I could scarcely reply. My mouth was swollen, my lips cracked. I was shaking. "Come up," I finally croaked. The pulses in my temples banged like a drum and my fingers fumbled as I tried to comb my hair.

He walked in. "I've made you my assignment for the day," he announced cheerily.

"Assignment?"

"Easy does it," he said, as he had the night before. "Let's get out in the air." He took me to a cafeteria and brought a small glass of orange juice.

"It won't stay down," I faltered.

"Sip it little by little and you'll get it down if we have to stay here an hour."

How much had I eaten in the last two days? Three days?

"I don't remember eating anything." I said. "I just remember drinking."

"All right. Get that orange juice into you, then."

I sipped, I gagged, I staggered to the ladies' room and threw up, and staggered back. After the third try I managed to swallow the remainder.

"Now we'll walk," John said. And we walked. I stumbled along with him, half-falling, tripping, getting dizzy spells. My knees buckled, I clung desperately to him. Several times he put his arm around my waist and supported me. "It's going to be all right, Lillian. It's going to be all right," he repeated. "Nothing can happen to you. I am with you. Just ask God to help you get through this hour."

"Get through this hour!" I cried. "I've been asking all my life for help. What do you mean this hour!"

I started to cry. "You're taking me on streets where people will recognize me."

"You're just as good as anybody else," he said. "You're just sick. Stop worrying about what people will think of you. Don't be so conceited. That's one of the troubles with an alcoholic—a swollen ego."

I cried at that. He had hurt my feelings.

He led me into an air-cooled movie on Broadway. I ran to the ladies' room and drank what seemed gallons of ice water. I kept giving that back, too. Somehow he managed to keep me in the theatre two hours, while I turned and twisted.

Then we walked some more. "Oh, God," I moaned. "John, I've got to have a drink. I won't be able to live through this day."

"In half an hour," he said. He held my arm firmly, and we walked up one side street, down another. A half-hour passed—and no drink. "You're torturing me," I wept. "It's not a half hour, it's an hour. For God's sake, get me a drink."

"In another 20 minutes," he said inexorably. But when the 20 minutes had elapsed, we were in the AA clubhouse, and I was seated at a table, and being fed hot coffee and talked to, talked to and being fed hot coffee.

So the second day passed, a repetition of the first. Julia sat with me through the night. The third morning I was again in the company of my new friends.

"We're driving you to an AA meeting," John said. I was put into an automobile.

My eyes played tricks on me. The roads were weird white ribbons in tunnels of darkness: now I was on a merry-go-round, now on an elevator, rising, dropping down, rising again. "You are going to hear a talk by Bill, the founder of AA." John's voice was in my ear. Now I was helped up a staircase, and then I was in a large room among many people, with the hum of voices and cigarette smoke all about me.

I was introduced to a man from the Hal Wallis studio. "I'm making a picture about alcoholics," he said. "Let's talk."

"Why talk to me?" I demanded. "I don't know anything about all this."

"Wouldn't you like to see a picture made that would help alcoholics?"

"Yes, but I don't want anybody to know who I am. I've been keeping my alcoholism a secret for years. Please don't bother me."

A thin, tall gray-haired man began to speak and the hum of voices subsided. I tried to control my trembling hands. The speaker's words were without meaning. Suddenly his voice broke through a haze: "There are three kinds of alcoholics in this room tonight. First, those who have already found the peace and happiness that comes with sobriety. Second, those who have been sober only a

short time, and wonder if they'll ever reach that goal.
And finally, those who have the sweat breaking out all
over as I talk, sitting on their hands so no one will know
how they are shaking. Those are the ones I'm talking to
now. You can look at the fellow on one side of you, and
the woman on the other, and you, too, will eventually
have their serenity, if you will keep on this program,
one day at a time."

Like a shock of icy water thrown in my face, the words
registered: *That man standing there knows exactly what
I am feeling. I don't have to tell him what I am suffering.
I'm not alone.*

But gain serenity? Have peace? That's ridiculous. Even
if I stop drinking, what have I to be happy about? The
sixteen years of life I threw away? How could I get them
back? I know I've got a voice, but how would I get my
glamor back? Nobody would want to watch a hag on
the stage, a has-been . . . What was he saying now?
Try to follow the 12 steps. Turn your will over to a
Higher Power. Do they mean God? Haven't I turned my
will over to God? What happened? I'm still suffering.
What do they mean, a Higher Power would restore my
sanity. Wasn't I sane when I came out of the hospital?
And yet I drank again . . . I heard Bill's voice again:
"Try to have a conscious contact with God."

The sentence remained in my mind, and after the
meeting, as they drove me back, I turned to John. "That's
it, John. I've lost my contact with God."

"Easy does it, Lillian," he said. "God or a Higher
Power, whatever you feel or think, is what is meant. How
you believe in what you need will gradually come to you
—God as you understand Him. But—one step at a time.

Take it cafeteria style. What you don't like, let alone. Remember—we do it here one step at a time."

They left me off in front of my apartment building, and placed a pamphlet in my hands.

"This explains the 12 steps," John said. "Don't try to do them in one day. It took you 16 years to destroy yourself. You can't mend overnight." He held my hand for a minute. "Put as much effort into this program as you put into your drinking, Lillian, and you'll make it."

Again Julia stayed through the night with me. I struggled to read the pamphlet. It listed 12 steps to sobriety. In substance they were:

One. Admit you are powerless over alcohol and that your life has become unmanageable.

Two. Believe in a Power greater than yourself.

Three. Turn your will and your life over to the care of God as you understand him.

Four. Make a searching and fearless moral inventory of yourself.

Five. Admit to God, to yourself and to another human being the exact nature of your wrongs.

Six. Be entirely ready to have God remove all these defects of character.

Seven. Humbly ask Him to remove your shortcomings.

Eight. List all the people you have harmed and be willing to make amends to them all.

Nine. Make direct amends to such people wherever possible, except when to do so would injure them or others.

Ten. Continue to make personal inventory and when you are wrong, promptly admit it.

Eleven. Seek through prayer and meditation to im-

prove your conscious contact with God as you understand Him, praying only for knowledge of His will for
you and the power to carry it out.

Twelve. Having had a spiritual experience as a result
of these steps, try to carry this message to other alcoholics, and to practice these principles in all your affairs.

"Oh, Julia," I said. "Now that I've read it, I'm not sure
I understand. Especially the religious part."

"Honey, this isn't a religious program. This is a spiritual
program," she said. "If you accept the first step, you're
on your way."

Yes. I was powerless over alcohol. My life had become
unmanageable. But make a moral inventory of myself?
Why, if I looked over my past, I'd only be driven to
drink again. I wanted to forget what had happened. How
would I handle all that?

"Honey, one step at a time."

The fourth day I was with my new friends again. That
night John said, as he and Julia escorted me to my apartment door:

"Lillian, you've gone through 72 hours without alcohol.
That means it's out of your blood stream by this time.
But you will still want to drink. Your thinking hasn't
changed this quickly. For some time now you'll be
physically sober but still mentally drunk. And it won't
be easy. If you want to continue this program, we want
to continue to help you. But from now on, you're on your
own."

"I want to continue," I said humbly. But would my
shakes ever leave me?

There was a remedy for that, John said. They would
take me tomorrow to a clinic where I would be given

vitamin and liver shots. They would help tremendously. "But remember—it's up to you now."

He and Julia left their telephone numbers, if an emergency rose, and departed.

After they had gone, the realization came to me, beyond all doubt, that if this man, or whoever was helping me, man or God, gave me up, the last door was closed to 1e. I was in AA now. If I left it, nothing waited outside ut insanity or death.

I walked into the kitchen, took the bottle with two ounces of gin still in it, and poured the contents down the drain. I did now know it then, but I was never to take another drink.

Now I lived and breathed AA. I neglected my mother, Minna, Edna, everyone I had known, for I dared not go without an AA member at my side, lest someone I meet, some situation arise, that would upset me and send me to the nearest bar. The true alcoholic takes the first drink for the person, or situation, or insult, that upsets him. He takes the rest of the drinks for himself.

I began to understand the importance of moral inventory and the listing of persons I had hurt. So long as I continued to believe that others hurt me, I would feel anger, resentment, bitterness—all emotional states which called for liquor to assuage. If I accepted my shortcomings instead of fighting their existence, once more I was removing an emotional stimulus to alcoholism.

First thing I awoke, I hurried to the clubhouse and breakfasted there (thus avoiding the temptation of the morning drink). "We stay sober 24 hours at a time," John explained. "You don't know what's coming tomorrow, and neither do I. All you can hope for is the best today. We never forget one thing: we're just one drink away from a drunk again."

Over and over he repeated: with us, alcoholism is a disease. It's an allergy of the body coupled with an obsession of the mind. It is no more disgraceful than diabetes or tuberculosis. We will never be cured of it. Though we never drink again, we are still alcoholics—dry alcoholics. Our alcoholism has been arrested, not cured.

An important part of the program consisted in thinking less of I and more of *you* and *they*. Printed cards were distributed at meetings. One read, "Just for today, don't say a harsh word to anyone." Another: "Today try to do a good deed for someone which no one else will know about." A third: "Just for today, I will try to adjust myself to what is, and not try to adjust everything to my own desires."

It was like learning to live all over again. "You'll have to let us do your thinking for you for a little while," John had said. I acquiesced. It was reminiscent of Bloomingdale, for I was being helped to organize my thinking. I would wake each morning and ask myself, "What will I do today?"

A glance at a card. "Today try to do a good deed for someone which no one else will know about." I walked along the Bowery until I found a poor drunk asleep in a doorway. I looked in my purse. I had 75 cents. I took 40 cents and put the money in his pocket. That act made me glow more than anything I had done in my Charlanna League days.

The next day: what shall I do today? Again, the card. "Today, think and act your best. Look your best." That was a difficult job—but that day I was a lady. I tried to look my best. When I mounted a bus, I said, "Thank you!" to the driver so warmly that he stared, then grinned back. "Don't mention it, ma'am." My courtesy to everyone bowled them over. But I was doing and acting my best.

With Maggie, an AA who spent much of her time helping alcoholics, I visited the Bellevue alcoholic ward, the one place I feared most. I went among raving alcoholics in straightjackets, their eyes black, their noses bloody, their faces blue with bruises from their drunken falls, and I talked to them, tried to soothe them and make them feel they were not alone.

I read a great deal of AA literature, and I learned the appalling statistics of alcoholism. I placed the little cards about my room and kept the literature at my bedstand so that I could read it when I woke in the dark hours of the night.

At meetings various members rose and spoke on their personal experience with alcohol. Once I was asked to speak. I stood up. I had faced many audiences without qualms. This was the toughest appearance I had to make. I couldn't act. I had to be. I was no longer a stunning actress with the camouflage of clothes, beauty and reputation. This was the real me on display for the first time in my life.

Stammeringly I tried to tell about myself. These are all my blood brothers in the audience, I thought. We all suffer from the same illness, and these talks we give are our blood transfusions to one another. We all have an incurable disease—alcoholism.

"I can't get up here and tell you I'm a happy person," I said. "But I am sober. I am trying to contact God as I understand Him. I don't yet have the peace of mind I know many of you have, but I'm told that if I hold on, it will come.

"The other day I read in the Bible Paul's words to the Romans: 'For I am persuaded, that neither death, nor life, nor angels, nor principalities, nor powers, nor things present, nor things to come, nor height, nor depth, nor any other creature, shall be able to separate us from the love of God.' "

I was convinced, I added, that no matter what happened, the fact that I was now with them meant that I must in some way be connected with God.

I was limp when I sat down. "What a beautiful talk," one woman said. A girl approached me. "This is my first meeting," she confided. "You don't know how you've encouraged me. I have such a terrible alcoholic problem. I looked at you and I thought, 'If she can do it, after what she's gone through, I can do it, too.' "

Her words left me with a warm glow. Was this what they meant when they said I would be happy again? Because I had helped someone?

I wrote a friend: "Do you know what it is like to be well? Why, I've only now begun to appreciate the beauty of the world. It's been so long since I could look out with comfort into daylight, or face a bright sky.

"I always had to have the blinds down in my room, and to wear sunglasses when I went out. I could not stand the light; it threw me into the shakes. Even the sound of birds drove me mad. Daylight was horror. All alcoholics must wait until sundown before they can begin to live.

"It was like a pig going down in the mud of its pigsty," I wrote her. "You need dimness; your room is always gloomy; you live in darkness and in your blindness.

"Now, for the first time, I see the world as it is. I live again. I am a new human being."

Yet it was not easy. Sleeping became a problem, and I turned to sleeping pills. At the end of my first month in AA I was drinking coffee by day and taking sleeping pills by night. Soon I was visiting doctor after doctor, telling them I had just come out of the hospital and needed sedatives for my nerves. I became so accustomed to them that they lost much of their effect, and I slept only in fitful snatches through the night.

One morning, when I woke about nine o'clock, I wanted liquor. For no ascertainable reason, every nerve in my body demanded it. My imagination tortured me. I tasted liquor, smelled it, inhaled it, desperately desired it.

I knew if I rose and dressed and went out, I would succumb. I telephoned John's number. "Come over right away, for God's sake," I begged him.

I hung up. I began trembling as though I had a chill. If only someone were there to tie me to the bed—

There was a knock on the door. It was Minna who, coming to town to shop, had dropped in on me. She saw at once that I was not myself.

"Are you all right?" she asked, alarmed.

"Make me coffee," I said, "Please, hurry."

As she brewed it, John arrived. He understood. "Have your coffee, Lillian, and then we'll take a long walk."

"Minna," I said. "You ought to know. I was headed straight for a bar."

CHAPTER XXIV

KATIE wouldn't believe me.

I had been in AA six weeks. Katie had attended a meeting with me, but the same fear remained in her eyes. "You sure you're not drinking, Lilly?"

"Mom, I'm not. I swear I'm not. Honest to God, Mom, I haven't touched a drop in six weeks."

"All right, Lilly," she said. "I believe you. I want to believe you. And if these people can keep you from liquor, God bless them."

She continued to live with Ann, and from time to time, when she could, she gave me a little money. Edna and Minna attended several AA meetings with me. They, too, wanted to believe, but they felt sometimes they were hoping against hope.

One afternoon I sat quietly at my table in the clubroom. I glanced about the room idly, and my eyes caught those of a good-looking blond young man who was seated alone, too, drinking coffee. I thought, he's entirely too young, too clean and fresh looking, to be here. He can't be more than thirty. Was he a fellow sufferer? I glanced at him again, and when our eyes met a second time, I smiled. He rose and came across the room to my table, walking with a slight limp.

"I've been watching you since you first came in," he said pleasantly, "but you've always been surrounded by so many people I never got the opportunity to talk to you. How are you getting along?"

He introduced himself. His name was Burt McGuire. I thought, I wish this fellow had seen me in my good days. I bet I look awful to him now.

He *was* handsome—slender, blue-eyed, cultured in voice, quiet in manner.

After a little while he asked, "Would you like to go to the movies tonight?" Suddenly I felt like a school girl. I said, almost in confusion, "I'd love to."

That afternoon we tuned in a dance band on the club-house radio, and some of us tried to dance. I attempted an old buck-and-wing, and in my clumsiness sprained my toe and threw out my sacroiliac. Combined with a bad cold I picked up, I was an unhappy figure by nightfall.

"I'm not much to take out this evening," I apologized, when Burt called for me. "Funny, too. When I was drunk, these things never happened to me."

He laughed. "They did, but you couldn't feel them. Anyway, come on. A picture will do you good."

As we walked, he chatted easily. Had I noticed that hardly anyone in AA seemed to get to sleep? People there all hours of the night? "I've been in about a year now," he said, "and it takes a long time before you sleep normally. We keep the same hours as when we were drinking, live the same life, only we do it without liquor."

"You mean, instead of sitting in a bar all night, we go to all-night movies?"

"That's right," he laughed.

I was very much aware of Burt seated next to me in

the theatre. I remonstrated with myself. This is silly Lillian. You're an old bag. He's only being kind, carrying out his twelve-step work helping an alcoholic—that's all. Don't get silly ideas.

After the show we stopped for hamburgers. My appetite was slowly returning; at least I could handle food without nausea. When Burt took me to the entrance of my hotel, we talked for a few minutes. Then, as he left me, he said, "Lillian, remember, from this moment on, you'll never walk alone again."

What a line, I thought, as I went up the elevator. He couldn't possibly mean it. But if he didn't, why did he say it? In the past the men in my life stood to gain by complimenting me. I had youth, glamor, money, then. Now I possessed nothing. I was 140 pounds of buxom woman, bloated, my complexion blotched with fine networks of broken blood vessels, testament to my innumerable drunks; my eyes were constantly bloodshot; I wheezed from inflamed sinuses; my hands still trembled. What had Burt to gain?

I could hardly wait, however, until the next day to see him. But before he appeared at the clubhouse, John approached me. "Lillian," he said, "I want to talk to you. As a friend." He went on, after a moment, "I don't want to hurt your feelings, but you ought to know something about Burt McGuire before you fall for him. He's from the Four Hundred, kid. His family has homes in Southampton and Palm Beach and Park Avenue. He's real society. He's here only because of his alcoholic problem. He's had trouble with his family and they've disowned him until he gets out of it."

I understood what I was being told. *You've been*

through the mill, kid. This family won't have any part of you.

Now I remembered. I'd read it in a Broadway column. This was the T. Burt McGuire, Jr., who helped Sherman Billingsley of the Stork Club select pretty debutantes for public events. He knew rich, young, beautiful girls. What kind of fairy tale was I building up for myself? To him I was just another broken-down, pitiable drunk that had to be helped, that was all.

Burt, arriving a few minutes later, greeted me warmly. How did I feel? Would I like to take a walk? He'd been thinking, he said. Oughtn't I think about resuming my career? Maybe rehearse a few songs? He would like to discuss my future with me.

"Please," I said. "I don't feel like talking about impossible things." I went to another table.

When I rose to go, hours later, Burt approached me. "Can't a few of the gang walk you home?" he asked. "Let's all go over to your place and scramble some eggs and bacon."

The others chimed in. "Come on, Lillian." I had to agree. About ten of us pooled our money to buy bacon, eggs and coffee cake, and later we sat around at my apartment until nearly three a.m.

Presently only Burt remained. "Lillian," he began "aren't you going to let me really help you?"

"That's the only reason you're here, of course," I retorted bitterly. "It's to help me. It couldn't be any other reason."

He went on calmly. "You're taking sleeping pills, aren't you?"

I was shocked. "How did you know?"

"I could tell. You always have a bovine expression on your face."

Oh! Bovine! That's how he saw me. As a big cow. Naturally. Him, and his pretty, young, slim debutantes.

"I'd like to tell you something for your own sake, Lillian," he was saying in his quiet, pleasant voice. "I like you. You are a nice person. I think you could be a wonderful person again. You know I observed you for six or seven weeks before I talked to you. I never thought you'd be able to stick it out. I thought you'd be on the street long ago. But you've stuck with it—and that's why I'm saying this to you. If you're going to take sleeping pills, you might as well go back to drinking. Because if you continue the pills, you'll get involved with dope, and then you'll really be on a merry-go-round."

"I know all about sleeping pills," I said impatiently. "But liquor always meant more to me. Pills never bothered me."

"Yes, but now you're using them as a substitute. That's something different, and more serious." He shook his head. "I'm not telling you what to do, I'm telling you what you're up against if you continue." He sat there looking at me, very sweet, very earnest—and very right.

"But what will I do now?" I asked contritely. "How can I stop? I can't sleep. I can't get through the nights— I never could."

"If you'll let me, I'll stay here every night until you can sleep without pills," he said. I looked up at him quickly. "I promise I won't bother you in any way."

He did not leave that night. Night after night he sat by my bed. Hour after hour he talked to me. "You know

God is really watching over you and trying to see that you go to sleep. You know it. You're on the road up, and nothing's going to stop you now—nothing."

Sometimes I slept, but there were nights when, toward dawn, I could endure it no longer. Then I said, "Excuse me, Burt," hurried into the bathroom and swallowed a sleeping pill as once I had sneaked a drink of liquor. Within five minutes Burt knew what I had done. He said nothing. It was a struggle, and we both knew it.

In August, 1946—I had been sober for eight weeks—Burt left to spend a month with his family in Southampton. He was invited to see them from time to time. I had learned by then that his parents were devout Catholics, and known for their Catholic philanthropies. His grandfather had contributed heavily to the building of Maryknoll Seminary near Ossining, N. Y., one of the largest and best known for the education of foreign missionaries. Burt had all but broken his mother's heart in two ways—his alcoholism, and the fact that he had virtually left the church, attending services only when in Southampton so as not to embarrass his family there.

Before he left, he said, "You must try to get back to your career. Why not call on Milton Berle again? You're well enough to make a real try now." I followed his advice, but it was one of my most difficult steps. I called on Milton in his Brill Building office. I was accompanied by John, for in case of an emotional setback, his was the practiced hand that would keep me from the nearest bar. He waited downstairs in the lobby as I went up.

I sat for half an hour outside Milton's door. Show

people came and went. Lillian Roth, the has-been, coming to her old friend Milton for a handout. I sat there and took it.

Milton greeted me with all his old exuberance. "Come on," he said, "let's go to Lindy's for a bite and then we'll talk." For a wild moment I wanted to scream. Why had it always to be Lindy's! Why had I always to be put on display! We walked down Broadway, John trailing discreetly behind. Our journey was a steady succession of "Hi, Bill—Hi, Sammy—you remember Lillian Roth, don't you?" I wanted to sink through the sidewalk. They saw me, Lillian Roth, fat, purple-faced, cheap dress, cheap shoes, *she who got socked*—When we entered the restaurant, John lounged outside with a cigarette, pretending to be absorbed in the autographed photographs which filled Lindy's Broadway window.

When I emerged, I had a booking. Milton had proved a friend in need. An agent whom he knew would give me a one-shot chance, at a fee of $100, in a Catskill hotel— the Borscht Circuit.

I rehearsed in my room to the accompaniment of a phonograph. Florence Lustig, who had been a member of the Charlanna League, and who owned an exclusive apparel shop, fitted me with a dress. "I can't afford an expensive gown," I told her. She let me have a $150 dress for $30. Katie gave me money to buy a pair of shoes. I was ready.

I stood in the wings, trembling, clutching John's hand. Through my performance he would stand in the wings, where I could see him, to give me courage, as Burt was to stand at every performance through the years to come. A roll of drums—and the announcement by the master of ceremonies: "And now—folks—someone you'll all remember—a great singer and a great personality—Lillian Roth!"

I was before an audience again, and one in which virtually every man and woman knew my story.

I sang the numbers I had practiced to records, and I closed with "You Will Never Walk Alone," because these were Burt's words. The applause rolled toward the stage. I realized that it was sympathetic applause. The men in the audience were sorry for me, even as they were contemptuous, as perhaps every man is secretly contemptuous of a woman who has so far lost her femininity as to become a sprawling drunk. As for the women seated beside their men—no envy was in their hearts this night. They could applaud without reservation. I certainly wasn't competing with them. No husband watched me covetously, and every wife knew it. I was just a girl who had lost a good man in Judge Shalleck, a girl who had messed up her life.

I sang automatically. Years of training came to my support, so though I cringed inwardly, outwardly I sang unconcerned.

"Very good, Lillian," were the words that greeted me as I came off the stage. If I wanted additional proof, here were two more bookings later in the month. Meanwhile, I held in my hand an envelope with $100 in cash. I sent $50 to Katie at once; and, back in New York, spent most of the remainder taking a group of AA's to dinner. Dad would have done that, too. With $15 which was left, I bought a pair of beautiful shoes. I was on the way to becoming a woman again.

I was booked at the Coronet Club in Philadelphia by Mickey Alpert, at $500 for a week's engagement—more than I had dreamed of in years. Bobby Kroll turned out a number of tunes for me and I borrowed money from Milton Berle to buy two gowns,

Again at the Coronet Club, as I stood on the stage, I thought, what is the audience thinking? They're thinking, *see that dame up there? Remember her? She used to be a big star. She's been a lush for years. . . .*

When I came off the stage, the fumes of liquor overwhelmed me. A dry alcoholic in a nightclub is like a diabetic in a candy factory; temptation—and breakdown—are an arm's length away. One of the club owners was a jovial type. "Lil, you did a swell job. Don't you want to celebrate," he urged me. "Let's have a drink."

"No, thanks, I'm on the wagon," I said politely.

He wasn't satisfied. I raised a glass of orange juice to my lips and my nostrils were assailed by the unmistakable odor of bourbon. I felt the rush of blood to my face. "Oh, no," I exclaimed.

He grinned. "Oh, I thought I'd fool you. One little drink can't hurt you."

I almost wept. "It's poison to me!" I cried. "You might as well give me carbolic acid!"

I sniffed every drink thereafter, but by the time my engagement was over and I returned to New York, I had almost succumbed. Only the presence of a few AA's who dropped in at the club enabled me to get through the engagement. When Burt came back from Southampton a few days later, I exploded. "I can't stand it," I shrieked. "I don't want to sing again. People don't think of me any more as a talent. I'm just a freak to them!"

Burt tried to soothe me. "It's all in your mind," he said.

He took me to AA meetings; he took me to movies, night after night; he played bridge with me; and he talked, and talked, and talked.

"Don't be afraid of people," Burt said. "You're just as important to God as they are—maybe more, because you're one of the sick ones."

To the one place I feared most—Lindy's—I went again, at its most crowded hour. After a sandwich and coffee, on my way out I passed a woman I had known all through my married life with the judge. Her husband was a judge of the New York Supreme Court; she had been our guest many times; they had often taken part in my charity affairs; we, in turn, had visited their home. We were old friends.

I went over to her and slid into the booth, next to her. I put out my hand. "Hello, Dorothy, how are you?"

She looked through me. "I don't know you," she said icily, ignoring my hand.

I was stunned. "Why, Dorothy, I'm Lillian, I was married to Ben Shalleck. Have I changed so much?"

"I don't know you," she repeated coldly. "Please leave my table."

I barely managed to stand up. The room started to spin. Hot and cold waves came over me: I couldn't swallow. All these people about me, who saw or heard or must know what had been said: the clatter of dishes; the movement of waiters—I had to get out that door. So Burt said I was as good as anyone else! Somehow I pushed my way out and paid my check.

My eyes blinded with tears. I made my way to the

clubhouse, to sob out my story to Burt. "You see, I'm not like other people! Decent people won't have anything to do with me!"

"Don't let it throw you," he said, comforting me. "You didn't drink. You came here. That's the important thing. You didn't allow self-pity to drive you to a bar. As for her—she's sicker than you are." And so be buoyed me up again.

But there were other experiences. A few days later, driven by a will I had believed long since broken, I walked into Lindy's again. I'd show these people how I could take it.

An elderly waiter came to my table. "How are you today, Miss Roth?" he asked. I smiled at him. "I'm fine, thank you."

"I hear you're going to try to make a comeback," he whispered. "Maybe you don't remember me, but I know you well. I've watched you through the years. I knew you when you were a little girl, and I waited on you when you came in here with your mother and sister." He paused, and leaned closer. "Look, Miss Roth, if you—well, if you ever need money for gowns or traveling, I can always loan you a few hundred—even more if you need it."

Tears stung my eyes. How good people *could* be! But I couldn't let him know how badly off I was. Instead, I said, "Oh, thank you, that's sweet of you and I appreciate it, but really I don't need a thing." My heart overflowed.

"Burt," I said one afternoon, "remember the day you first came over and talked to me in the clubhouse? What did you really think of me?"

[292]

He smiled, his blue eyes crinkling with amusement. "You won't be flattered," he said.

I put my hand on his arm. "Tell me, anyway."

"Well, you were sitting there when a fellow came up to me and said, 'Burt, when are you going to twelve-step Lillian Roth?'

"I looked over at you again. I thought, she isn't very pretty," he went on, his voice belying his words. "The thought that came to me was, she looks so woebegone with those huge, sad, swollen eyes. I used to watch you then—I guess we all did. I never figured you'd make it. You were so high-strung and you seemed to pay no attention to what was being said. You had lost so much, and you had so little to gain, I thought, because it didn't appear as if you'd ever go anywhere in show business even if you became sober." He stopped. "I remember asking you how old you were, and you said thirty-four. I thought you were lying. 'She's closer to fifty-four,' I said to myself."

"Oh, Burt!" Then I said, "Am I beginning to look better?"

I was losing a year a week, he said, laughing. He went on seriously, "I mean it. You're coming back and you're going to be a big success again."

"Oh, please," I said, almost impatiently. "Even if my complexion ever clears up again, even if I got the right songs and a chance to sing, I'm still thirty-four. I could never be a glamor girl again."

"You're the type of woman who becomes more glamorous as she matures," he said stoutly. "Think of Mary Martin, Ginger Rogers, Joan Crawford—"

"Oh, Burt. You're a man. It isn't so hard for you."

A few days later I said, "You don't see much of your family, do you, Burt? Where do you live now?"

He replied, "At the Pennsylvania."

One day, wanting to reach him, I telephoned the Pennsylvania Hotel. No Burt McGuire was registered there, nor had been for months. Why did he lie to me? Perhaps he didn't want me to know where he lived. But wasn't honesty basic in the AA program? Too embarrassed to press him, I checked with John.

John looked at me for a moment. "Did he say Pennsylvania Hotel?"

"That's how I understood it," I replied. "Pennsylvania."

"Well, he was right as far as he went. He probably would have told you sooner or later," John said. "Burt, you know, is broke most of the time and he's too proud to borrow. He used to spend most of his nights at the Pennsylvania Turkish Baths, until his family closed his account there. Now and then he sleeps in the waiting room of the Pennsylvania Station, with a ticket stub in his hat so they won't kick him out."

I looked at Burt differently after that.

He had his own overwhelming problem. He had been stricken with polio as an infant. It almost completely paralyzed him until he was nine years old. He was in braces until he was 16. His family tried to compensate him: he had his own ponies, his own boat, he travelled widely. Despite all this, he became an alcoholic at eighteen. "Liquor opened a world of fantasy to me," he told me later. "I wasn't the boy who always stumbled and fell, who couldn't play baseball or football, whose speech nobody could understand until I was twelve . . ." During the war he tried to enlist, but was rejected. He volun-

teered to become an ambulance driver for the American
Field Service attached to the British Army. He saw
eighteen months' service overseas. He was in action in
El Alamein, in Eritrea and Syria. In Africa he was almost
continuously drunk. Once, after the war, he awoke in a
Toronto hotel with no memory of how he had gotten
there. "The last thing I remembered had occurred *five
weeks* earlier!" The shock of that sent him to AA. When
he met me, he had been sober for nearly thirteen months.
Meeting me, he said, gave him a new hold on himself.
Now, he felt, he had someone at his side who made the
fight against alcohol worthwhile.

Later, he told me that in those months though the
principle of AA was working for him—he *was* physically
sober, but without spiritual understanding—he had
prayed, hoping there was a God who would hear him,
who would send him someone whom he could love and
who would love him, for he was very lonely.

We began to read the "Runner's Bible" a collection of
excerpts from the Old and New Testaments, studying
the words of sages and prophets, seeking to find a philosophy to live by. We read together an hour a day.

One evening we spoke seriously about our feelings for
each other. I had thought it was love too many times
before. I wasn't sure now. I knew that I was very fond of
him, and felt lost when we weren't together. He, too, was
not sure what the actual meaning of love was; but he
was content and happy with me. Yet it all seemed quite
hopeless. I was a Jewess, he a Catholic. The gulf between
us was widened not only by religion but by my past. I
could understand why his friends cut him when they
saw him with me. In only one respect were our back-

grounds alike: we'd both once had money—he because he'd been born to it, I because I had earned it—and now we were both broke. Both of us had been at the top: now both were at the bottom, given up by those who once loved us.

"But the differences aren't so terribly important," Burt said earnestly. Then he added, with a rueful smile, "Of course, with this bum leg I couldn't take you dancing, or do any wild gallivanting. I'd slow you up too much."

"Oh, Burt," I said, aghast. "Believe me, I never think of your affliction. To me you are perfect. I'm the one who is not complete. Even if we married, I could not have children. I'm the one's who's not whole. I'm only a shell of myself."

Now he was taken aback. "That's a terrible way to think!" he exclaimed. "I see *you* as perfect. I see you in God's image. I see amazing things happening to you. I've seen the change in your personality for the better—gradually you've gone from negative to positive thinking. I know it by your search for knowledge, by the way you study the various philosophies and try to reach God as you know God. Why," he went on, suddenly, "Lillian, I wouldn't be surprised to hear you speak in churches some day. I can just see you challenged by people who won't understand in the beginning."

As I regained myself, he said, I would reach the top again. I would be in the public eye. "By then" he continued, "you will have built yourself a glass house, and it will be good for you, because it will keep you firm in your belief and keep you studying. Remember," he said, and he put his hand on mine, "you're going to be back in your career, on the top."

I thought, now, wasn't he wonderful? Maybe he really is in love with me, because he must be slightly mad to believe I could become all that. And how would someone like me be asked to speak in churches? And what would I speak about? And reach the top again. . . .

No one could ever know how Burt rebuilt my deflated ego, and what confidence he instilled in me. When a woman is down as far as she thinks she can descend, and a man meets her and sees potentialities and a beauty which she thought long since gone . . . When a man has such dreams about what a woman can be again, and places her on a pedestal, she must try to attain that goal. She can do no less. I had thought everything in me had disintegrated, deteriorated, vanished. But not in Burt's eyes.

"We have to decide what you and I can accomplish together," he said. "But we have to start with you. Suppose I try to get you some steady bookings." He leaned over and kissed me on the tip of my nose. "Not suppose," he said. "I will."

So we pooled our interests and our efforts. Burt took me to Werner's of Switzerland, on Fifth Avenue, a beauty parlor to which he used to take aspiring models when he was associated with John Robert Powers. "We're going to redo you," he said. He made me change my dark hair to blonde. "It'll help you feel like a new person," he explained. He borrowed money to buy me a few dresses. At every turn he was there to advise, encourage, counsel.

As for marriage—perhaps, we thought, that had better wait a little while. Katie had met Burt and liked him. "But Lilly," she said, when she realized how I felt about him, "don't rush into this marriage. So many mistakes so far, so many mistakes!"

In late 1946 Burt booked me into a small nightclub, the Chateau Madrid, in New York. For the first time in years I was singing again in the Big City. My photograph, blown up, big as life, was outside. With Katie, Burt, Minna and Edna in the audience, I sang songs from "The Vagabond King"; I sang, "Sing, You Sinners!" "Ain't She Sweet," and other numbers I had introduced, as well as many new tunes. And one rainy day in January, 1947, Burt, escorting me home from the AA clubhouse, said casually, "Let's get married." I hesitated. "Come on," he said, "let's get married. This one is for keeps." I could not—I did not—want to say no again.

We went to West New York, a sleepy New Jersey town, and were directed to the marriage bureau by two men, a little the worse for drink, who were lounging aimlessly in front of City Hall. After we obtained our license, we emerged to find the men still there. We looked at them, Burt and I, and knew them for our own. Burt said gently to them, "Would you boys do us a big favor and be our witnesses?"

They came into the clerk's office and stood at our sides as we were married.

CHAPTER XXV

IT DIDN'T FOLLOW, just because I had been sober for six months, that bookings fell into my lap. Burt's job as my manager was no easy one. I had been out of sight too long.

The Chateau Madrid was followed by La Martinique, one of New York's top nightclubs. I was held over for four weeks. Then I was invited to the Five O'Clock Club in Miami. Audiences and critics were enthusiastic.

Then silence. No bookings. Our money dwindled.

Burt checked into it. "This is how it shapes up," he said, after making the rounds. "They're afraid of you, Lillian. In some places they're afraid to book you because if you're successful, you might get drunk. Others fear that if you fail, you'll turn to liquor. Still others won't engage you because when your name comes up, someone says, 'What do we want an old bag like that? She must be sixty by now.'"

We looked at each other, and I must have appeared so woebegone that he laughed and kissed me. "We've had tougher times," he said. "It won't be easy, but we'll make it."

Apparently, it was going to be tougher before it would be easier. New complications arose because of an article about me in *Look* magazine, which traced my return to sobriety and attributed it to my association with a group of ex-alcoholics.

I had wished to remain anonymous, but after consulting some AA friends, they agreed that my story would help others. In addition, as Burt put it: "You weren't anonymous when you were drinking. If the press could print stories and pictures about you beaten and disgraced, it's only right to let people know you're sober again."

Yet I was criticized. Some said I was glorifying a drunken career. Others accused me of using AA for personal publicity, although in the *Look* article I made no mention of the organization by name. Still others, meeting me on the street, if they did not turn aside (this still brought tears to my eyes) tried to joke about my sobriety. "Don't kid us, Lillian," they'd say. "Once a lush, always a lush. You'll be back on the bottle again." One erstwhile friend said laughingly, "I wish you luck, kid, but you were sober when you came out of the hospital and it didn't take long before you were pie-eyed again."

For the first time since my sobriety I felt almost despondent. Again, it seemed I'd hit a stone wall. Then an invitation came. The Tivoli Theatrical Circuit in Melbourne, Australia, wanted me for a six months' tour through Australia and New Zealand.

We were broke. The adverse criticism of the few became magnified in my mind; I was heartsick about it. Burt and I agreed it would be helpful to get away for a while and obtain a new perspective. A final argument was that the tour would enable me to earn enough money to take care of Katie as I wanted to.

We accepted.

Burt hadn't seen his mother since our marriage. "We're going on a long journey," I said. "I think you should visit her. I can't blame her for not understanding our problem, or for being unsympathetic toward our marriage. She doesn't know me, I'm of a different religion, and what she's read about me can't make her feel very happy about us."

Burt made the visit, and returned beaming. His mother wanted to meet me. I went to her Park Avenue apartment, my heart in my mouth. I knew I could never be the girl she had envisaged as her son's wife.

She took me in her arms when we met, and embraced me. "Can you ever forgive me for waiting so long?" she asked. She was a slight, gentle woman, not at all the formidable dowager I had expected. "I'm surprised you even asked me to come," I replied. "My record doesn't look very good in print."

"We must forget all that," she said. "We should be great friends." Later she added, "You know, our Lord is a Jew, the greatest Jew that ever lived." When we left, she kissed me again and gave me a small book entitled, *Prayer and Intelligence.* "Some day you may want to read this," she said, almost shyly. "It was translated by a Jewess."

A week later we boarded the ship at San Francisco, only to be told that it had been a troop carrier, and was still divided into separate quarters for the sexes. Burt and I would have to be separated.

I became panicky. I had not been apart from Burt since our marriage, and very little before then; and on those occasions, an AA had been with me nearly every hour. I was physically sober, but, without Burt, might I not suffer the dry jitters . . .

I became even more frightened when I saw my bunk, one in a tier of bunks in a barracks-like lower hold with nearly 30 women and children. And my first night was almost as bad as my first night at Bloomingdale's. There was scarcely six inches between me and the bunk above. I suffered from claustrophobia. My bunk was over the engine room, and I lay alone, almost smothering, the engines droning in my ears. Somewhere an electric fan whirred weirdly. I began to gag; I broke out into cold sweats: all the symptoms of my alcoholic insanity seemed to come back. The awful thought beat at my brain: *maybe I wasn't sent to Bloomingdale's for alcoholism, but for insanity!* Hadn't I been sober for months, and wasn't I lying here, suffering the agony all over again? . . . I lay weakly, and the engines seemed to spin out the words, "Holy Night, Silent Night," over and over again: a steady drone. And finally I fell asleep.

In the morning, Burt comforted me. "It will take time, darling. You're still thinking alcoholically. But easy does it . . ."

That day the voyage was brightened by the meeting with a minister, the Rev. William James of Melbourne, who was returning home after a visit to the United States. We told him about the work being done by AA. Perhaps he could pass the word along in his church.

"It helps us, you know, when we can help other alcoholics," I told him. "If you ever meet any one with a drinking problem, will you send him to us when we're in Melbourne?"

"I have one back home I'll give you as a gift," he said, with a half-smile. "I can't do anything with him.

He drinks up my collection box. God help him, he's been a hopeless drunk for twenty years."

"We'll do our best," I promised.

His Majesty's Theatre representative who met us when we arrived in Auckland in July, 1947 made no attempt to conceal his surprise. "I expected to see a much older woman," he confessed.

I perked up. He said it as if he meant it.

I did well in New Zealand, although I was never certain about the applause. For the theatre was so cold that people wore overcoats and carried blankets. Often I wondered if their applause was for me, or to keep themselves warm.

A charming gray-haired little woman dropped in one day to see us backstage. She introduced herself as Karen Wilson, a member of Parliament. She'd heard that I was a member of Alcoholics Anonymous, she said; New Zealand knew nothing about the organization or its work, she added, and she felt that a group similar to AA was desperately needed in the country. Were we prepared to help start such an organization here?

I explained my wish to remain anonymous. In the States my membership had become known and I didn't want to risk further criticism. "Of course, each member decides for himself whether he wishes anonymity," I pointed out. "In my case I want people to think of me as an artist, not as a kind of freak who's overcome a problem. But I'd be glad to work behind the scenes with you, and Burt and I will help you in that way to form a group."

Miss Wilson, who masked an iron will and a tremendous amount of energy behind her frail appearance, understood. Quietly she introduced us to her associates, among them a film producer, a newspaper man and an advertising executive who had attended AA meetings in the States. With them we launched the nucleus of an AA group in Auckland.

Alcoholic fumes still tantalized me. I resented the fact that others could drink with impunity. A considerable amount of social drinking went on around us, wherever we were. Now and then some of our heartier friends pushed a huge brandy glass under my nose and said with heavy jocularity, "Take a sniff!" At a dinner party one man remarked with some impatience: "Oh, you Americans and your isms. Americanism, radicalism, Momism, and now alcoholism! No such thing. It's all absurd."

We had been only a few days in Melbourne, Australia—where I opened at the Tivoli Theatre—when the doorman rapped on my dressing room. Distaste was written on his face. "There's someone here called Jack and he says the Rev. Mr. James sent him to see you."

The Rev. Mr. James? Of course—the minister we met on shipboard.

At the stage door stood an emaciated, unhappy man. His frayed sleeves were too short, his trousers looked as if they had been taken from a rubbish heap, the soles of his shoes flapped. He stood there, shaking. He managed to get out a few words: "The Reverend said you could help me, ma'am, and I need help very badly."

I looked swiftly at Burt. This man needed a drink, as I had needed one my first day in AA. We had a bottle in our trunk. Perhaps we had taken it with us so I would know it was there: perhaps we had taken it with us in anticipation of such a case as we had now. But we had it.

I took the man's arm. "Come on in, Jack, I know just what's bothering you." We led him to a chair in our dressing room. "How'd you like a little drink to stop those shakes?" He looked up gratefully, his teeth chattering. He was too far gone to speak again.

I poured the drink, and held the glass for him. But my hand shook, too, and Burt had to steady my hand with his as I held the glass to Jack's mouth. Little did our visitor know how I felt as the liquid went down his parched throat and the fumes went up my nose—if only that were going into me! But *he* needed it—and he needed me.

He still trembled, but he knew he was among friends now.

I was due on stage in ten minutes. We had to keep Jack under surveillance. He had to be talked to, watched, comforted.

Adjoining our dressing room was that of a dance team, Cabot and Dresden, a married couple who had been friendly to us. I hurried into their room. "You must do something for us," I said. "We have an alcoholic in a bad way in our room. I'm due on stage now and Burt has to stand in the wings. Would you pretend that you're alcoholics? Because usually when we have something to do, we pass him on to another AA. If he thinks you're alcoholic, he'll feel at his ease."

Of course they would, said Mrs. Cabot. She led our new friend to their room, and began unfolding a fantastic story of alcoholism. Later we gave Jack a dollar and told him to return whenever he wished. We knew he would buy liquor with it, but he could not buy much. We had planted a seed, however small. He would be back.

Next evening, at the stage entrance, Jack was there—with another man. Both stood, shaking. "My buddy here," Jack said with a weak grin, "he needs help, too."

Undoubtedly Jack told his friend he had found two soft-hearted Americans who were good for a touch of a dollar, and even a free shot of liquor. All you had to do was to listen to them talk.

Burt and I conspired together. We asked Jack's friend to go into Cabot and Dresden's room. While I spoke to him there, Burt spoke to Jack in our room. I told our newest friend: "Jack had a fair amount of sobriety for one day, but I can tell that you know more in one hour than he knows in a day. Now, Burt and I have a dinner engagement we can't break. I want you to take care of Jack. Here's some money and you take him to dinner and see that he doesn't touch a drink."

Then I took Jack aside. "Jack, you're a little shaky yet, but you're the stronger one. You've had nearly a day of sobriety. Take care of your friend. See that he doesn't drink."

Two hours later they returned. Each told me separately how he had watched the other. Neither had taken a drink.

After that we kept one with us, in our room or that of our friends', while the other sat in a box to watch the show. Thus neither one was able to get a drink.

Meanwhile, a third candidate arrived. The word was out. By week's end, we were dealing with six alcoholics, and had an AA nucleus. We knew three would make it; the statistics never failed. Fifty per cent would become sober; twenty-five per cent would leave, but return; the remaining twenty-five per cent would be lost.

Presently we were holding meetings in our dressing room. Alcoholics were with us sometimes until three a.m. Then we left for the hotel, and back again the next day. We spoke with them for hours; we went through the DTs with them, walked miles with them, poured black coffee in them—what had been done for me nearly a year before, and for Burt two years before, we now did for them.

In the midst of this activity, a ruddy-faced heavy-set man who exuded strength and good humor, called on us. He was the Rev. Irving Benson of All Souls Church. He conducted a national radio program from his church each Sunday, called "A Pleasant Sunday Afternoon," to which he invited distinguished guest speakers. Recent visitors had included Winston Churchill and General Montgomery. Would I be good enough to come to his church next Sunday and speak to his congregation, and to the listening audience throughout Australia? On alcoholism?

Speak from a pulpit? Burt was prophetic! I was overwhelmed. Awkwardly and in embarrassment I had talked before small AA meetings in the States. But to speak on the air to millions. . . . "It's against the principles of AA," I protested. "I will be criticized. I might be accused again of seeking publicity."

Mr. Benson was silent for a moment. Then he said earnestly:

"Please, please do think it over, Mrs. McGuire. There are instruments in the Lord's work, and you may well have been chosen to be such an instrument. The criticism you may receive from a small minority must be measured against the help you will give to countless others who hear you."

I agreed, finally, and Burt with me.

We spoke, not of ourselves but of alcoholics: of the 5,000,000 and more in America out of a population of 160,000,000. We cited the grim statistics: five per cent of all persons who drank were alcoholics. At least 12,000 died annually of alcoholism, but the true mortality figure was many times larger, for heart attacks were usually given as the cause of death because of the wholly unjust stigma attached to alcoholism. We pointed out that alcoholism was no respecter of persons: social registerites and laborers, Senators and members of Parliament, princes and paupers, high bottom or low bottom drunks—all were as one.

We told of the National Foundation for Alcoholism which provided hospitalization for alcoholics. We paid tribute to Marty Mann, citing her long, successful struggle to have legislators recognize alcoholism as a disease.

The results were staggering. We were inundated with hundreds of telegrams, letters and invitations to speak. Alcoholics converged upon our stage door. As long a line waited there as waited outside the Tivoli Theatre box-office in front. But in the queue backstage there were weeping mothers and wives, sometimes entire families, praying that we could help their sons and husbands.

From waking to sleeping we had no rest, either at the theatre or our hotel. We made appointments at seven a.m. and at two a.m. the following morning. We talked with men and women in our dressing room, in clubs, in private homes. And one morning another minister approached us—the Rev. Gordon Powell, of Melbourne's Independent Church. He would be deeply indebted if we would speak at his church: but he wanted something more than statistics. I must speak out of my experience and out of my heart. He pushed aside my doubts. Finally I agreed: and since it was evident we could no longer handle both stage work and alcoholics, I took a three-week leave from the theatre.

When we arrived Sunday morning at Independent Church, and were seated on either side of the altar, Dr. Powell introduced us, saying that we were giving away what God had given to us. No woman had ever spoken from his pulpit before, but one would today. His introduction was eloquent and moving.

I was deeply affected. The infinitely peaceful atmosphere of the church, the majestic organ music, the tenderness and sincerity of Dr. Powell's words . . . It is a difficult thing to express, but a profound sense of the religious came upon me. I thought, I wonder what God wants me to say.

I had no notes. I was not a public speaker. I had a limited education. What was I to say to these people? As I stood before them, I prayed silently, "God, please put the words in my mouth." And the words came.

When I finished, I saw tears in the eyes of many in the front pews. And Dr. Powell, moving slowly forward to the pulpit, turned and gave his blessing to me, and to Burt, and to all in the church.

I returned to the hotel tremendously moved. I felt I had a soul, that it was reaching forward to the unknown, not a dark, frightening unknown, but a warm, friendly otherworld. I was elated, yet serene. Burt sat in a chair and began to read. I threw myself on the bed, turned on the radio next to me, and tried to relax.

I closed my eyes. The BBC, from London, was broadcasting a presentation of Our Lady of Fatima, relating the story of how she appeared to three shepherd children in Portugal, on a Sunday morning in the last year of World War I, while all the world prayed for peace, and revealed to them things that were to come. The narrator's voice was soft, his words eloquent, and I listened.

No one believed the children. Instead, the Mayor ordered them to jail as punishment, and refused permission for them to go to the grotto where the Lady promised she would reappear and speak to them again, and cause a miracle so non-believers would believe.

Thousands flocked to the grotto. And a miracle did come to pass. It was attested by correspondents from anti-religious newspapers who came to scoff. Some had seen one thing, others had seen other things, but all had seen something not explainable in ordinary ways. Those who were religious saw the Infant Jesus on the lap of Mary. Some saw the Blessed Mother. Some gazed without hurt directly into the molten, whirling core of the sun, which spun and danced on its axis, then hurtled toward the earth, then halted midway. It poured rain, and yet none were wet. And again and again, month after month, strange events took place in the grotto where the shepherd children first saw the Lady of Fatima.

A great hope took hold of me. If God had allowed the Blessed Mother to appear, it meant that every loved one who had died, still continued on: for surely if He allowed one to exist, He must allow all to exist. It proved the promise in the Bible: *I shall give you life eternal.* God surely must love what He creates, as a father loves his children. Many thoughts went through my mind. I thought of my father, and the understanding I could have given him and did not, because I did not understand alcoholism until I suffered from it myself. But here was hope. He knew I was sorry. Here was an answer. There *was* eternity. Human struggling and suffering were not for nought . . .

"Oh, Burt," I said, almost dreamily. "That story rings so true to me. It must be wonderful to be a Catholic and have such strong beliefs. I'd like to know more about Catholicism."

My words must have sounded startling to him, spoken without warning, although he knew I believed in God, though I had found no spiritual contact with Him.

After a moment, Burt said quietly, "Well, you know Lillian, it takes a long time to study Catholic doctrine, and it's not easy."

"I know," I said, thinking aloud rather than speaking the words. "But I must try. I won't be satisfied until I do. I've been searching for a long time—maybe this is what I've been searching for. Maybe," I added, "if I found a Jew who understood Christianity or a Christian who understood Judaism, it might clarify my thinking."

Burt rose and walked slowly to the window. "It's odd that you should speak of a Jew who understands Christianity," he remarked. "As a boy I was taught my catechism by a priest who was born a Jew. Mother told me later he'd gone to Australia." He paused. "Australia's a big country, and Lord knows where he is—"

He began to thumb through the telephone book on the stand between our beds. "If I recall, he was in the Order of the Blessed Sacrament," he said, almost to himself. He found the page listing churches: there was a listing for Blessed Sacrament Church. He rang the number. I heard him speak into the mouthpiece. "I knew a priest in America many years ago who came to Australia," he said. "He'd be quite an old man now. Do you suppose you would know where I might find him? His name was Father William Fox."

He listened for a moment, then slowly replaced the receiver.

"Father William Fox is a priest in the church I just called," he said, in a strained voice. "It's three blocks from here."

Father Fox was a tall, thin stooped man with warm brown eyes and a gentleness that won me to him at once. Burt explained the strange coincidences which led us to his study.

"Sit down, my child," the priest said to me. "What is it you want to know?"

I felt utterly inadequate to answer him as I wanted to. I was on the edge of an awakening which I sensed, or experienced, rather than understood. But I tried to reply.

"Father, there's so much I want to know! But I'm really confused. There's something in me urging me to break through, telling me that there is something to be known, a great truth—and I'm frightened of it."

"Frightened of what?" he asked gently.

I searched for words. "I guess, just frightened of consequences. I love my people, but what will they think of me if I turn to Christianity? Will they think that I am disowning my birthright as a Jew? On the other hand, will Christians think I'm trying to escape persecution by hiding behind Christianity?" I spoke as honestly as I knew how. "But I do have this feeling, this yearning, and I must find out what it is."

Father Fox shook his head slowly, and smiled. "Patience, Lillian, patience. It is wonderful that you feel you want to become a Catholic, but you must *know* it. Feeling is emotion: knowing is logic. For truth's sake, you must not worry about the consequences or what people think. If they love you, they will love you no matter what your faith. It's only important to know what God wants of you."

"But how would I know?"

He said, "Pray to Him. Pray to God. He will direct you in His own good time."

Before I left, he told me: "Remember, Lillian, you can be proud of your heritage. For Christ was a Jew. Judaism is the trunk of the tree, Christianity the branch. I advise you to pray—and wait."

We departed, with a promise to attend Sunday Mass.

"What does he mean, I will be directed in God's good time?" I asked Burt as we walked out. "There are so many things I want to know. How will I go about it? Is prayer the way?"

Many people, Burt said, had read their way into the Church. But prayer was important, too. Prayer opened a door for them. It might open a door for me.

As we passed through the foyer of the church, I took from the Readers' Shelf a number of pamphlets. When we returned to our hotel, I said a little prayer to God.

"I don't know what You want from me, Dear God, but

[315]

I hope that as the Jews in the Bible asked for a sign, You will give me one so that I will know what to do when the time comes."

I prayed, not quite sure what I was asking for, but I prayed as Father Fox had told me to.

Next morning the telephone rang. It was the desk clerk. "There's a parcel down here for you from America. Shall I send it up?"

When I opened it, I found two copies of *Our Lady of Fatima*. They had been sent by Burt's mother, one for each of us. They had been mailed two weeks before.

Had I been given a sign?

CHAPTER XXVI

We HAD many talks with Father Fox. He was extremely interested in the interpretations of AA written by ministers in the United States, which we had brought along with us, and particularly one brochure published by a Catholic priest which called attention to the similarity between the Twelve Steps of AA and the Fourteen Points of St. Ignatius.

Both stressed turning your will over to God; confiding in another; making amends, and helping others. Father Fox had hundreds of reprints made, to be distributed in the Catholic churches of Australia. He also arranged for Burt to meet with a group of priests so that he could speak to them on AA. They, in turn, would discuss the subject from their pulpits.

What especially pleased us was to learn that the Rev. Gordon Powell and Father Fox—distinguished Protestant and distinguished Catholic men of the cloth—had met, and now worked together to help alcoholics.

Our days were crowded with speeches. One of our talks was made before the Australian Society of Psychiatrists, which invited us to address its annual convention in Melbourne. Dr. Powell introduced us.

Many in the audience were critical. They doubted the

efficacy of the Twelve Steps. They doubted the success of
AA. One man stood up and demanded:

"Miss Roth, have you had special training in psychiatry?"

"No, sir," I said.

"Do you have a degree in psychology or related subjects?"

I shook my head.

"As a matter of fact," he went on, "you have no university degree of any kind from any recognized institution?"

For a moment I was tempted to say, "Bloomingdale's,"
but this was not the occasion.

"As a matter of fact," I replied, "I never went to college.
My formal education ended when I was fifteen."

There was a moment of silence, then cries of "Hear!
Hear!" and applause.

Dr. Powell closed the meeting. "I hope that you will
all keep us of AA in mind when you deal with patients
who may need the help and counsel of an organization
like AA," he concluded.

At the invitation of a group of Methodist ministers in
Adelaide, we flew there, where we spoke to the Mayor,
members of the City Council, and the Director of Prisons.
I made clear that we spoke not as AA representatives, but
only as alcoholics whose cases had been arrested.

One evening an intense young man came to me as I
left the platform. "I'm a newspaperman, Miss Roth. Could
I speak to you in your room?" We invited him up.

He asked many questions, thanked us and departed.

Next morning a special delivery letter arrived. It was
from our friend of the night before. He was not a reporter:

he was a printer, and an alcoholic. He was on the verge of committing suicide, he wrote, when he had spoken to us. All he wanted now was our forgiveness. Would we telephone him and let him see us once more?

A few hours later he was in our room again.

"I'm a fallen-away Catholic," he began. "I find it hard to believe in God."

I told him I could not help him in this. I was still in search myself. And my husband, I said, had been away from his church since childhood. But why could he not believe in God, I asked?

"I was a flyer in the war," our visitor said. "I was assigned to bomb a schoolhouse—a retaliation raid. I dropped my bombs while the children played in the yard. That was my order, and I carried it out."

As he zoomed away, he looked behind. He held his hands over his eyes as he spoke. "It's haunted me. Never, to my dying day, will I believe in God again, nor will I be able to erase the sight of those children—what I did, knowingly."

I racked my brains for the right words to comfort him. What could *I* tell him? I could say only that all of us may be chosen as instruments in ways we cannot understand. "You came to me for help," I went on. "Perhaps I can't help you as I should. But I need *your* help. I have a little book on the Mass. I don't understand it. Even if you don't believe any more, won't you explain it to me?"

So we sat that night. He did not drink. He explained the Mass to me. These, he said, were the psalms of David. I had not known that. And this was taken from the Jewish Passover service: the breaking of the bread, the drinking of the wine. As he expounded, earnestly and with increasing calm, I thought: now we three have something in common. He and Burt were not attending their church, yet they were helping me, a non-Catholic, to understand their faith. By the same token, Burt and I had his trust.

When we left Adelaide, he was using his presses to reprint AA literature, and working with local clergymen to organize an ex-alcoholics group there.

In Brisbane, an attorney, a taxi-driver and an actor formed the first nucleus of ex-alcoholics to carry on the work we began in that city.

Katie's letters, which had been following us, caught up with us at our final stop, Sydney. They were letters of love and encouragement, full of homey gossip. Once I had told her of Burt's wild dream that I would "speak in churches." Now she reminded me of it.

One of my last talks was in North Sydney. A Jesuit priest, who introduced himself as Father Richard Murphy, chatted with me when I finished. "There was something universal about your talk," he said. "But if you will forgive me—you seemed a bit uncertain as to the spiritual aspects of your struggle." He looked thoughtfully at me. "When I said 'universal,' I meant universal in the sense of Catholic," he added.

I found myself telling him what I had told Father Fox.

"If God wills it, it would be wonderful," he said. "It would mean much to both of you if you could be married in the Church."

He suggested that I read "Faith of Our Fathers," by Cardinal Newman who, he said, was a convert. We had long talks on faith and God.

Before we left Sydney, Burt and I were invited to visit

the prisons. We were shocked to see that alcoholics were jailed in the same cell blocks with murderers, and locked behind iron doors from four p.m. until six a.m. "They don't understand how cruel that is," I explained to our guide. "An alcoholic is a desperately lonely person. To lock him up so long is pure torture."

We were invited to make our observations formally to the Ministers of Health, Education and Prisons. In doing so, we explained how alcoholism was handled in the majority of the States. Later we learned that more liberal methods of treatment were introduced in Australia.

Our last tea in Sydney saw us as guests of the warden of the women's prison. We chatted in friendly fashion. A pretty, apple-cheeked girl, wearing a tiny apron, served me my tea, asked me charmingly if I took milk or sugar, and deftly presented me with napkin and muffins.

"Is she one of the prisoners?" I asked, when she was out of hearing. "She seems so lovely and sweet."

The warden smiled.

"Oh, yes," he said. "An excellent prisoner, too."

"What did she do? What is she in here for?"

The warden looked at me for a moment. "She poisoned her husband," he said blandly. "She put arsenic in his tea."

I must have set my tea down sharply, for it spilled over.

We had now been away from home for eight months— the longest period Katie and I had yet been separated. I longed to see her. We wired her money to meet us in Los Angeles, and in May, 1948, we returned to the States.

On the boat Burt and I had time to look through hundreds of letters that had come to us from all parts of

Australia, from churchmen, from leaders of missions, from men who had campaigned, as they put it, "against John Barleycorn" all their lives. There were reports on alcoholics who had been helped by AA, notations which summarized so much in so little:

"Percival started on a job at the shoestore Friday last. He's really on the beam now."

And again:

"Have I written you about Stan Lewis? He was the advertising fellow from Auckland, who got the shakes the night Lillian spoke. Well, you wouldn't know him today. He's chairman of his group, and he's been sober for a month straight—the first time in years."

Or:

"Harry Carlote thought one day he would so much just like 'one,' and after a lot of fiddling about, he went into a bar and one of his old cobbers said, 'Good old Harry—have a drink?' He said, 'No, thanks,' and walked out before he realized what he was doing. For a time he just couldn't make out why he had done it. 'Where'd I get the guts to say "No, thanks?"' he keeps asking me. He can't understand it, but he accepts it."

And one letter from a young Australian writer with whom I had discussed, rather doubtfully, the idea of writing a book on my life. For again I was torn: a book would open the door to the accusation that I was glorifying my drunkenness, that in some perverse manner I enjoyed the ignominy of it. My friend wrote:

"Lillian, you must get started on that book! The sooner the better. The literary critics mayn't rave over it, but that doesn't matter. If it lifts just one person out of the abyss of alcoholic mire, it won't have been wasted. Maybe this very minute some poor unfortunate is waiting, in desperate need of help. In some distant country, or perhaps just around the corner from where you and Burt are reading this, there may be someone, maybe a lovely young girl, perhaps a fine, otherwise decent and respectable young feller, or perhaps even a grizzled two-bit bum, in need, in terrible need, of you both, but in particular in need of the thoughts and experiences you have locked in your heart. *Don't let anybody defeat your purpose, Tony.* Remember when you gave me that message in my darkest moment? I made use of it, and now I give that message back to *you*, Lillian. Write your book, for good or for bad. That's all that counts now."

At Los Angeles Katie greeted us. "Baby, I'm so glad to have you back!"

Burt and I took a little house in Santa Monica. Burt obtained a job with an advertising agency and I received my first booking—at Ciro's, in Hollywood!

Now, I thought, things are beginning to work out. I looked up the addresses of the stars I'd worked with, those who had seen me climb to the heights and tumble down again. To each I sent a wire: "I am opening at Ciro's. I haven't been among you for a long time and I'd be so thrilled if you'd come to my opening."

The big night arrived.

But the stars were not out that night. . . .

The critics were highly complimentary. My evening was "a triumphant return." One wrote, "We came to sympathize, we remained to cheer."

One night Mary Pickford and Buddy Rogers came to see my show. Mary said simply, "You know, Lillian, I rarely go to night clubs. But the minute Buddy heard you were playing at Ciro's, he got all excited. He's admired you for years and I must say, so have I. And after hearing your wonderful performance, I'm so glad we came." Another night Gene Raymond and Jeanette MacDonald were on hand to see the show—Gene, with whom I'd gone to school, Jeanette, with whom I'd worked in "The Love Parade" so long ago. Others who came were Alice Faye, Phil Harris, the Ritz Brothers, and Jimmy Durante.

There had been a time when Jimmy had rather rough going, too. When I was married to Mark Harris, Jimmy was working at the Earl Carroll Night Club in Hollywood. The beautiful girls received first billing—not Jimmy. Mark and I came to see him.

"Thanks for coming," he said, then. "So few have shown up." Now he kissed me: "I'm returning your visit, kid," he said, flashing that inimitable grin. "Good luck. I'm telling you, you're going to make it again."

My hopes were high. I *was* coming back.

I bought new gowns, new musical arrangements, and a big ad in *Variety*, and waited.

Again, nothing happened. No calls from agents. No offers. Three months passed. I was booked to replace the ailing Tony Martin at the Biltmore Hotel at Lake Tahoe, Nevada. The press reviews were good. One critic compared me to Ethel Merman. Then weeks passed without a call.

We did the best we could to make ends meet on Burt's salary. Mother, who had enjoyed me at Ciro's as she had not enjoyed her Lilly for many years, found her health improved by midsummer. She felt it was time to return to New York to see Ann and her baby—and she knew our finances were low. Burt and I saw her off. "Don't worry, darlings," she said. "We'll be together soon. We're never separated for long."

CHAPTER XXVII

DURING these first few months back in the States, I had much time on my hands and read a great deal. I was particularly impressed by Lecomte du Nouy's *Human Destiny*, and its emphasis upon collaboration with God to achieve personal dignity. I also read carefully an article by Clare Boothe Luce, who had recently been converted to Catholicism, entitled, "Apologetics For the Convert." My reading encouraged me in the search for a way of life that would meet the needs of the Lillian Roth who had experienced what I had experienced, who had come the road I had come.

I spoke to several priests, each time in some embarrassment, for my motive was not always understood. They tried to be helpful, but they were not too encouraging. "Your case is difficult. And the Church looks on these matters very seriously."

Burt's mother wrote me frequently. In one letter she enclosed a gift of two rosaries, and passing the Church of the Blessed Sacrament in Hollywood of an afternoon, Burt and I went in to have them blessed.

The priest who performed the ceremony was a dark-haired, dark-eyed man whose calmness struck a responsive chord in me. I felt he was a man who would understand my problem. "Father, there's something personal I'd like to discuss with you, if I may," I told him.

He invited me into his study. He looked at me for a moment, a smile playing about his lips, then said surprisingly, "Mrs. McGuire, was your maiden name Lillian Roth?"

I stared. Had he recognized me from photographs? How would a priest know the name of a nightclub entertainer?

"We received a letter some time ago from Father Richard Murphy in Sydney," he explained. "We thought you'd be along one of these days." Father Murphy had written to Father Joseph McCloy, pastor of the Hollywood church.

I spoke later with Father McCloy. "Anyone who has knocked so often deserves to have the door opened," he said. He suggested that I begin instruction in Catholicism. "If, after studying it, you find it is your will to enter the Church, then it will be so. When you become a Catholic, we shall present your case to Rome for a ruling as to whether you can marry in the Church."

From whom was I to take instruction?

From the Rev. William Swager of St. Monica's Church, Santa Monica—my parish church.

"Why do you want to be a Catholic?" Father Swager asked.

He was tall, bespectacled, enormously learned.

"I just feel—well, I just know that God wants me to be a Catholic."

He looked at me quizzically.

"How do you know there is a God?"

This overwhelmed me. Wasn't this a question he should answer for me? I believed in God, but I had never tried to define how or why. I looked about almost in confusion. My eyes fell on the window of Father Swager's study, looking out on the church lawn. It was a bright, sunny day: the world outside was green and lovely.

"I just feel it," I said. "Everything's that made, all the beauty about us—the trees, the grass, the birds—why, the entire universe, you and I—we just couldn't have happened! I read Lecomte du Nouy and he speaks of 'chance and anti-chance.' He explains God as anti-chance. It's hard for me to believe that everything about us, all this beauty, all the growth and birth and wonders about us—that all are chance. There must be a God."

Again, in the same quiet, schoolmaster's way, Father Swager asked:

"Do you have any proof?"

Once more I searched for words. "Well," I said lamely, "in school I learned that there is a cause for every effect. I was taught that the greatest scientific minds, who can tell you all the mysteries of cells, are baffled trying to explain how life began, or what it really is. But life exists —and there had to be a cause—and the cause is God."

He shook his head. "That is not enough proof," he said. He looked out the window for a moment, then turned to me. "Do you know why God made us?"

My answer was childlike, but I could think of no other at the moment. "He must have been lonely," I said.

The priest smiled. "God made us to love Him and to serve Him and to be happy with Him eternally." He rose and put out his hand to me. "I believe you are sincere, Lillian. We will begin our course of instruction at once.

There will be books for you to study. We will move slowly. You must have proof that convinces you there is a God. You must learn, too, how to defend your belief through the proof you have."

Through the long, hot summer of 1948 I took my instruction. Four afternoons a week I sat in Father Swager's study for sessions which lasted from two to three hours. I pored over books on science, history, theology. When I found it difficult to understand, or to accept, Father Swager was patient. "You must not accept anything unless you believe it," he repeated. "Otherwise, it is hypocrisy. You are not *forced* to believe."

Burt called for me each afternoon.

One sweltering day he arrived quite early. Our session was only half-completed. I asked Father Swager if I might invite my husband into the cool of the study.

"Certainly," the priest said. Burt came in, a little diffidently, and took a chair in a curtained alcove. "I'll just read a magazine until you're finished," he said.

Next day he called for me a little earlier, and the day after still earlier. "You might as well sit in the room with us," I suggested. "You'll get more air."

As he drove me home later, he said suddenly, "I've been listening to your lessons."

I smiled. "I know," I said.

He grinned sheepishly. "You know, I never realized the logic in Catholic doctrine. After all, I stopped studying as a youngster. All I knew were the childhood fears of hell and damnation. I never really grew up in my religion."

Presently we were taking instruction together, and it seemed strange, yet inevitable, that I, a Jewess, entering a faith which was based upon my own Judaism, should be instrumental in bringing my husband back to the faith into which he had been born.

For that is how Burt returned to his church.

On August 14, 1948, I was baptized.

"Father," I said, "I am frightened now. I will have to go to confession. And, Father—I have so much to confess!"

He took my hand in his. "No, Lillian," he said, "there is no confession for you. With your baptism you have been reborn. In the eyes of the Church you are without sin. All that is in the past. Put it out of your mind. It is as if it has not been."

On August 15, the following day, I took my first communion.

I prayed to God. *Help me to love You and do Your will.*

Later that afternoon, I sat meditating; and it occurred to me that all my life I had lived with anxiety, so great that until this moment I had carried sleeping pills with me, fearing that some unexpected crisis might upset me beyond control. In my mind sleeping pills substituted for the drink I might take if something too overwhelming to endure came upon me.

Now I felt an inner peace. What was there to be frightened of? Whatever happened, there was God to go to, to understand you, to give His love to you. I knew, with this peace I had found, that I would have no need for the pills: and by doing away with them, I would destroy all the subtle, unknown fears that had been my companion for so many years.

I missed Mother. I wanted to return to New York and see her. She had not been feeling well. Burt and I worked our way eastward, Burt taking any job he could obtain to pay our train fare from town to town. Then, finally, we were in New York. When we introduced our mothers, they threw their arms around each other, and Mrs. McGuire cried, "Oh, my dear, the Irish and the Jews have always got along well, haven't they!"

CHAPTER XXVIII

Iᴛ ᴡᴏᴜʟᴅ ɴᴏᴛ be honest to say that my conversion to Catholicism did not puzzle many friends. When I had first written the news to Katie, her reply had been characteristic: "You know I don't know too much about religion, Lilly, but if it makes you happy, then it's right for you."

But many friends accused me of forsaking Judaism. I had to confess that though Mother and Dad believed in God, we had no religious ritual in our home. Looking back, I can say that I felt I was a spiritual person, that I had even a sense of the mystical, that I was convinced of the existence of good and evil, and that I wanted to be good, but I knew no church.

I am not an authority on Catholicism. I am ignorant of many of its profound aspects. I can not say to others: do as I have done. I am only telling my story as I lived it. I hope that those who will, will understand. As to the others, I leave it to God.

We were now living in the McGuire home in Southampton, which Burt's mother had loaned us for the winter. Katie, living with Ann, was not too well. We had little money, but whenever we could, I gave her small

sums. It seemed to me that she was more delighted when
I gave her $2 for Bingo than when I had given her $10,000
to play roulette at Monte Carlo. I was well again, and
that was the important thing.

Each time I saw her, however, she seemed more frail.
Ann and I took her to a physician, who reported that she
had a mild heart condition, but would be all right if she
took care of herself.

The night of February 6, I awoke, as I had years before,
the night Arthur died, with a strange sense of foreboding.
I went downstairs and wrote a letter to Minna:

"You know how worried I am about Katie. I'm going
into New York tomorrow to bring her back here. Please,
Minna, come down to Southampton and stay with us for
the weekend. I am going to lose Katie and I will not be
able to stand it. You must stay with me."

When Burt and I brought Katie to Southampton we
put her to bed in a large upstairs room. She was in wonderful humor, confiding in Minna that she could not
understand "why Lilly is fussing so."

Sunday morning Minna and her husband decided to
return to New York. I begged her to stay one more night.

"Now, don't be silly," said Minna, hugging me. "You
just love your mother so much and you're crazy with
worry, but there's no sense to it. Your mother feels fine."

The moment she left I became panicky and hurried
upstairs. Katie was reading "John Brown's Body." Oh, I
thought, she must not read that: it is full of graveyard
scenes.

"Let's talk, Mom," I pleaded.

"All righty," she said. She put down the book and
smoothed the folds of a blue bathrobe I'd ironed for her

earlier. It seemed to me that with her fresh face and the lipstick she had put on, twenty years had dropped from her.

"We could pass for sisters, Mom," I said gaily. "Did you fix yourself up for me?" And I kissed her.

I had to say what I had to say, and now was the moment. "You know, Mom," I began. "I suppose you've often wondered how I came to join the Church. How do you really feel about it?"

She shook her head. "Darling, you know whatever makes you happy is what I want for you. Naturally I wonder sometimes what our friends think, but you know I just believe in God. I'm sorry I don't know more about religion, but whatever people believe that gives them happiness, then that's it."

"Maybe you'd like to hear the story, anyway." I told her how I had listened to the broadcast about the Lady of Fatima as I lay in my hotel room in Australia, and all that happened afterwards. She listened quietly. "Do you really think there is a heaven, Lilly?" she asked.

"Don't you, Mom?"

"I don't know. Sometimes I think that when you die you die, and that is the sum and substance of it. You have lived—and you die. I know I wouldn't want to be too old when I go."

"For goodness' sake, Mom," I said. "I'll be gone before you. In fact, I'd better tell you about heaven now. Whoever gets there first will prove it."

"I'd like to believe that," she said wistfully. The urge was strong in me: *you must tell her there is a heaven.* I told her as eloquently as I could. If I were not certain there was an eternity, a hereafter, I would have been unable to come out of the particular hell I found myself on earth. I wanted to be always with those I loved. There was a heaven. "You'll see," I said. "It will be just as I said. I'll get there before you and make arrangements." And I laughed, holding back my tears, and hugged her.

She said, "Well, if you say so, it must be so. You know, Lilly, you're the boss. You're always right."

I kissed her again. "I'm going downstairs now, Mom, to see about dinner."

When I came up a few minutes later, she was reading a newspaper article on heart disease. How can I get that paper away from her, I thought. I served her dinner, and quietly took the paper downstairs. I made myself a cup of tea, and read the graphic description of a coronary attack.

Suddenly Burt screamed, "Lillian! Lillian!"

I rushed upstairs. She had suffered an attack. I whispered frantically to Burt, "Get the doctor!" I knew what it was. Hadn't I just read all about it?

Then the doctor was there, and an ambulance, and she was taken to the hospital.

I remained at her bedside, hour after hour. As in the old days, I became hysterical. "If they don't save her, I'll kill myself. Don't talk to me about God!" I screamed at the priest. "What is God doing? She's dying!" But a moment later I was on my knees, praying. Why could she not be spared a little while longer? I had so much to atone for, I wanted so much to make her last years happy and proud . . .

They placed her under an oxygen tent. I sat with her. A nurse brought a Sunday newspaper and said, "Would you like to read it?"

I opened the papers and the comics were on my lap. My mother, under the oxygen tent, opened her eyes. "You have your funnies, Lilly?" she asked. "That's good. You always liked them. I used to read them to you as a baby, do you remember?"

"Yes, Mom," I said brokenly. "I'll read Dick Tracy to you." And I read it aloud.

She fell asleep. I looked at her, and grew nervous. Minutes passed. She slept, peacefully. I hurried out of the room to find a nurse. I went into the next room. Coffee was being served. I said, trying to be nonchalant, "I'll have some black coffee, please." Then I went back into my mother's room and she was dead.

I looked at her, dazed. A nurse came in, and vanished, and returned quickly, a hypodermic in one hand, a small glass of brandy in the other. "I thought one of these might help you," she said gently. "The doctor ordered them for you."

I said, "No, thank you." How silly of her to think that, I thought dully. If my mother could endure sixteen years of pain watching me destroy myself, certainly I could take the pain of losing her as she would expect me to. I knew, in this awful hour, that nothing could ever hurt me again.

CHAPTER XXIX

THREE LOVES I had: David; my father; my mother.

To whom, now, was I to atone?

In the night I prayed and wept. Why could I not have had a little more time to do the things I wanted to do for my mother: to buy her lovely clothes, to make her happy, to have her see me a success, to watch her face light up and hear her say again, "That's my Lilly!"

Why could He not have spared her for a few more years so that I might, in some way, try to make up for all the suffering I had caused her? If only she could have seen me regain my dignity and courage, to balance in some way those sixteen years of watching her child disintegrate before her eyes, to balance all her shame, and humiliation, and tears, and mother's anguish!

Burt thought a change of scene would help, and we moved to a New York hotel. I became withdrawn and introspective, and Burt worried. But one night, as I lay in bed weeping for Katie, I remembered something she used to say which for these many years I had forgotten. When I was little, if I fell down, or if some other child hurt my feelings, or, later, if some great disappointment came to me, and I cried, she would say, "Lilly, baby, don't cry tonight—cry tomorrow." And I would try to control

[335]

myself and say, "All right, Mom. I'll cry tomorrow." Now, fighting my hysteria, after Burt fell asleep, fighting the panic, I pretended that Katie was in the room with me, talking to me as she did when I was a little girl. "Lilly, baby, it will all be different tomorrow."

I thought, yes; nothing can be decided as you lie in the dark, and even if you reach a decision, there is nothing you can do. You must wait for tomorrow. I'll put off the tears until tomorrow, and tomorrow everything will be changed, for God will have given us a new day.

And still I cried.

I prayed, and tried to visualize my mother as a little child would visualize her, in heaven. I saw her, with her shy smile and her warm eyes and all the love for me that is in her heart, seated with the Blessed Mother, near the throne of God; and through my tears I saw them together, the Blessed Mother and my mother Katie, their arms about one another, each taking care of the other, and as mothers taking care of all the world, and saying to all the lost, and frightened, and bereaved: "Now, that's all right —have no fear—have no fear any more, my darlings. Have no more fear, my darlings."

It was June, 1951. Burt and I were alone in our house, and I was nursing my old sacroiliac, when the telephone rang. The pain had sent me to a chiropractor, and now I lay almost doubled up on the sofa, unable to move.

I heard Burt's voice. "No, she couldn't," he said firmly. "She's ill. Tomorrow? No, I'm sorry. But I'll take your number."

I asked weakly who it was.

"Al Paschal, who handles Ralph Edward's show, 'This

Is Your Life,'" he replied. "He's doing the life of Nacio Brown." Paschal wanted me to fly to Hollywood and surprise Nacio by singing a few bars of "Eadie Was a Lady," one of the many song hits Nacio had written, and which I sang in "Take a Chance."

A miracle got under way. "What?" I demanded. "What did you say?" With each word my back straightened a little. "Tomorrow?" I asked, straightening up a little more. "Of course I'll do it. Give me that number." My back forgotten, I hurried to the telephone.

Burt stared at me, and chuckled. "If you hams aren't something! There you are, all but passed out, but someone asks you to sing—"

I didn't deny it. Burt and I flew to Hollywood next morning and a day later I took part in Nacio Brown's story. A great song writer received his due, and I was happy to be in the show.

At the customary party given later by the Hazel Bishop lipstick people, sponsors of the program, Ralph Edwards said, "You know, some day your life should be done. Your husband, Al and I were talking about it."

"My life? Oh, Mr. Edwards, what have I accomplished!"

Now that I had been in the public eye again, big things were predicted for me. But predictions no longer excited me. I had begun my comeback in 1946, and now, in 1951, the road seemed just as long as before.

I appeared in a musical in Santa Fe; I was booked into the Mocambo and the Bar of Music in Hollywood. Mike Connolly, columnist on the *Hollywood Reporter*, gave me a farewell party in Hollywood when I was about to return to New York. Robert Taylor was there, and Zsa-Zsa Gabor,

Father Keller, Louella Parsons, Mary Pickford, Florabel Muir, Harrison Carroll, the Duncan Sisters, Gilda Gray, and many others. Cobina Wright, Sr., heard me sing several numbers. "My dear child," she exclaimed, "where have you been hiding yourself? You can't leave this town yet."

I told her, "I've been working right along, Miss Wright, not too steadily, but it seems I just haven't hit the proper vibration."

At her suggestion I was booked into John Walsh's Deauville, on Sunset Strip. One night a small, dark-complexioned woman who was seated with six or seven young men asked Mr. Walsh if I would care to come to her table.

He introduced us. "Lillian, do you know Miss Polly Adler?"

It was the New York madam. She was delighted to see me "coming along fine," she said, with a smile. She'd watched my career and felt she knew me. She wanted to tell me about something.

"Once, when you had your trouble drinking, I was walking down Park Avenue on a rainy day when I saw a doorman shove you into the street. I guess you had gone into his doorway to get out of the rain. I bawled him out. I said, 'That is a lady, and you had no right to do that!'"

I smiled, too, but my heart was not in the conversation. "Let's talk about happier times," I suggested. She said, "Do you know, we have something in common?"

"We do?"

"Oh, yes. We both have a past, and we're both writing a book. But mine is psychological."

I was held over for six weeks at the Deauville. Press and public were warm and cordial. And again, silence.

[338]

June, 1952, found us in New York, down to our last
$100. We were living on credit in a smart Park Avenue
hotel. The owner, a widow whose husband had been an
alcoholic, assured us that we could pay her when we had
the money.

Whatever we had earned, we invested in my act, in
order to keep it up to date—new gowns, new songs and
new arrangements. The public generally has no inkling
of how expensive a singer's appearance can be. I could
not present songs or orchestrations already on the market.
A special arrangement, for example, of a popular song,
costs from $300 to $1,000. A special piece of lyric material
can cost $1,500. To be beautifully gowned also demands
considerable sums of money.

Thus, at the fees I received, I might have to work
several months to pay for a few songs, a few arrangements
and a few gowns. Since my bookings were at long intervals, we were almost always broke. In addition, we continued paying back friends who had aided me during my
illness.

Now, with debts beginning to accumulate, I grew discouraged. "Burt," I said one day, "let's not fool ourselves.
I've gone as far as I can with my career. I'm forty-two
years old and if it hasn't come by now, I don't think it
ever will." I thought ruefully for a moment. "I'm not
retiring from the profession—the profession is retiring me."

Burt laughed, but shook his head. "I wanted to surprise
you," he said, "but I might as well tell you now. Mother's
released a portion of my trust fund that I was to receive
later, and I've got a plan." We would buy a motel in
Florida, build a little cottage for ourselves next to it. With

an income assured, I could continue to sing without financial pressure.

"Oh, no," I said. "I've tried since 1946 to make a go of
it. Each time I see an agent, he asks, 'Are you serious this
time?' I tell him, 'You people book me so seldom that
every time I work it's called a comeback.' No. I've had it.
Lillian Roth's retiring—by unpopular demand!"

I felt fine, I admitted: I could face people again. I felt
I had regained my dignity, and a degree of serenity. I
was tremendously grateful, but enough was enough.

"Buy the motel, Burt, and I'll help you run it. *Mr. and
Mrs. Burt McGuire, Your Hosts.* I smiled. "I'll still have
my name up in lights." Neither of us thought that was too
funny. Yet I think we both knew in our hearts that we
still hadn't called it quits.

We drove to Florida. Yes, Florida was booming. But
motels? Friends discouraged us. We'd lose what little
money we had.

Stymied, Burt obtained a position with Imported
Motors, a firm which sold European cars. And instead of
buying a motel, we bought a small home on the harbor
in Fort Lauderdale, a part of Florida which enchanted
me.

One morning I read that Martha Raye, Harry Richman,
Danny Thomas and Joe E. Lewis were all in Miami, working. The sense of challenge rose in me. Well, I thought,
I really don't *have* to sing—but I can do it, just for the
enjoyment of it. I looked through the classified telephone
directory and chose an agent's name at random. "I'd like
to do a little work while I'm down here," I told him over
the wire. "Do you suppose you can book me?"

"Come down to Miami this afternoon," he said. "We'll talk about it."

I drove to Miami, an hour and fifteen minutes from Fort Lauderdale, and arrived on time for our appointment. The agent had left, his secretary informed me. Any message for me? None.

I thought, this is as much as the name Lillian Roth means today. Glumly I drove back to Fort Lauderdale.

"Don't let it get you," Burt said. "I have a job. We have each other. You can busy yourself in other ways. You can take a hand in the various charities down here. You can swim and boat and make new friends. Enjoy yourself."

Why not? That was the original plan, anyway.

Yet—

One night we went to see Martha Raye's show. She was terrific. Here, I thought, is one of the world's greatest comediennes. Inspired, I hurried home, dug up a scrapbook and sought out Harry Kilby, an agent I knew. The profession was in my blood. Maybe I hadn't learned my lesson, but I was sure my talent remained. Audiences and critics liked me. Here was the proof. Why, then, couldn't I come back?

"I don't need to look at your scrapbooks," he said. "I know what you can do. And you look wonderful—as you did fifteen years ago. I can get you jobs if you'll take the kind I can get you—one-night stands—not much money. Trouble is, people haven't seen you work lately."

Had nothing trickled down to Florida about my appearances through the country?

"Yes—ss," he said, a little doubtfully. "But people don't know what you look like down here. They think you're an old woman. Let them see you."

I accepted, and began working the big hotels, a different one each night. "I'll be able to buy a lamp or a chair or something else for the house," I reasoned. "Anyway, I'll keep my hand in."

Then, a telephone call. A girl who was co-headlining with Myron Cohen for the Christmas Week at Miami Beach's beautiful Casablanca Hotel became ill. I replaced her, and was held over for two weeks. In January, 1953, Al Paschal telephoned me from California.

"Lillian," he said, "Ralph Edwards would like to do your life. You remember he once mentioned it to you. How do you feel about it?"

Feel? I was stunned. It was an honor to be chosen, but —*my* life? It certainly wasn't the life of a great woman. It was the life of an alcoholic, and her return to living again. If the world wanted a fairy-tale ending—there wasn't one. Spiritually the ending was lovely, for I had found a way of life. But—

"Think of the good this will do," Al said. "Nothing like it has ever been portrayed before."

I had been trying to live down my past. I knew people wouldn't forget that I was an alcoholic, but I wanted them to think of me as a person, not as a glorified ex-drunk. That had always been my concern since I'd attained my sobriety.

Burt and I discussed it. Ralph called and spoke to me. Finally, when Ralph called again, I accepted.

We flew to California two days before the show. Al, waiting for us at the airport, hurried us quickly into a car, so no one would see me, and literally smuggled us into a suite at the Hollywood Knickerbocker Hotel.

"Do what you want, Lillian—sleep, rest, read, listen to the radio—but you can't leave this room," Al instructed me. "You can't use the telephone. You can't communicate with anyone but Burt. Now, you know that our show will be about you, but that's all I can tell you."

I was consumed with curiosity. What questions would I be asked? What guests would appear? Had they brought Minna to California? Edna? Mrs. Berle? Perhaps even the Rev. Gordon Powell, from Melbourne, because he had just written a book on personal peace and power, and dedicated it to us?

"No, no, no," said Al, grinning. "I'm telling you nothing."

I spent a long, lazy day listening to the radio. I tried to keep my mind off the show. I was accustomed to appearing before cameras, but behind the one I was now to face sat 40,000,000 people—and they would be my jury.

Burt came in. "I've seen the script," he said. "Don't worry about anything." Beyond that he refused to say more.

Next morning I was hurried around the corner to the NBC Radio Theatre and pushed into a dressing room. Someone shouted, "All right—keep out of sight, everyone. She's coming out to rehearse her songs."

I rehearsed on the empty stage, unable even to see my pianist, who like everyone else, was hidden behind a screen.

Then I was rushed upstairs to the makeup room. When it was time for me to go on stage, I prayed, as I had always prayed before I spoke. The prayer soothed me and I stopped worrying about myself and tried to think of those in the audience who might be helped by my story.

[343]

Suddenly, I was given the cue, and I came through the curtain. I tried to avoid the camera. As the rough outline of my life was presented by Ralph Edwards, I thought, had all this happened to me? I was shocked. Could this horrid, fantastic life have been mine? But it was my life. Nothing I could do would eradicate it. Here it was, revived and made fresh to me and to the public.

At that moment, seated on the stage, I would have liked to have been anybody else but me, the camera on me and this story unfolding.

I sang a number I had rehearsed, but I had no idea of what it was. I thought only, what will I be asked next? How will I answer it? Will I say the right thing? Will the public understand?

Then the program was over, and the telephone calls and wires poured in. They were warm and understanding. The mail continued long after we returned to Florida. Ralph Edwards forwarded thousands of letters, many from priests, ministers, rabbis, telling me how their congregations had witnessed the show and felt great hope; and letters from men and women appealing for help for themselves or for those they loved. It was as though the program had suddenly opened a thousand secret doors, and from them came pouring men and women who suffered as I had suffered, and hoped against hope that they could find a way out.

I read each letter and answered them, at the rate of hundreds a week. Where help was needed, I tried to suggest how and where it could be obtained.

Later, I was invited to the Clover Club in Miami for a two week engagement. The public's acceptance led Jack Goldman, the proprietor, to hold me over for sixteen weeks. The club was filled nightly; the audiences were so warm, so encouraging, that sometimes it was hard for me to start my song because my throat was choked with tears.

Perhaps that is the way people really are—warm, and generous and ready to give of their hearts and affection, if only we open our hearts to them.

It was the same thrilling reception later at the Sans Souci, in Miami. And then, at last, after seven years, my return to New York, and the announcement in December, 1953, in Walter Winchell's column:

"Lillian Roth, who made it the hard way, and Julius La Rosa, who made it the easy way, open at La Vie en Rose on Christmas Night. . . ."

The critics came out in full force. Their reviews were excellent.

Offers came in, from all parts of the country. I was invited to record for Coral Records. Monte Proser asked me to return to La Vie en Rose. Other nightclubs bid for my services.

All this, happening in my new lifetime, I thought. It was true: God works in a mysterious fashion. This was what I had labored for all these years—to be welcomed back as a human being, to know that I was privileged to use my voice—my gift from God—as He intended it, to make people happy. It pleased me when men of my own age, who knew me in their college days, came up to say, "We used to call you our pin-up girl. And here you are, a pin-up girl again." Boys and girls who knew me in their teens now bring their teen-age children to see me. "Mother tells me she was your fan, and now I'm your fan."

It is good to be welcomed back by the public.

On one occasion a young man introduced himself. "Miss Roth," he began, a little embarrassed, "I hope you won't think I'm forward, but I loved the way you sang, 'I'll Cry Tomorrow.' I've never seen you before but your name is so familiar. Where have I heard it before?"

I smiled at him. "Ask your father," I said.

One quiet Sunday afternoon Burt and I were seated on the lawn of our Fort Lauderdale home, sipping cool lemonades and talking idly. It was a time for reminiscence.

"Do you realize, Burt," I said almost dreamily. "It was seven years ago that we first met."

He grinned. "They were seven lean years, weren't they, darling?"

I leaned over and kissed him. "If you're going to quote the Bible," I said, "what about the next seven?"

Burt shook his head. "I won't try to prophesy, but I will say—they seem to be starting off beautifully."

I was silent for a moment. "You know, Burt, it's a good thing one can't foresee the future. If I'd had any idea seven years ago of the struggle ahead of me, I think I would have given up then. But I know now that God was always at my side—"

"Yes," Burt said. "You really never lost faith. You did it— one day at a time."

There was a pause. Burt put his hand on mine in his old, familiar gesture. "It wasn't so difficult, was it?"

Difficult? Would anyone—could anyone but Burt—know how difficult it had been? Into my mind came a line from the writings of François Mauriac: *"We are moulded and remoulded by those who have loved us; and though the love may pass, we are, nevertheless, their work, for good or bad."* Burt's love had been so sure, so constant, so self-less, it had sustained me; and what had happened to me in the past had strengthened me to look with hope to all the unknown tomorrows.

I looked at Burt and I loved him very much.

"No, Burt," I said. "It wasn't so difficult."